TEP ®
TECHNOLOGY
ENHANCEMENT
PROGRAMME

technology
in practice

TEP®
TECHNOLOGY
ENHANCEMENT
PROGRAMME

technology
in practice

JOHN MURRAY

Acknowledgements

The Technology Enhancement Programme, funded by the Gatsby Charitable Foundation, exists to enhance and enrich technology education and training. For further details contact:

Gatsby Technical Education Project
4/7 Red Lion Court
London EC4A 3EB

Photo acknowledgements

Cover: © Tony Stone Images; **pp.**18, 45, 46, 47, 48, 49, 54, 68, 69, 70, 142, 165, 166, 167, 168 © John Townson/Creation; **p.**211 NASA/Science Photo Library.

© Technology Enhancement Programme/John Cave/Andy Bardill 2000

First published in 2000
by John Murray (Publishers) Ltd
50 Albemarle Street
London W1S 4BD

Reprinted 2001

Layouts by Wearset
Artwork by Jim Wilkinson, Wearset
Cover design by John Townson/Creation

Typeset in 10½ on 13pt Eras Book by Wearset, Boldon, Tyne and Wear
Printed and bound in Italy by G. Canale

A catalogue entry for this title is available from the British Library

ISBN 0 7195 7179 0

Contents

■ Section 2 Data 101

■ Section 3 Small miracles of technology 169

■ Section 4 Projects   205

1 Mechanisms   206

2 Control   215

3 Electronics   221

4 Structures   224

5 Materials   229

Introduction

This book is based on the very successful Young Technologist's Handbook published by the Gatsby-funded Technology Enhancement Programme (TEP).

It is designed primarily as a resource for design and technology at Key Stages 3 and 4 of the National Curriculum. But it is also suitable for post-16 work, and supports elements of Standard Grade and Higher Still courses. The original material has been revised and greatly extended. The new book contains a wealth of look-up information and gives special attention to the application of science and maths in design and technology. Implicit throughout is the belief that pupils should use, if and where appropriate, quantitative methods and standard reference data to help them solve problems. For both emphasis, and ease of reference for any user working from the index, all key terms within the text are in **bold** and clearly cross-referenced. In Section 4 Projects, terms given in **bold** indicate that more information can be found on this topic in Section 1 Background information and/or Section 2 Data.

This book has several unique features – not least the 'Small Miracles of Technology' section. This is premised on the belief that pupils can better understand their made world by looking closely at manufactured products. It assembles a number of case studies of products normally thrown away without a second glance. Each of these, however, is capable of telling a fascinating story about both design and manufacturing.

The book also contains a number of project outlines drawn from fifty or so TEP publications. These can be treated as starting points, adopted as focused tasks, or contextualised to provide more rounded design and make activities.

There is no simple prescription for using **Technology in Practice**. It provides wide-ranging information on materials, systems and processes to support creative endeavour in an increasingly demanding subject.

SECTION 1

background information

1 Mathematics

Why use maths?

Designers and engineers often use mathematics to solve problems. This is because it is more accurate than guessing the answers to problems. It is much safer when the design of something, like a parachute, has to be just right. When you look up information on materials, it is usually given in the form of numbers. If these are applied correctly, designers can predict the performance of materials in things such as buildings or aircraft. A lot of the maths used by engineers, even though it might look complicated, is in fact very simple.

Symbols

A **symbol** is a letter or sign that stands for something else. Symbols are used in technology in three main ways: as shorthand, to name something, and as a means of simplifying.

As a shorthand or abbreviation

As well as using common maths symbols such as '+' and '−', engineers often use symbols instead of words. For example, > means 'greater than'. If you think about the shape of the symbol (and its opposite), you can probably guess why it is the shape it is.

THIS > THIS

As the name of something

Letters of the Greek alphabet are often used in technology to name things. ρ (rho) stands for density; Ω (omega) stands for electrical resistance. Ω is in fact the unit of resistance. The Greek letter π (pi) stands for a very special number (3.141 593) which enables us, for example, to calculate areas of circles, volumes of cylinders and many other things.

As a means of simplifying

electronic symbol for a transistor

Symbols are used in diagrams and drawings to stand for parts and components that do not have to be drawn every time as accurate pictures. In circuit diagrams, electronic components each have a symbol – some of which look a little like the real thing. When they are used in diagrams, they make the diagram easier to draw and easier to read, and, like all symbols, they are part of a language which everybody can understand.

Big numbers

The maths and science used in technology and engineering often uses very long numbers. Instead of writing or saying these numbers, we can use several types of shorthand.

Prefixes

A **prefix** is added to the front of a unit as a multiplier or divider. 'Kilo' always tells you to multiply by a thousand: 1 kilogram is 1000 grams; 1 kilowatt is 1000 watts. 'Milli' tells you to divide by a thousand: 1 milligram is a thousandth of a gram.

Table 1.1   General mathematical symbols

+	Plus, positive or add		>	Greater than
−	Minus, negative or subtract		≥	Greater than or equal to
×	Multiply		<	Less than
÷ or /	Divide		≤	Less than or equal to
=	Equal(s)		±	Plus or minus
≠	Does not equal		$\sqrt{n}$	Square root of n
~	Approximately		$\sqrt[3]{n}$	Cube root of n
≈	Approximately equal(s)			

Table 1.2   Greek alphabet (many of these are used as symbols)

α	A	alpha		ν	N	nu
β	B	beta		ξ	Ξ	xi
γ	Γ	gamma		o	O	omicron
δ	Δ	delta		π	Π	pi
ε	E	epsilon		ρ	P	rho
ζ	Z	zeta		σ, ς	Σ	sigma
η	H	eta		τ	T	tau
θ	Θ	theta		υ	Y	upsilon
ι	I	iota		φ	Φ	phi
κ	K	kappa		χ	X	chi
λ	Λ	lambda		ψ	Ψ	psi
μ	M	mu		ω	Ω	omega

Symbols

Long numbers also have symbols. k stands for kilo or 1000. Instead of writing 0.000 001 metre, we can write μ, which is 1 micron (one millionth of a metre, or one thousandth of a millimetre). For example, an average human hair is 100 microns (100 μ) thick; you may see this printed as 100 μ or 100 μm.

Exponents

To abbreviate long numbers, engineers often use **exponents**. An exponent is a number that tells you how many zeros are on the end of a number. Many calculators now have an engineering function key that allows you to key in numbers with exponents and do maths with them. This avoids keying in – and possibly becoming confused by – very long numbers.

2 Maths and formulas

Using mathematics will help you to find design solutions quickly and easily. Some of the most common problems are to do with areas and volumes.

Area and volume

The top figure on page 5 tells you how to work out the **areas** of a number of common shapes. For example, you may need to work out the cost of a circular disc of material, such as silver, which is priced in pence per square centimetre. On a calculator, you simply multiply the radius of the blank by itself (r^2) and then multiply the result by π, which on most calculators means pressing the π key.

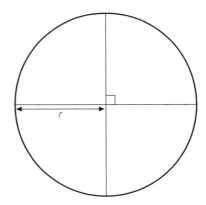

The bottom figure on page 5 tells you how to work out the **volumes** of a number of different 'containers'. This is only slightly more complicated than working out areas. For example,

Volume of a cylinder = area of the base (identical to calculation on area of a disc) × the length

This simple calculation is often used for estimating how much liquid a container will hold. With a bit of thought, you can work out the dimensions of different container sizes needed to hold a specified amount of liquid. For example, you make an assumption about (guess) the diameter of the base, and divide its area into the volume of liquid to give the length.

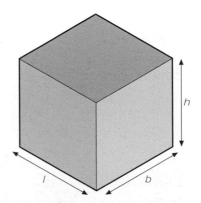

To estimate the volume of a complicated container shape, break it down into a number of simpler shapes. For example, the volume of a cylinder with a hemispherical dome at both ends is the volume of the cylinder + the volume of a sphere.

area of a rectangle

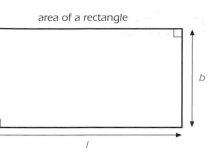

$$\text{area} = l \times b$$

area of a circle

$$\text{area} = \pi r^2$$
$$\text{circumference} = 2\pi r$$

area of a parallelogram

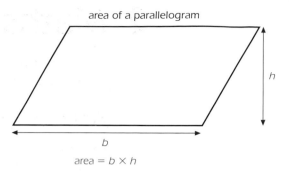

$$\text{area} = b \times h$$

area of a sector of a circle

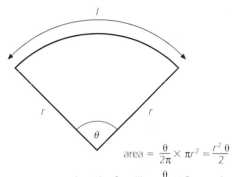

$$\text{area} = \frac{\theta}{2\pi} \times \pi r^2 = \frac{r^2 \theta}{2}$$

$$\text{length of arc}(l) = \frac{\theta}{2\pi} \times 2\pi r = r\theta$$

Note: θ is in radians
$$1 \text{ radian} = 57.3°$$
$$1° = 0.0175 \text{ radian}$$

area of a trapezium

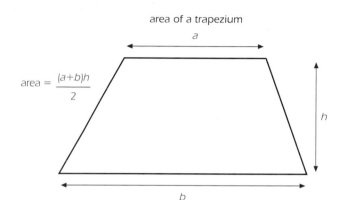

$$\text{area} = \frac{(a+b)h}{2}$$

area of an ellipse

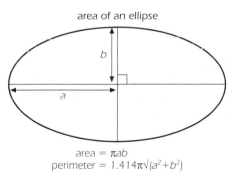

$$\text{area} = \pi ab$$
$$\text{perimeter} = 1.414\pi\sqrt{(a^2+b^2)}$$

area of a triangle

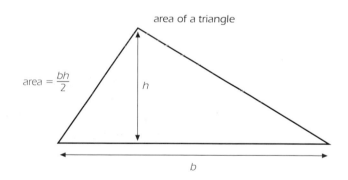

$$\text{area} = \frac{bh}{2}$$

If you know the volume of a piece of material, such as your design for a paperweight, you can work out its overall mass by multiplying the volume by the **density** of the material. Density values can be found in Table 1.6 (see page 20).

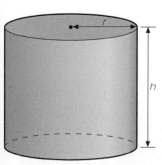

volume of a cylinder $= \pi r^2 \times h$

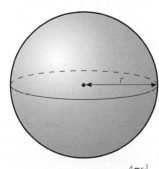

volume of a sphere $= \frac{4\pi r^3}{3}$

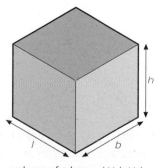

volume of a box $= l \times b \times h$

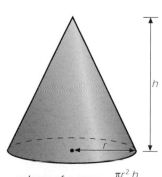

volume of a cone $= \frac{\pi r^2 h}{3}$

Uses of pi

Example 1. Paper feeder feed rate

This example shows how you can work out the speed of paper emerging from a small paper feeder when the speed of the rubber driving wheels is known. (See Gearboxes, page 148.)

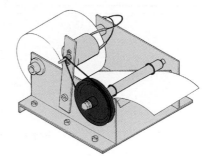

Assume a ten-tooth pinion gear on the motor spindle, a 60-tooth driven gear, rubber driving wheels turning at 1500 r.p.m. (revolutions per minute), and 8 mm diameter wheels on the driving shaft.

$$\frac{\text{Speed of driven gear}}{\text{Speed of driver gear}} = \frac{\text{number of teeth on driver gear}}{\text{number of teeth on driven gear}}$$

$$\frac{\text{Speed of driven gear}}{1500 \text{ r.p.m.}} = \frac{10}{60}$$

$$\text{Speed of driven gear} = \frac{10 \times 1500}{60} = 250 \text{ r.p.m.}$$

The driving shaft wheels also rotate at 250 r.p.m. Therefore:

Paper feed speed = 250 rev/min
  × circumference of the 8 mm diameter drive wheels (mm/rev)
  = 250 × πd mm/min
  = 250 × 3.142 × 8
  = 250 × 25.136
  = 6284 mm/min

This equals approximately 6.3 m/min or 105 mm/s.

Example 2. Length of paper needed for roll-tubes

This example shows how you can work out the length of paper needed for making a roll-tube. Roll-tubes are used in designing and making structures and can be bolted together.

The inside diameter (I/D) of a roll-tube is the diameter of the mandrel, providing the tube is tightly wound.

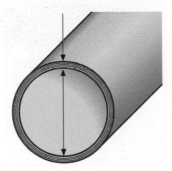
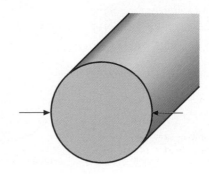

The outside diameter (O/D) of a roll-tube depends on the number of turns of paper. For a required O/D of roll-tube, the number of turns of paper required is given by:

$$\text{Number of turns} = \frac{\text{required O/D} - \text{mandrel diameter}}{2} \div \text{paper thickness}$$

For example, if the required O/D of the roll-tube is 8 mm, the mandrel diameter 5 mm and the paper thickness 0.1 mm (ordinary photocopier paper),

$$\text{Number of turns} = \frac{8 - 5}{2} \div 0.1 = 15 \text{ turns}$$

The *approximate* length of paper needed for a required O/D of roll-tube is given by:

Length = number of turns × diameter of mandrel × π

For example, if there are 15 turns and the mandrel diameter is 5 mm, then

Length = 15 × 5 mm × 3.142 = 236 mm approximately

A much closer approximation is given by:

Length = number of turns × average diameter of tube × π

For example, if there are 15 turns, the mandrel diameter is 5 mm, and the tube O/D is 8 mm,

Length = 15 × 6.5 mm × 3.142 = 306 mm approximately

1 A cycle has wheels with a diameter of 60 cm. How much ground will the cycle cover if the wheels revolve 100 times?

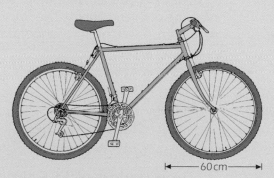

2 A cycle generator has to rotate at a minimum speed of 1000 r.p.m. before it generates enough current to supply the lights. The cycle wheels are 60 cm in diameter and the friction wheel driving the generator is 15 mm in diameter. What is the minimum speed, in metres per minute, that the cycle has to travel at in order to operate the generator?

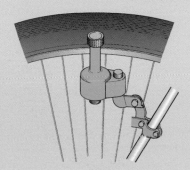

See

- Tumbler unit, page 208
- Paper feeder, page 214

Other useful formulas

1. Ohm's Law

Ohm's Law states the relationship between current (*I*, measured in amps), voltage (*V*, volts) and resistance (*R*, ohms) in an electrical or electronic circuit:

$$V = I \times R$$
$$I = V \div R$$
$$R = V \div I$$

If we know two of these, we can work out the third. For example, if we connect a component whose resistance is 10 ohms across a typical car battery (12 volts), how much current flows?

$$I = V \div R$$
$$= 12 \text{ volts} \div 10 \text{ ohms}$$
$$= 1.2 \text{ amps}$$

2. Power equation

The equation for electric power gives us the power (*P*, measured in watts) from the voltage (*V*, volts) and current (*I*, amps):

$$P = I \times V$$

For example, if we measure a current of 1 amp from an electric motor running from a 6 volt battery, the power is given as:

$$P = 1 \text{ amp} \times 6 \text{ volts}$$
$$= 6 \text{ watts}$$

The power of electric motors in appliances, such as drills and vacuum cleaners, is usually expressed in watts.

Components, such as resistors, are given a maximum power rating. This is a measure of the amount of heat they can safely get rid of before burning out. A 10 ohm, 5 watt resistor connected to a 12 volt battery will seriously overheat:

$$I = V \div R$$
$$= 12 \text{ volts} \div 10 \text{ ohms}$$
$$= 1.2 \text{ amps}$$

$$P = I \times V$$
$$= 1.2 \text{ amps} \times 12 \text{ volts}$$
$$= 14.4 \text{ watts (nearly 10 watts over the maximum power rating!)}$$

3. Time period of 555 timer

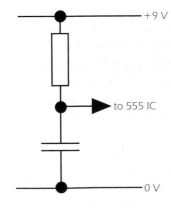

+9 V

to 555 IC

0 V

The 555 timer is the most frequently used chip for making timing circuits. Two components, a capacitor and a resistor, set the time interval. They are connected in series as shown in the figure.

It is possible to calculate the time period of the 555. If *C* is the capacitance (measured in farads) and *R* is the resistance (in ohms), then

Time period (seconds) = 1.1 × *C* × *R*   (where 1.1 is a constant)

In the case of a 1000 μF capacitor and a 1 kΩ resistor,

$$C = 1000 \text{ μF} = 0.001 \text{ farad (F)}$$
$$R = 1 \text{ kΩ} = 1000 \text{ ohms (Ω)}$$

Time period = 1.1 × *C* × *R*
$$= 1.1 \times 0.001 \text{ F} \times 1000 \text{ Ω}$$
$$= 1.1 \text{ s}$$

Remember always to convert ratings and measurements to their basic units: farads, ohms, volts, watts, and so on.

3 Measuring

Where do units come from?

Whenever we measure length, mass, time or any other quantity, we use base **units** such as the metre, kilogram or second. These are examples of Système Internationale (**SI**) units which most countries have adopted. Nevertheless, you will still come across **imperial** units, such as inches and feet, which were universally used in this country until 'metrication' in 1968, after which time it was intended that all measurements would be in SI units. Many people, including engineers, 'think' in imperial units and many measuring instruments such as simple rulers are still marked in metric and imperial units.

The important thing about measurement is that the units are **universal**, so that a metre as measured in Australia is the same as a metre as measured in the UK. We need to know that we are talking about the same quantities when we exchange goods, for example. In technology and engineering, it is very important that we use common standards so that when parts for something are made in different places, they fit together. Parts of cars, for example, are made in different European countries and need to fit together. The idea of interchangeable parts is based on accurate universal measurement.

The instruments we actually use to measure length are marked out or **calibrated** from reference standards. These are very accurately calibrated 'rulers'. These in turn are checked against more accurate standards until, ultimately, we check against a single primary standard. The standard metre used to be a single bar kept in a vault in Paris. This has been replaced by a definition based on the wavelength of light which can now be measured by special instruments in different places. It is worth noting that the primary standard for mass is still a block of platinum kept in a vault in Paris. There is some concern because for reasons unknown it seems to be losing 'weight'!

Conversion between imperial and SI units

It is often necessary to **convert** from imperial to SI units and vice versa. Table 1.3 (see page 10) gives the formulas and figures to use.

Measuring things

Designers may need to measure very small and very large things. For example, small machines which one day might travel inside the human body to repair damage are measured in billionths of a metre. A billionth of a metre is called a nanometre – hence the term 'nanotechnology' to describe engineering on a very small scale. Designers of buildings, on the other hand, typically measure things in metres. In both examples, there is a need to measure accurately. All parts in a car can be exchanged for new ones only because they can be manufactured to great accuracy.

The most common form of measuring device is the **ruler**. It allows you to compare a marked scale against the thing being measured. Rulers work well for many measurements but are not good enough, for example, where we need to measure to within ±0.01 millimetre or less. We have a vast array of accurate measuring tools, the most common of which are **vernier callipers** and **micrometers**. Both of these tools are now available in electronic versions which have easy-to-read number displays.

Table 1.3 Metric and imperial conversions

		Metric = ( ) × imperial	Imperial = ( ) × metric
Area	square miles : square kilometres	2.59	0.386
	square miles : hectares	258.999	0.0039
	acres : square metres	4046.86	0.00025
	acres : hectares	0.4047	2.47
	square yards : square metres	0.8361	1.196
	square feet : square metres	0.0929	10.76
	square feet : square centimetres	929.03	0.0011
	square inches : square millimetres	645.16	0.0016
	square inches : square centimetres	6.4516	0.155
Capacity	gallons : cubic decimetres (litres)	4.5461	0.220
	US barrels : cubic metres (for petroleum)	0.159	6.29
	US gallons : cubic decimetres (litres)	3.7854	0.264
	quarts : cubic decimetres (litres)	1.1365	0.88
	pints : cubic decimetres (litres)	0.5683	1.76
	gills : cubic decimetres (litres)	0.1421	7.04
Fuel consumption	gallons per mile : litres per kilometre	2.825	0.354
	miles per gallon : kilometres per litre	0.354	2.825
Length	miles : kilometres	1.6093	0.621
	yards : metres	0.9144	1.094
	feet : metres	0.3048	3.28
	inches : millimetres	25.4	0.039
	inches : centimetres	2.54	0.394
Mass	tons : kilograms	1016.05	0.00098
	tons : tonnes	1.0160	0.984
	hundredweights : kilograms	50.8023	0.020
	centals : kilograms	45.3592	0.022
	quarters : kilograms	12.7006	0.079
	stones : kilograms	6.3503	0.157
	pounds : kilograms	0.4536	2.20
	ounces : grams	28.3495	0.035
Speed	miles per hour : kilometres per hour	1.6093	0.621
	feet per second : metres per second	0.3048	3.281
	feet per minute : metres per second	0.0051	196.08
	feet per minute : metres per minute	0.3048	3.281
	inches per second : millimetres per second	25.4	0.039
	inches per minute : millimetres per second	0.4233	2.363
	inches per minute : centimetres per minute	2.54	0.039
Volume	cubic yards : cubic metres	0.7646	1.308
	cubic feet : cubic metres	0.0283	35.336
	cubic feet : cubic decimetres	28.3168	0.035
	cubic inches : cubic centimetres	16.3871	0.061

The vernier calliper

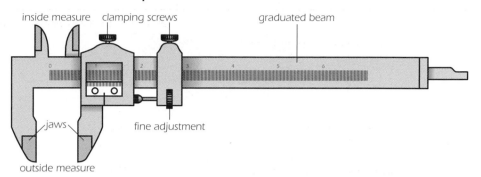

inside measure   clamping screws   graduated beam

jaws

fine adjustment

outside measure

You will see first of all that the small scale is1/10 mm shorter than it should be. This shortening is the key to the vernier principle.

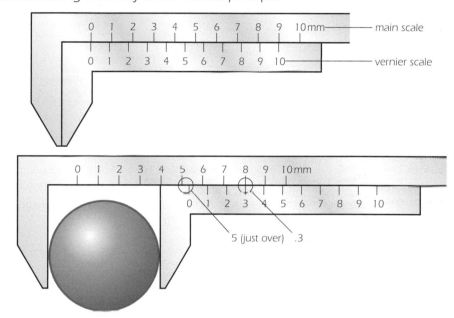

0 1 2 3 4 5 6 7 8 9 10mm —— main scale

0 1 2 3 4 5 6 7 8 9 10 —— vernier scale

0 1 2 3 4 5 6 7 8 9 10mm

0 1 2 3 4 5 6 7 8 9 10

5 (just over)   .3

When you measure something, the '0' graduation on the small scale moves to a point on the main scale. The example shows that we are measuring something just over 5 mm across. How much is it 'just over'? Look along the small scale until you come to the point where a graduation coincides with one on the main scale. This figure is the additional length in units of 1/10 mm. The overall reading in the example is therefore 5 mm + 3/10 mm = 5.3 mm.

On a real vernier calliper, the divisions on the two scales are finer than those shown in the example.

The bottom jaws of a vernier calliper are used to measure outside dimensions.

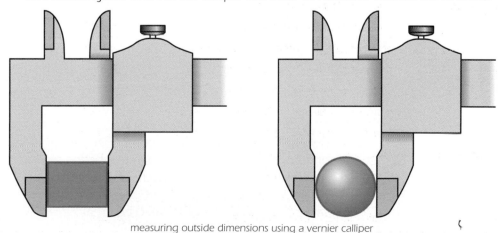

measuring outside dimensions using a vernier calliper

The same instrument may also be used to measure internal dimensions using the jaws on the top of the instrument. Their use in this way is illustrated below left.

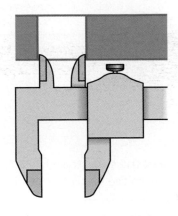

measuring inside dimensions using a vernier calliper

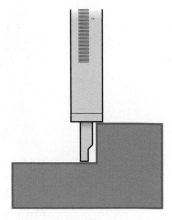

using a vernier calliper to measure the depth of a hole or a step

Measuring depths is another form of linear measure and this too may be done on some vernier callipers. These have a depth rod which passes through the main body of the instrument and is attached to the movable jaws. This rod may be inserted into the hole or down to the surface to be measured, and the distance read off.

When a vernier calliper is used in this way to measure a step, it is limited by not having an adequate flat surface which may be used as a datum surface. This problem is overcome in the vernier depth gauge, which is a specially adapted instrument for measuring depths and steps.

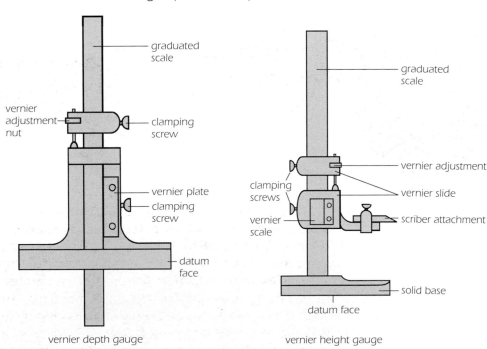

vernier depth gauge

vernier height gauge

Another linear dimension which is commonly measured is height. This is generally measured with the component and the gauge on a flat surface. In other applications, such as when machining a casting, it may be necessary to mark out a height prior to machining. For these applications, another vernier device is used, a vernier height gauge. This is simply another variation on the same theme with the graduated beam mounted on a solid flat base which forms the datum for measurements.

In an electronic vernier calliper, the distance moved by one of the jaws is sensed electronically and this distance is displayed on a small LCD screen.

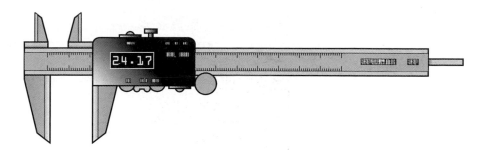

The micrometer

While vernier callipers and their derivatives are flexible and reasonably accurate, many people prefer to use the **micrometer** (the 'mic') for everyday use. Indeed, for accurate measurement of a diameter to less than a 'thou' (a thousandth of an inch, 0.001") or about 20 microns (0.02 mm) the vernier calliper is probably not really accurate enough. The micrometer relies on a very accurately cut screw thread which is wound in and out, the position being noted on a scale on the barrel of the instrument. The jaws of the instrument have hardened faces which offer a much larger area with which to line up the piece to be measured. Part of the skill of using a 'mic' is in sensing the pressure with which the component is gripped by the jaws. In the hands of an experienced worker, the 'mic' is an extremely accurate device.

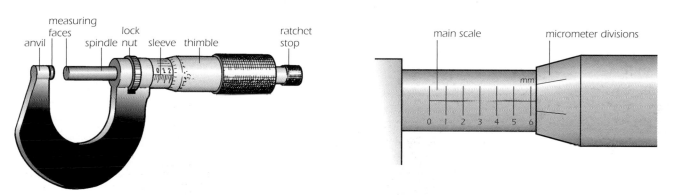

The enlargement of a simplified micrometer illustrates how it works. The main scale is divided into millimetre divisions and the thimble into 1/10 millimetre divisions. Because the micrometer's screw thread has a pitch of 1 mm, the thimble will move 1 mm along the scale for each complete revolution.

In the example shown, we first read off the number of complete millimetres moved along by the thimble. This is just over 6 mm. How much is it 'just over'? Look at the graduations on the thimble and read off the number that coincides with the centre line on the main scale. This figure is the additional length in units of 1/10 mm. The overall reading is therefore 6 mm + 3/10 mm = 6.3 mm.

On a real micrometer, the divisions on both the barrel and thimble are finer than those shown in the example.

While the micrometer is a more precise instrument than the vernier calliper, it suffers from the disadvantage that it has a much smaller range. A well-equipped workshop, therefore, would possess an entire family of micrometers from 0–25 mm (0–1"), 25–50 mm (1–2"), 50–75 mm (2–3"), and so on, up to a range which covers the largest components that the workshop handles.

Ultrasonic measuring

Undoubtedly the most common devices for measuring distances are the ruler or tape measure. Such is the rate of progress in electronics that even these simple devices are now challenged. For instance, measuring between two objects such as walls is increasingly done by means of **ultrasonic rulers**. In these, a pulse of ultrasound is sent from the electronic device and is reflected back by the far wall. The electronic circuit then calculates how long the process took and, knowing the speed of sound, can calculate the difference.

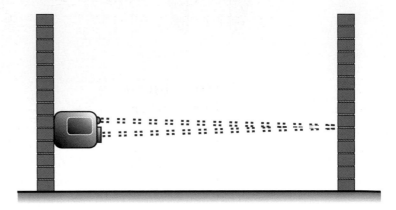

Example

The sensor shows that the sound took 0.1 second (100 ms) to travel to the far wall and back to the sensor. As we know that sound travels at 340 m s^{-1} at ground level in still air, we can calculate the distance travelled:

$$\text{Velocity of sound} = \frac{\text{distance travelled}}{\text{time taken}}$$

$$\begin{aligned}
\text{Distance travelled} &= \text{velocity of sound} \times \text{time taken} \\
&= 340 \text{ m s}^{-1} \times 0.1 \text{ s} \\
&= 34 \text{ m} \\
\text{Therefore width} &= 17 \text{ m}
\end{aligned}$$

4 Materials

The elements

Elements are the basic 'building blocks' of the materials from which we make things. Some elements, such as the metals **aluminium** and **copper**, can be used in their pure form. Other elements are combined. A small amount of **carbon** added to **iron** gives us **steel**. Instead of using the full name of each element, we can use just one or two letters. Table 1.4 lists these.

Table 1.4   The elements

Ac	actinium	Hf	hafnium	Pm	promethium
Al	aluminium	He	helium	Pa	protoactinium
Am	americium	Ho	holmium	Ra	radium
Sb	antimony	H	hydrogen	Rn	radon
Ar	argon	In	indium	Re	rhenium
As	arsenic	I	iodine	Rh	rhodium
At	astatine	Ir	iridium	Rb	rubidium
Ba	barium	Fe	iron	Ru	ruthenium
Bk	berkelium	Kr	krypton	Sm	samarium
Be	beryllium	La	lanthanum	Sc	scandium
Bi	bismuth	Lr	lawrencium	Se	selenium
B	boron	Pb	lead	Si	silicon
Br	bromine	Li	lithium	Ag	silver
Cd	cadmium	Lu	lutetium	Na	sodium
Cs	caesium	Mg	magnesium	Sr	strontium
Ca	calcium	Mn	manganese	S	sulphur
Cf	californium	Md	mendelevium	Ta	tantalum
C	carbon	Hg	mercury	Tc	technetium
Ce	cerium	Mo	molybdenum	Te	tellurium
Cl	chlorine	Nd	neodymium	Tb	terbium
Cr	chromium	Ne	neon	Tl	thallium
Co	cobalt	Np	neptunium	Th	thorium
Cu	copper	Ni	nickel	Tm	thulium
Cm	curium	Nb	niobium	Sn	tin
Dy	dysprosium	N	nitrogen	Ti	titanium
Es	einsteinium	No	nobelium	W	tungsten
Er	erbium	Os	osmium	U	uranium
Eu	europium	O	oxygen	V	vanadium
Fm	fermium	Pd	palladium	Xe	xenon
F	fluorine	P	phosphorus	Yb	ytterbium
Fr	francium	Pt	platinum	Y	yttrium
Gd	gadolinium	Pu	plutonium	Zn	zinc
Ga	gallium	Po	polonium	Zr	zirconium
Ge	germanium	K	potassium		
Au	gold	Pr	praseodymium		

Uses of some elements

Aluminium (Al)   The most abundant element on the Earth's surface, a light white metal. Widely used for its light weight in aircraft, cars and lorries, it is about a third of the weight of steel and very malleable. Also used for its high electrical conductivity and ductility in electrical cables, particularly in high-voltage power transmission; and its high corrosion resistance in decorative and architectural metalwork, as in the statue of Eros in Piccadilly Circus, London. Used in sheet form in the manufacture of drink cans, etc., and for baking foil. Widely used as alloys, principally with copper (Cu) in *Duralium*. (For further explanation of alloys, see page 17.)

Carbon (C)   A common element of which most life forms are largely composed. An important constituent in oil and gas and, hence, in most polymers.

Helium (He)   A light gas used in balloons and to make artificial 'air' for divers. The second most common element in the Universe.

Iron (Fe)   A malleable metal in use as wrought iron since the Iron Age, but now rarely seen in its pure form. Used as cast iron since the Middle Ages. Its principal use is in steel alloys where it is combined with carbon and other materials.

Titanium (Ti)   A metal used for its strength and lightness in aircraft and for its resistance to corrosion in marine applications.

Materials we use

foam polyurethane — aluminium — PVC — titanium alloy — chromium — rubber — steel

Many of the materials we use consist of several elements. **Organic** materials such as wood and plastics contain **carbon**. Metal elements are usually mixed together to give better properties. Copper is added to gold in jewellery to make it harder wearing.

Most products we buy consist of many different materials. A modern bicycle with accessories can contain over 100 different types of material.

1   Name other materials used in making a cycle or its accessories. What are the main elements making up these materials?

2   What materials are used in the following products:

See

- Ergonomic handle, page 229
- Cool container, page 232
- Mirror, page 239
- Kaleidoscope, page 240

Although the elements will never change, we are continually discovering and inventing new materials. Plastics and metals can now be 'designed' for different uses – hence the term 'designer materials'. Within the last few years, designers have been able to use **smart materials** – materials that seem to behave and respond intelligently. Lenses in spectacles and sunglasses and window glass can be made to darken in bright sunlight. Metals can be given a 'memory' so that they change shape at different temperatures. They are known as **shape memory alloys**.

The main groups of materials

Metals

Metals are used either in their pure form or as **alloys** – mixtures of metals. Chromium, for example, is used in its pure form for protective metal plating, and lead is used in its pure form as roofing sheet. Most metals we use are mixed together as alloys to give different properties. For example, silver and gold are usually mixed with copper and other metals to make them harder and more durable. Brass is a mixture or alloy of copper and zinc. One of the most important metals we use – **steel** – is a mixture of iron and a small amount of carbon. Tool steel contains small amounts of other metals such as chromium to make it tough and hard. A mixture of titanium and nickel gives an alloy called **nitinol** which has a 'memory' (see Shape memory alloy (smart wire) page 146).

Polymers

Polymers (commonly called **plastics**) are produced from carbon-based materials such as oil and coal. Polythene, one of the most common plastics, consists of carbon and hydrogen atoms grouped together in a special way to form long **molecules**. Polythene is used for plastic bags and electrical insulation. Very often, plastics are mixed together to give **co-polymers** (like metals mixed to give alloys). One of these is an **acrylic**, polymethyl methacrylate, known commonly as *Perspex*, one of its trade names.

Polymers fall into two main categories: thermoplastic and thermosetting (see Manufacturing techniques for plastics, page 39). **Thermoplastic** materials such as polythene can be heated and moulded into shape over and over again. **Thermosetting** materials such as melamine can be moulded only once. Sometimes both thermosetting and thermoplastic polymers are reinforced with **fibres** such as **glass** or **carbon fibre**.

Wood-based materials

Natural **wood**, sawn directly from trees, is still used in large quantities for building work and some furniture. **Softwood**, which grows quickly and can be managed as a renewable resource, is still the main material used in house roofs and general woodwork. Increasingly, sheet materials are made from wood products such as chips or fibre. Plastic-faced **chipboard** is used widely in self-assembly furniture, and **MDF** (medium density fibreboard) is also used in furniture construction. Like another important manufactured board, **plywood**, these materials offer low-cost, all-round strength and stability.

Ceramics

high technology ceramics used in high temperature jet engines

Ceramic materials, in the form of fired clay, have long been important for manufacturing goods ranging from cups to electrical insulators. Like polymers, ceramics have now become a 'designer' material. The correct combination of ingredients, processed correctly, can be used for making engine parts, jet engine components and even 'soft' materials that can be machined on a lathe. It is predicted that the all-ceramic car engine is not far away.

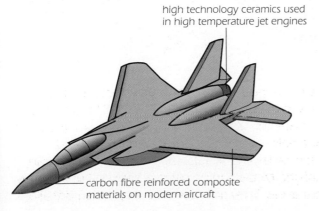

carbon fibre reinforced composite materials on modern aircraft

Silicon

Silicon is the most abundant of minerals and is used for manufacturing **integrated circuits** (ICs) or 'chips' for short. Chips have revolutionised electronics and computing and made possible products such as mobile phones. Silicon is specially melted and then 'grown' as a single crystal which is then cut into flat circular sheets. These are processed using photographic and other methods to form groups of connected components. Millions of components forming complete circuits can be made on a piece of silicon a few millimetres square. The same techniques are now being used to make 'micro-machines' such as electric motors that will fit on to the head of a needle.

See

- Radio, page 222
- Mirror, page 239
- Kaleidoscope, page 240

Properties of materials

Materials have many different properties. It is incorrect, for example, to describe a material as just 'strong' or 'weak' because it can be strong or weak in different ways. Concrete is very strong when it is compressed, but quite weak in tension (when it is pulled apart) (see Types of forces, page 71).

When a material is selected for a product, all its different properties need to be considered, such as hardness, melting point, strength in tension (tensile strength), and resistance to sudden impacts. Clear *Perspex* is a good choice of plastic for see-through displays but a poor choice for containers because it breaks easily.

The various properties of materials can be compared by looking at tables. The following pages give some example look-up tables. The complete tables can be found in larger reference books.

See

- Space frame, page 224
- Re-inventing the paper-clip, page 245

1. Applications of materials

Table 1.5 groups materials by their most useful **properties**. If you wanted a material for heat insulation, you might choose hardboard rather than, say, copper.

Table 1.5   Special properties of materials

Some metals with high melting points
Chromium
Heat-resisting alloy steels
High-speed steel
Nichrome
Nimonic alloys
Stainless steel
Stellite
Tantalum
Titanium
Tungsten
Vanadium

Corrosion resistant metals
Cupronickel
Lead
Monel metal
Nickel
Pure aluminium
Stainless steel
Tin
Titanium and alloys

Coating metals
Brass
Bronze
Cadmium
Chromium
Copper
Gold
Lead
Nickel
Platinum
Silver
Tin
Zinc

High strength to weight ratio materials
Carbon fibre reinforced plastics
Duralumin
Glass reinforced plastics
Magnesium alloys
Nylon
Polycarbonate
Some aluminium alloys
Spruce
Titanium
Titanium alloys

Good conductors of heat
Aluminium
Bronze
Copper
Duralumin
Silver
Zinc

Good conductors of electricity
Aluminium
Beryllium copper
Brass
Copper
Gold
Magnesium
Phosphor bronze
Silver

Good electrical insulators
Ceramics
Ebonite
Gases
Glass
Insulating papers
Mica
Shellac
Silicone rubber
Soft natural and synthetic rubber
Thermoplastics
Thermosetting plastics
Tufnol

Good heat insulators
Cork
Cotton wool
Expanded polystyrene
Felt
Glass fibre and foam
Glass wool
Hardboard
Insulating wallboard
Mineral wool
Plywood
Polyurethane foam
Rubber
Sawdust
Urea formaldehyde foam
Wood

2. Density

Table 1.6 shows the **density** of some important materials. Density is mass per unit volume, shown here in kilograms per cubic metre (kg m^{-3}). A dense material is very heavy for its size. A block of lead is much heavier than a similar-sized block of wood. Aircraft need to be strong but as light as possible, so aluminium is a good choice among the metals.

Table 1.6   Density of materials (ρ) for normal pressure and temperature

Metals	ρ (kg m^{-3})
Aluminium	2700
Aluminium bronze (90% Cu, 10% Al)	7700
Antimony	6690
Beryllium	1829
Bismuth	9750
Brass (60% Cu, 40% Zn)	8520
Cadmium	8650
Chromium	7190
Cobalt	8900
Constantan	8920
Copper	8930
Gold	19320
Inconel	8510
Iron: pure	7870
cast	7270
Lead	11350
Magnesium	1740
Manganese	7430
Mercury	13546
Molybdenum	10200
Monel	18900
Nickel	8900
Nimonic (average)	8100
Palladium	12160
Phosphor bronze (typical)	8900
Platinum	21370
Sodium	971
Steel: mild	7830
stainless	8000
Tin: grey	5750
rhombic	6550
tetragonal	7310
Titanium	4540
Tungsten	19300
Uranium	18680
Vanadium	5960
Zinc	7140

Wood (15% moisture)	ρ (kg m^{-3})
Ash	660
Balsa	100–390
Beech	740
Birch	720
Elm: English	560
Dutch	560
Wych	690
Fir, Douglas	480–550
Mahogany	545
Pine: Parana	550
pitch	640
Scots	530
Spruce, Norway	430
Teak	660

3. Hardness

Hardness is measured in different ways. The main tests involve pushing something into the surface of the material and measuring the size of the indentation. The Brinell hardness number (BHN) is found by pressing a hard ball into the surface of a material and measuring the diameter of the 'dent'. The load applied in this test is a standard 3000 kg. The Vickers test measures the depth of penetration of a sharp point. The load applied in this test is either 5, 10, 50 or 150 kg depending on the hardness of the material being tested. Table 1.7 lists some typical Brinell hardness numbers and shows, for example, that polythene is very soft indeed compared with cast iron.

Table 1.7 also explains one of the reasons why steel is used for garden tools rather than brass. What are some other reasons?

Table 1.7   Typical Brinell hardness numbers (BHN) for metals and plastics

Material	BHN
Soft brass	60
Mild steel	130
Annealed chisel steel	235
White cast iron	415
Nitrided surface	750
PVC rigid	20
Polystyrene	25
Acrylic (*Perspex*)	34
Polythene (high density)	2
Epoxy resin (glass filled)	38

See

- Emergency ice scraper, page 231

4. Tensile strength

The **tensile strength** of a material is its capacity to resist being pulled apart. This is very important because materials in both small products and large structures are subjected to tensile forces. Plastic carrier bag handles often stretch and break because polythene has quite low tensile strength. The same thing can happen to any other materials in other products if the forces are too high. Entire buildings have collapsed as a result.

Looking at Table 1.8 you will see why steel wire is used for crane lines and suspension bridge cables as opposed to aluminium, for example. Wood is much stronger if 'pulled' along the grain than across it. You will also notice that an unlikely material, spider's thread, has a much greater tensile strength than some other materials. Scientists have recently found out how to make a synthetic version of it.

Table 1.8 Comparative tensile strengths of materials (approximate tensile strengths for a range of materials for purposes of comparison)

Material	Tensile strength ($MN\,m^{-2}$)
Steel piano wire	3000
High tensile steel	1500
Titanium alloys	700–1400
Mild steel	400
Aluminium alloys	140–550
Traditional wrought iron	140–280
Modern cast iron	140–280
Copper	140
Brasses	120–400
Pure cast aluminium	70
Flax	700
Cotton	350
Silk	350
Spider's thread	240
Bone	140
Wood (along grain)	100
Tendon (muscle)	100
Hemp rope	80
Leather	40
Glass window or wine glass	30–170
Ordinary brick	5
Cement and concrete	4
Wood (across grain)	3

See
- Emergency ice scraper, page 231

5. Friction

When one surface moves against another, the resistance that opposes movement is called **friction**. The coefficient of friction is a number that tells us how easily one material will slip against another when a force is applied. The smaller the number, the less friction there is. Table 1.9 shows the coefficient of friction for pairs of materials in contact. The lowest number partly explains why people can skate on ice so easily. Rubber on a road surface has the highest number. Why is this important for cyclists and motorists?

Friction between materials is a bad thing when it interferes with machines running. We use lubricants such as oil and grease to help overcome friction. Friction is a good thing when we do not want materials to slip over one another, such as in drive belts on pulleys, brakes on cycles, or clamps.

Draw up a table of instances where friction is (a) wanted, and (b) unwanted.

Table 1.9   Frictional characteristics of different materials

Material	Lubrication	Approx. coefficient of friction (low pressure)
Metal on metal	None	0.20
Cast iron on hardwood	None	0.49
Cast iron on hardwood	Some	0.19
Metal on hardwood	None	0.60
Metal on hardwood	Some	0.20
Leather on metal	None	0.40
Rubber on metal	None	0.40
Rubber on road	None	0.90
Nylon on steel	None	0.3–0.5
Acrylic on steel	None	0.50
Teflon on steel	None	0.04
Metal on ice	None	0.02

6. Stiffness of sections

When materials are shaped they can become much **stiffer**. Folding paper into a number of 'V's converts it from a 'floppy' sheet to a stiff section. Modern cars and many other products are made from thin 'floppy' metal sheet that becomes stiff when folded.

Materials are available as sections, some being stiffer than others. The figure on page 24 shows how they compare (assuming each has the same cross-sectional area). A larger diameter tube with a thin wall is stiffer than a small diameter tube – and both are stiffer than a solid rod.

If we take the same sections and compare them by trying to twist them, the results are very different. In engineering, we call 'twisting' **torsion** (see Types of forces, page 71). A flat plastic ruler can be twisted easily if you hold the two ends. A tube is much more difficult to twist like this and this is the reason, for example, why lorry drive shafts are made from tubes. Designers have to work out what they want from materials supplied in sections so they end up with the strongest product.

See

- Hanging shelf system, page 226
- Packaging for survival, page 227

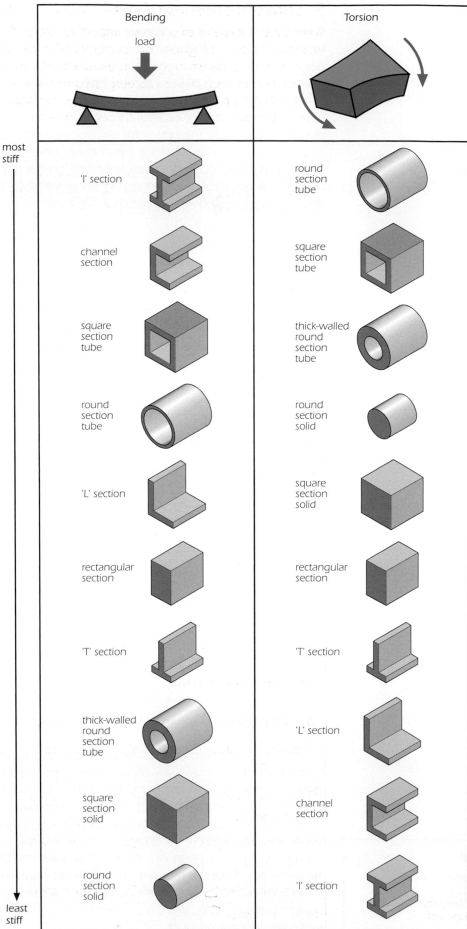

7. Some properties of plastics compared

Sometimes it is useful to compare important properties within a **class** of materials. Table 1.10 gives four properties of some common plastics. Impact resistance, as its name suggests, is the ability of a material to stand up to sudden 'knocks' and impacts. Glass has very little impact resistance unless specially treated. Polypropylene has very high impact resistance and is used for plastic cases and boxes that might get thrown around.

Many people think of *Perspex* (acrylic) as a 'strong' plastic. How does it compare with others in the table?

Table 1.10   *Physical properties of some plastics*

Properties of plastic	Tensile strength (N mm^{-2})	Impact resistance	BHN	Machinability
Thermoplastics				
PVC rigid	48	Good	20	Very good
Polystyrene	48	Average	25	Average
PTFE	13	Very good	—	Very good
Polypropylene	27	Very good	10	Very good
Nylon	60	Good	10	Very good
Cellulose nitrate	48	Average	10	Very good
Cellulose acetate	40	Average	12	Very good
Acrylic (*Perspex*)	74	Poor	34	Very good
Polythene (high density)	20–30	Average	2	Very good
Thermosetting plastics				
Epoxy resin (glass filled)	68–200	Very good	38	Good
Melamine formaldehyde (fabric filled)	60–90	Very good	38	Average
Urea formaldehyde (cellulose filled)	38–90	Very good	51	Average
Phenol formaldehyde (mica filled)	38–50	Very good	36	Good
Acetals (glass filled)	58–75	Very good	27	Good

BHN = Brinell hardness number

See
- Emergency ice scraper, page 231

8. Some properties of metals compared

Table 1.11 compares some important properties of different metals other than strength. Metals are often selected for use where they can stand up to high **temperatures**, such as tungsten filaments in bulbs. They are also used for **electrical power** and in **communications**. Copper is most commonly used for electrical wires and cables, but aluminium is also used in larger sections to compensate for its higher resistance.

What would be the best metal in the table for a saucepan? Is it used for this purpose?

Table 1.11 Some physical properties of metallic elements

Element	Density (g cm^{-3})	Melting point (°C)	Boiling point (°C)	Thermal conductivity (W m^{-1} °C^{-1})	Coefficient of linear expansion (10^{-6} °C^{-1})	Electrical resistivity (nΩ m)	Main uses
Al	2.7	660	2400	205	23	27	Electrical wire
Cu	6.96	1083	2580	390	178	16.8	Electrical wire
Au	19.3	1063	2660	310	14	23	Jewellery/ Electrical contacts
Fe	7.9	1535	2900	76	12	97	Castings
Pb	11.3	327	1750	35	29	206	Pipes
Ni	8.9	1453	2820	91	13	68	Plating
Pt	21.5	1769	3800	69	9	106	Jewellery/ Electrical contacts
Ag	10.5	961	2180	418	19	16	Jewellery/ Photographic emulsions
Ta	16.6	3000	5300	54	6	135	Capacitors
Sn	7.3	232	2500	64	23	120	Surface coating
Ti	4.5	1680	3300	17	9	550	Aircraft parts
W	19.5	3380	6000	190	4.5	55	Light bulb elements
Zn	7.1	420	907	113	31	59	Surface cooling

9. Some properties of different materials compared

Sometimes it is useful to compare the properties of a wide range of different materials at a glance. Table 1.12 would enable a designer, for example, to think about insulators (electrical and thermal) and compare them with their weight.

Table 1.12   Some physical properties of non-metals

Material	Density (g cm^{-3})	Melting point (°C)	Thermal conductivity (W m^{-1} °C^{-1})	Coefficient of linear expansion (10^{-6} °C^{-1})	Electrical resistivity (MΩ m)	Main uses
Alumina	3.9	2050	21	8	10^3–10^6	High temperature linings, etc.
Brick	14.4–2.2	—	0.4–0.8	3–9	1–2	Structure and cladding in buildings
Concrete	2.4	—	1.0–1.5	10–14	—	Structure and cladding in buildings
Dry ground	1.6	—	—	—	0.01–0.1	All sorts!
Glass	2.4–3.5	1100	0.4–1.1	3–10	5 × 10^3 –10^6	Containers, windows, insulation
Granite	2.7	—	2.4	6–9	—	Decorative cladding, working surfaces
Mica	2.8	—	0.5	—	10^3–10^6	Insulation, as used in small windows
Nylon	1.14	200–220	0.25–0.33	80–130	10^4–10^7	Textiles, engineering components
Paper (dry)	1.0	—	0.06	—	10^4	Newspapers, magazines, books
Perspex	1.2	85–115	0.19–0.23	50–80	—	Models, experimental construction
Polystyrene	1.06	80–105	0.1	60–80	10^{10}	Engineering components, packaging
Polythene	0.93	65–130	0.25–0.5	110–220	10^5	Engineering components, packaging
PTFE	2.2	—	0.23–0.27	90–130	10^9	Engineering components, non-stick surfaces
PVC (plasticised)	1.7	70–80	0.16–0.19	50–250	10^4–10^7	Protection of components, clothing
Porcelain	2.4	1550	0.8–1.85	2.2	10^4–10^7	Containers, insulation: heat and electrical
Quartz (crystal)	2.65	—	5–9	7.5–13.7	10^6– 2 × 10^8	Crystal oscillators
Rubber (natural)	1.1–1.2	125	0.15	200	10^7	Tyres, insulation: heat, electrical and vibration
Sandstone	2.4	—	1.1–2.3	5–12	—	Structure and cladding in buildings
Timber (along grain)	0.4–0.8	—	0.15	3–5	—	All sorts!

Using the look-up tables

Designers use tables of information to help make them make decisions about what materials to employ. These decisions often mean compromises. There are few materials which are ideal in all respects: cheaper steel tools go rusty; clear plastic CD cases break; trainers wear down, and so on.

Using the tables to help you, list what materials you would consider for:

- the door of an immersion heater cupboard
- a tool rack for small garden tools
- an outside letterbox
- parts of a candle-heated hot plate for keeping food warm
- a small push-along toy for young children
- a cycle lock
- skateboard parts.

5 Manufacturing

In contemporary society most products are manufactured rather than hand-made. **Manufacturing** is the process where products are made on a large scale, using machinery. Modern large-scale manufacturing methods allow affordable products to be produced. Before the industrial revolution most people could not afford to buy products. They either made them themselves or bartered (exchanged) other goods, such as crops, for them. Only the very wealthy could afford to commission people to make things for them. If you were to go down any high street today you would find it very difficult to buy any products that had been made by hand rather than manufactured. When products are designed the manufacturing methods available must be considered by the designer. Effectively designed products will exploit the range of manufacturing processes available and reduce the amount of 'hand-finishing' or assembly required.

Manufacturing processes

All manufacturing processes, whether they are for metals, plastics or woods, can be classified into one of four groups. Knowing about these groups can help you decide how an existing product has been made and how a new product might be designed for manufacture.

Casting/moulding

The material is **fluidised** and poured or forced into a **mould** or **die**.

- Metals – Sand casting, investment (lost wax) casting, die casting, sintering.
- Plastics – Injection moulding, blow moulding, compression moulding, rotational moulding.
- Woods – Compression-moulded MDF or chipboard components.

Wasting

The product or component is made by **cutting**, **grinding** or **abrading** the material. Abrading a material is done by using abrasives such as glass paper, silicon carbide paper, carborundum, and so on.

- Metals – Cutting by turning, milling, drilling, water jet, laser, flame, or sawing and abrading.
- Plastics – Cutting by turning, milling, drilling, water jet, laser, or sawing and abrading.
- Woods – Cutting by turning, routing, planing, drilling, or sawing and abrading.

Forming

The material is **bent**, **stretched** or **squashed** to form a new shape. Thermoplastics (see page 39) have to be **plasticised** by heating them. Metals can be cold formed or they are sometimes heated to aid the forming process.

- Metals – Shearing or stamping, drawing and ironing, press forming, elastomeric forming, hydraulic forming.
- Plastics – Vacuum forming, heat bending.
- Woods – Laminating.

Fabricating

The product or component is made by **joining individual pieces** of material together by using adhesives, welding or mechanical fixings.

- Metals – Riveting, welding, oxyfuel gas welding, electric arc welding, resistance welding, mechanical fastenings, adhesives.
- Plastics – Adhesives, mechanical fixings.
- Woods – Adhesives, mechanical fixings, joints.

Many products use a combination of moulding, forming, fabricating and wasting when they are manufactured. Section 3 of this book – Small miracles of technology – describes how many common products are manufactured.

■ Manufacturing techniques for metals

Casting/moulding

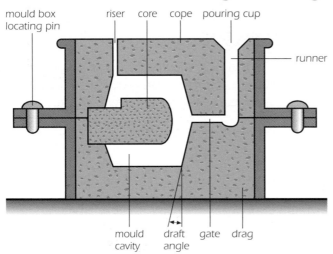

mould box
locating pin

riser   core   cope   pouring cup

runner

mould
cavity   draft
angle   gate   drag

Sand casting

Sand is the most commonly used material for creating expendable or single-use **moulds**. The process uses a **pattern** which is made from wood, aluminium or plastic. The pattern is made in the same form as the final component but it is slightly larger to allow for contraction when the metal cools. The pattern must have sloping sides (technically known as a **draft angle**) so that it can be withdrawn from the mould. Special sand is packed tightly around the pattern in a two-part case; the pattern is then carefully removed to form a **mould cavity**. The sand is normally mixed with a small percentage of clay or other binder to prevent it from crumbling. If the casting is to be hollow, a specially made sand core is suspended in the mould cavity and then knocked out of the final casting.

Molten metal is poured into the cavity through a **runner** which is drilled into the sand using a tube. When the mould cavity is full, often metal appears at the top of the second hole, or **riser**. Any shrinkage that takes place as the molten metal solidifies is drawn from the runner and riser.

Heavy machine parts, car engine blocks and vice bodies are among the many products manufactured by sand casting. For one-off castings, or castings that have a complex shape including undercuts, expanded polystyrene is sometimes used as the pattern which is left in the sand mould. It is burnt out as the molten metal is poured in.

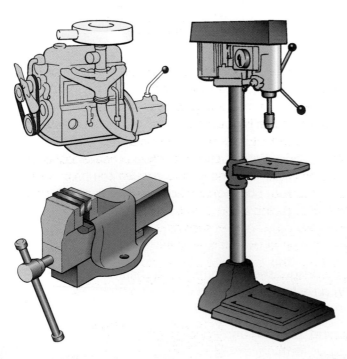

Lost wax (investment) casting

In this casting process, the form of the intended product is made as a **wax pattern** and placed in a mould material which sets hard around it. The wax is then melted out of the mould to leave a cavity for casting metal into. The mould material is usually a form of **plaster** which can resist high temperatures when it has set hard. The process is known as **investment** casting because the pattern is 'invested' in the plaster mould.

Investment casting has a very long history, but it is still commonly used to produce complex shapes in materials that are difficult to work in other ways and that could not be made by sand casting. Examples of products made by investment casting include cheap mass-produced jewellery, gold false teeth, and mascots for Rolls-Royce cars. The process is also used in some high-technology critical applications, including the manufacture of components such as jet engine turbine blades. The following sequence of illustrations shows the stages in casting a turbine blade using this method.

a Individual wax patterns produced by die casting

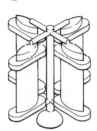

b Individual patterns assembled on to sprues (trees)

c Assembly placed in container and filled with ceramic slurry

d Flask heated to melt wax out

e Flask heated and molten metal poured in

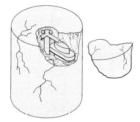

f Flask removed and investment broken away

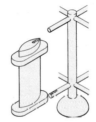

g Individual parts cut away from sprues, polished and machined

Die casting

In **die casting** a metal mould is used to cast low-temperature alloys based on zinc. The mould or die – which may be in two or more parts – can be made in a number of ways, including conventional machining or by a process called **spark erosion**. In **gravity die casting**, the metal is poured into the mould. In **pressure die casting**, the molten metal is forced into the die under pressure.

The die can be reused almost indefinitely. Dies can be costly to produce, but once the cost has been recovered the process is very cheap indeed when compared with sand or investment casting. Die casting is used to manufacture small metal toys, door handles, taps, small fixtures and fittings, and so on. It is also often used to produce the heavy rigid chassis, or base, needed by devices such as computer disk drives.

Note that as the number and type of polymers available increases, many **injection-moulded plastic** components (see page 39) are now used instead of die cast metal ones. Injection moulding is even cheaper than die casting.

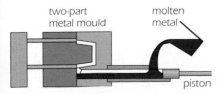

two-part metal mould | molten metal

piston

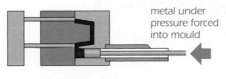

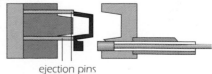

metal under pressure forced into mould

ejection pins

Sintering

Sintering is more of a moulding than a casting process. It uses a metal mould in the form of the intended product, which is filled with **powdered metal**. When this powder is subjected to both heat and pressure (below the melting point of the metal), the particles fuse, or sinter, together and form a solid mass. Sintering produces a porous metal material which can absorb oil, so it is often used for producing bearings and bushes. These components are normally made from a bronze powder which sometimes includes a graphite lubricant.

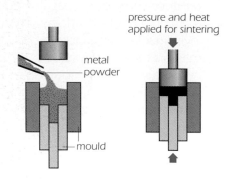

pressure and heat applied for sintering

metal powder

mould

Wasting

Lathe turning

Lathe turning is a very common manufacturing process in engineering. It normally uses a single-point cutting tool held in a tool post. The tool bit is specially shaped and angled. The tool can be made from high-speed steel (HSS) or tool steel with a very hard replaceable tip. There are several basic turning operations:

- longitudinal turning
- taper turning
- facing off
- parting off
- screw cutting.

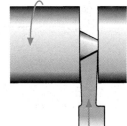
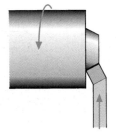
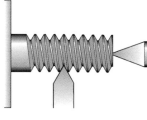

| longitudinal turning | taper turning | facing off | parting off | screw cutting |

In all lathe turning operations the rotating workpiece must be turning at the correct speed. This can be determined from a look-up table. In the case of screw cutting, the speed of the workpiece is synchronised with the speed of the moving tool. The tool is ground to the profile of the thread being cut.

Many lathes used in industry now use **computer numeric control (CNC)** (see page 45). A computer is programmed with machining instructions, and the two axes of movement of the tool and the speed of the workpiece are then controlled entirely by the computer.

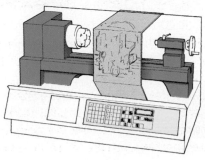

CNC lathe

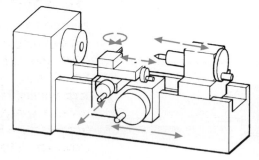

manually operated lathe

Vertical milling

A **vertical milling** machine uses a multi-point **cutter** held in a **chuck**. The head remains stationary while a moving table holding the workpiece moves along x, y and z axes. It is also possible to tilt the head of the milling machine at an angle in some cases.

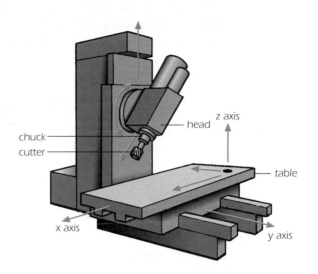

There are a wide variety of milling cutters for vertical milling machines but the most common ones are **end mills**. These can be used for a variety of surfacing operations or for cutting channels or slots. An end mill is not designed to drill down into a workpiece; holes have to be drilled prior to milling out a blind channel.

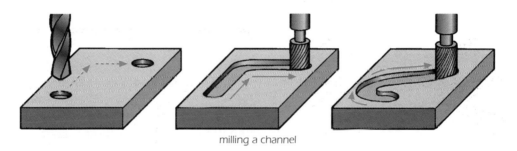

milling a channel

Alternatively a **slot drill** can be used. Slot drills have only two cutting surfaces, but these extend right to the centre of the cutter end. This allows them to be plunged into the surface of the workpiece. However, slot drills have the disadvantage that they cannot clear the waste material, or swarf, away as quickly as end mills as they have fewer flutes. This means that material feed speeds must be slower.

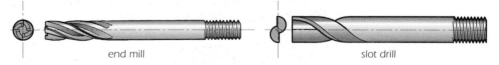

end mill   slot drill

Most milling machines used in industry now use computer numeric control (CNC) (see page 45). A computer is programmed with the necessary cutting information, including cutter speed, table feed rate, and x, y and z axes movements. The computer then controls the operation of the mill. It is a highly skilled and complex process to cut curved profiles using a vertical mill, which requires the addition of specialist devices like rotating tables and dividing heads. However, cutting curved profiles with a CNC mill is a very easy process.

twist drill   reamer

Drilling

This is perhaps the most common of all machining operations. However, the bulk of holes that we drill are produced to fairly wide dimensional tolerance. When a very accurately sized hole with smooth sides is needed, the workpiece is drilled slightly undersize and then finished by passing through a **reamer**.

A **twist drill** is made from high speed steel (HSS) and has a complex shape or geometry. The cutting is done by the drill tip and the waste material, or **swarf**, is cleared as it passes up the **flutes**. The drill illustrated is a large diameter type with a tapered **shank** or **quill**. This fits directly into the drilling machine or lathe tailstock in place of the chuck. Drills of less than 13 mm diameter have a parallel-sided shank which is held by a chuck.

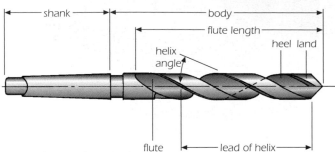

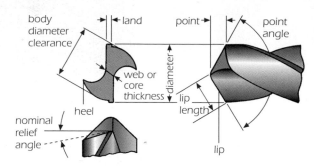

When a large drill is used, a smaller **pilot hole**, or series of pilot holes, is drilled first so that the core, or web, of the larger drill can pass through. The recommended speeds for drill diameter and material type can be found by taking a series of measurements, illustrated in the figure above. Look-up tables can be obtained which contain this information. Generally speaking, the larger the drill the slower the drilling speed.

Forming

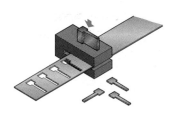

Shearing or stamping

A paper hole-punch performs a simple **shearing** operation to produce a hole. The same principle is used in industry to make holes of different shapes or to punch out, or stamp out, many identical flat shapes. Shapes that are punched out are very often then put through another forming operation to give them their final shape; for example the metal sliding cover on floppy disks and optical disks is stamped out from a strip and then bent around a former. The small tag that attaches to the spring is also formed at this stage.

Drawing and ironing

In a **drawing** operation, a punched-out blank of metal is placed between two tools and pushed into a cylindrical form. Aluminium drink cans are made by a combination of drawing and **ironing**. As the metal is forced into shape it passes through a series of very hard steel **ironing rings** which reduce the thickness of the cylinder and polish the material.

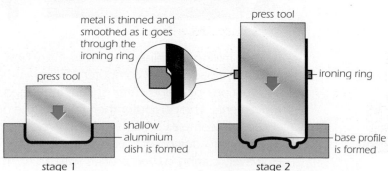

Press forming

Press forming tools normally have at least two hardened steel parts which are squeezed together with the sheet metal workpiece in between. A two-part press tool for making metal channel sections is illustrated. This tool can be operated in a large vice, but in industry a large hydraulic or mechanical press is normally used. Extremely large and expensive press tools are manufactured for car body components. Equally large presses are needed for the pressing operation.

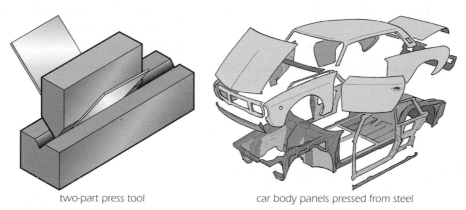

two-part press tool   car body panels pressed from steel

Elastomeric forming

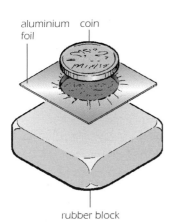

aluminium coin
foil

rubber block

In **elastomeric** forming, a special rubber block is used in place of one half of the press tool. As the workpiece is squeezed between the steel tool and the rubber, the rubber yields and the metal takes up the shape of the steel tool. Elastomeric forming avoids the cost of making the two intermatching steel parts needed in a conventional press tool. Elastomeric forming is very useful for producing small, detailed formings.

You can demonstrate the principle of elastomeric forming by using a pencil eraser as the rubber block. Place a sheet of aluminium foil over the rubber and then press a coin into it. The foil will take up the shape of the coin.

Jewellers and silversmiths sometimes use a small-scale form of elastomeric forming to produce domed shapes. A 'tool' is cut out from a piece of thick acrylic sheet. The metal is laid on to a layer of *Blu-Tack* and then the acrylic tool is forced down on to it, normally with a fly-press. The *Blu-Tack* forces the metal through the hole in the acrylic, forming the dome shape in the metal.

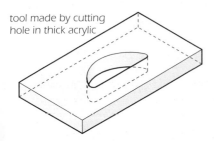

tool made by cutting
hole in thick acrylic

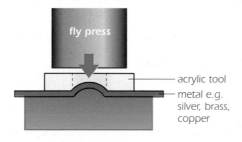

fly press

acrylic tool

metal e.g.
silver, brass,
copper

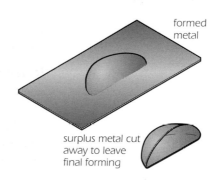

formed
metal

surplus metal cut
away to leave
final forming

Hydraulic forming

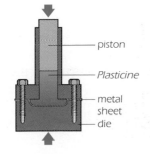

piston

Plasticine

metal
sheet
die

In **hydraulic** forming, sheet metal is pressed into a steel die or mould by means of fluid under pressure. Hydraulic forming is used to form large sheets of material and to reduce the cost of producing conventional press tools. A simple hydraulic forming press which uses *Plasticine* as the hydraulic 'fluid' can be made very easily to use this manufacturing process on a small scale.

Fabricating

Riveting

Various forms of **riveting** have been used for thousands of years to join two pieces of metal together. They produce a permanent fixing and so are used in applications where the components do not need to be easily disassembled. Rivets are still used today in many applications, ranging from large-scale structures like bridges down to small-scale objects like kitchen utensils.

In its simplest form a rivet is a metal rod which is passed through a hole. One end of the rivet may have a domed, flat or countersunk head already on it. However, in some applications, such as silversmithing, the rivets are made by the silversmith from the raw material. The metal rivet passes through the hole and a second head is formed on the plain end. This is achieved either with a hammer and punch or, more commonly, using a **rivet set**. A rivet set is a special punch with the profile of the domed head shape ground into its end.

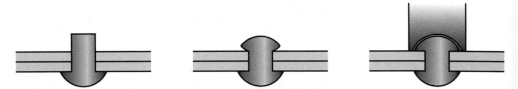

Recently there has been a general trend towards using special welding techniques in place of riveting. This is because welding uses fewer components, is less subject to stress concentration points and is more easily automated. However, new techniques of riveting have been developed for particular applications. One of these techniques involves pressing part of one sheet through a hole in the other sheet. This technique removes the need for a separate rivet. It is used to fasten the ring-pull on to aluminium drink cans. A similar joining method has recently been developed that simply pushes two sheet materials together in a similar way but without the initial hole.

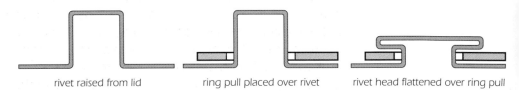

rivet raised from lid   ring pull placed over rivet   rivet head flattened over ring pull

Welding

In a **welding** operation, the metal from two or more parts to be joined is melted and run together. When the metal solidifies the parts fuse together. Welding produces a very strong permanent fixing. There are five main categories of welding.

- **Oxyfuel gas** welding – Processes where the heat from a gas/oxygen flame is used to melt the metals involved, for example oxy-acetylene.
- **Electric arc** welding – Processes in which an electric arc is used to generate the heat necessary to melt the metals involved.
- **Resistance** welding – Processes in which the electrical resistance of the metals involved generates the heat necessary when a current passes through them. Spot welding is a form of resistance welding.
- **Solid state** welding – Processes where the heat is generated internally in the metals involved by phenomena such as friction.
- Other processes – A range of other processes which use other physical phenomena to generate the necessary heat. Examples include the use of laser beams or electron beams.

Oxyfuel gas welding

In this process a gas is burnt in oxygen which generates an intensely hot flame. Today the gas **acetylene** is almost universally used, which gives rise to the term **oxy-acetylene welding**. The flame produced has two distinct zones, the tip of the inner zone being the hottest point in the flame and the part which is generally used for welding. The combustion at this point is complete and, as all of the oxygen has been consumed, the flame is neutral and will not oxidise the metals to be joined. In the outer zone the excess of acetylene causes some of the oxygen in the surrounding atmosphere to be used in combustion, thus further protecting the metal from oxidation. The joint is assembled and the flame applied to the weld area. When welding temperature is reached, a steel welding rod is fed into the joint, and both rod and flame are gradually moved together to run the weld along the joint.

Electric arc welding

In this process, an **electric arc** is created between an electrode and the workpiece. The electrodes are made of metal, generally being the same material as that to be joined, and are consumed by being melted to form part of the join. In some more specialised arc welding processes tungsten is used as an electrode, and this is consumed very slowly by evaporation.

Consumable electrodes are coated with a material which burns off to form a protective atmosphere around the weld. By preventing oxygen from contacting the hot weld surfaces, this greatly reduces the danger of oxidation of the weld.

Some forms of arc welding also use an inert gaseous shield to prevent contamination of the weld. The commonest gas used is **argon** which gives rise to the term **argon-arc welding**.

The arc generated during welding has a temperature in excess of 3000 °C and emits a very bright light. As with gas welding, the operator's eyes must be protected from the light by a dark-coloured translucent screen.

Resistance welding

This process relies on the heat released due to resistance when a large electric current is passed through the materials. The most common use of the technique at the present time is in **spot welding**. Spot welding (a form of **resistance welding**) is used in the motor manufacturing industry to assemble car bodies.

In spot welding, a current is passed through the two metals to be joined using a pair of cylindrical electrodes, one on each side of the sheet. These are clamped over the metal sheets while the current flows. Spot welding is a very appropriate process for automation. Robotic spot welding production lines are now often used in the motor manufacturing industries. The illustration shows the general assembly of a spot welding head in use, along with the form of the finished weld.

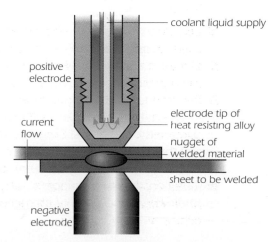

See

- Desktop furniture, page 242
- Construction system, page 246

Mechanical fastenings

Mechanical fastenings are a cheap and simple method to produce semi-permanent fixings. They are used in applications where the components need to be disassembled for maintenance, service or modification. There are thousands of different types of mechanical fastenings available for joining metals (and dissimilar materials) together. Some of the more common of these fastenings are illustrated. They all use a screw thread which results in a strong locking force. Screws, nuts and bolts are the most common and convenient to use of all **mechanical fastenings**.

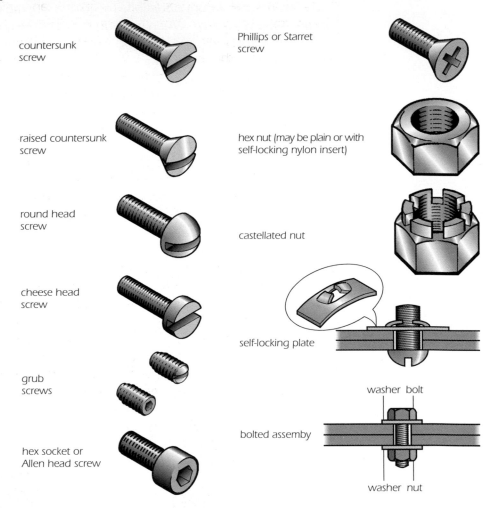

countersunk screw

raised countersunk screw

round head screw

cheese head screw

grub screws

hex socket or Allen head screw

Phillips or Starret screw

hex nut (may be plain or with self-locking nylon insert)

castellated nut

self-locking plate

bolted assemby

washer bolt

washer nut

Adhesives

Advances in the understanding of materials have resulted in a huge range of new engineering **adhesives**. Adhesives are now used to join metals and other materials in structural applications such as aircraft where previously the method was not considered permanent or safe enough.

The most commonly available adhesives for joining metals available in school workshops are **epoxy resins**, such as *Araldite*, and **double-sided tapes** and **pads**. An enlarged range of double-sided adhesive tapes from the 3M company includes a UHB (ultra-high bonding) tape which is currently used to fasten the body panels on to buses! Common double-sided tapes make an extremely strong joint if the surface areas to be joined are relatively large. As with any type of adhesive joint, the strength of the bond depends largely on the surface preparation. Any two surfaces to be joined must be chemically cleaned, for example by wiping down with methylated spirits. (See also Adhesives, page 158.)

Manufacturing techniques for plastics

Polymers used for making things can be divided broadly into two groups:

- thermoplastics
- thermosets.

Thermoplastic materials such as **polythene**, **polystyrene** and **acrylic** soften or become fused when heated. In this condition they can be formed into shape using a variety of methods. The shape remains permanent when the material has cooled down. The same thermoplastic material can be heated, softened, shaped and cooled many times. This explains how it is possible to recycle some plastics.

Thermosetting materials such as **epoxies**, **polyester resin** and **melamine** can be moulded into shape only once. The chemical process that takes place during the moulding or curing is irreversible and results in the **cross-linking** of molecules. Cross-linked molecules cannot 'slip' when heated as they can in a thermoplastic. Generally speaking, thermosetting plastics can withstand higher temperatures than thermoplastics. If they are heated excessively, the material simply breaks down.

Although it is still possible to divide manufacturing processes into those suitable for thermoplastics and those suitable for thermosets, the rapid emergence of new plastics, **co-polymers** and **fibre-reinforced** materials, together with new moulding techniques, has started to blur this distinction.

Casting/moulding

Injection moulding (thermoplastics)

Injection moulding is the most widely used commercial method for producing moulded plastic goods. Although the costs of the mould, or tool, are high, the unit cost for each moulding become very small if large numbers of goods are produced. Precision injection moulding has largely replaced the small metal parts that were once machined. It is also now being used for many small components that were previously die cast in metal. Large-scale injection mouldings, ranging in size from dustbins to complete boats, have also made many products much cheaper.

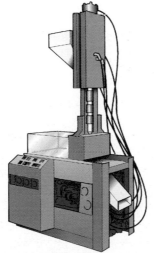
industrial injection moulding machine

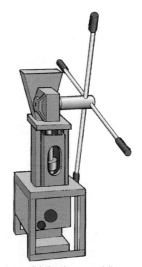
small injection moulding machine

Injection moulding is a fairly simple process, although moulds and mould making can be very complex indeed. Plastic granules are fed from a hopper into a heated barrel and forced under pressure into a mould. The smaller injection moulding machines use a ram to force plastic into the mould, whilst industrial machines use a slowly rotating screw (like a mincing machine).

See
- Space frame display system, page 225
- Injection-moulded product, page 243

Injection moulding can be carried out on a small scale using a **hot melt glue gun** to inject the plastic into a mould. Hot melt **glue sticks** are now available in a wide variety of colours. The mould can be made from a length of wire section trapped between two plates or at least three metal plates where the centre plate has a cavity cut out.

Note that if the glue gun method is used, you must coat the surface of the mould with a silicon release spray or a light lubricant such as *WD40*, otherwise the glue will stick the mould together!

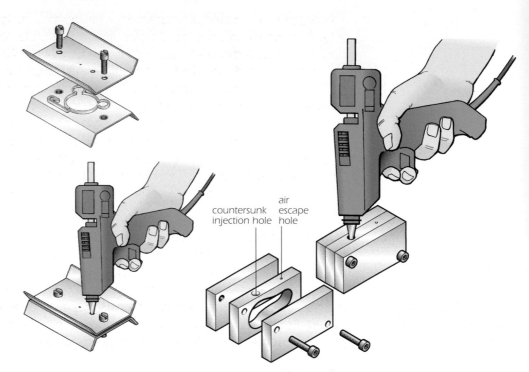

Note: can be more than one plate in centre to produce layered forms

Blow moulding (thermoplastics)

This process uses a thermoplastic polymer in a plastic state but, in this case, the material is **blown** into the mould. The majority of bottles and hollow containers are made in this way, starting off as a hot tube of polymer through which air is blown. Sometimes blow moulding begins with a fused mass of material which is converted into a tube by a mandrel. Sometimes the process starts at stage 3 with a length of tube introduced into the mould.

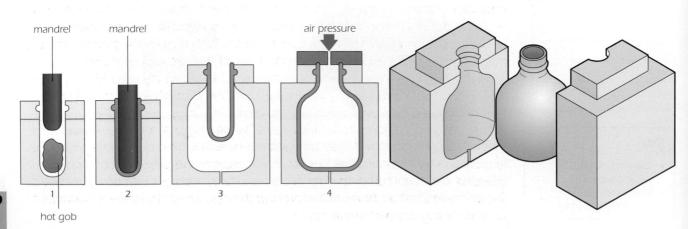

Compression moulding (thermosets)

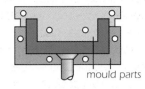
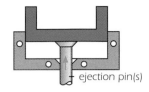

1 granules placed in open die   2 heated dies closed   3 finished component ejected

polymer   mould parts   ejection pin(s)

This process uses **powder** or **granules** of a thermosetting polymer. The polymer is loaded into the press either as granules or as a tablet-like 'preform'. Such preforms allow a measured quantity of the polymer to be compressed into a form which is easily handled and has a premeasured weight.

Once the powder or preform has been placed into the mould, the heated **plunger** is brought in to press the polymer into the mould. This plunger, which also forms part of the mould shape, fuses the polymer, enabling it to flow smoothly into the mould. In some processes the volume of polymer is accurately measured to enable the mould to be adequately filled but, in most processes, excess material is used and provision is made for this to flow over the edge of the mould, forming 'flash'. The flash needs to be removed after pressing and, as this is a further process, adds to the cost of the moulding.

See

- Ergonomic handle, page 229
- Clock, page 237
- Hi-tech pen, page 244
- Construction system, page 246

Rotational moulding (thermoplastics)

In this process the correct amount of thermoplastic paste, which is normally plasticised PVC, is put into a hollow mould. The mould is then placed into an oven and **rotated** in two directions at once. The plastic evenly coats the inside of the hollow mould. After cooling, the hollow plastic product is ejected from the mould. Rotational moulding is a simple way of producing cheap hollow plastic products such as footballs, toys and large containers.

Forming

Vacuum forming (thermoplastics)

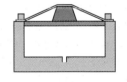
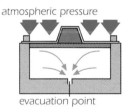

sheet plastic

mould

atmospheric pressure

evacuation point

1 heating   2 raising platen   3 pumping air out of chamber

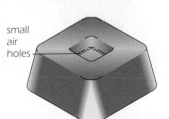

small air holes   draft angle

small air holes

In **vacuum forming** a sheet of thermoplastic material is clamped over a **vacuum chamber** containing a pattern which has the same shape as the component to be formed. Heat is applied by an electric heating element until the sheet becomes soft and pliable. The platen is lifted, which pushes the pattern into the plastic sheet, and then the air is pumped out of the vacuum chamber. Atmospheric pressure will then push the plastic sheet tightly around the pattern.

The cost of pattern making for vacuum forming is much lower than that of making tools for injection moulding. However, the moulding has the disadvantage of needing to be trimmed of waste material. Patterns should have a good surface finish and their sides should have a gentle slope, or draft angle. Undercuts should be avoided, as these will prevent the pattern from being released from the moulding. Any negative details, such as blind holes or cavities, should have small air holes drilled around their perimeter to prevent pockets of air from being trapped in the cavity.

Manufacturing techniques for wood

Modern mass manufacturing methods for wood-based products do not use many of the traditional woodworking techniques. Much use is made of manufactured board materials such as **MDF** and **chipboard**. These materials behave more predictably than timbers when they are machined, are readily available in large sizes and enable cheaper products to be produced. The majority of the timber used today comes from managed sustainable sources and is relatively quick to grow, such as pine, beech, birch, and so on. Again, this enables cheaper products to be produced and is less damaging to the environment.

Wasting

Machining

Modern woodworking machinery tends to be multifunctional and is often **computer numeric controlled (CNC)** (see page 45). For example, an industrial-scale **CNC router** can be programmed to undertake all of the cutting, drilling and shaping operations needed to produce the components for a kitchen cabinet from melamine-faced chipboard.

The machine itself is similar to a vertical mill except that the cutter rotates far more quickly. Industrial machines use a **vacuum table** to hold down the workpiece whilst it is being cut, drilled and shaped.

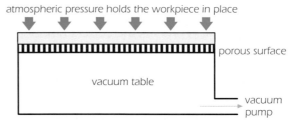

atmospheric pressure holds the workpiece in place

porous surface

vacuum table

vacuum pump

Although CNC routing is incredibly adaptable and capable of many individual operations, the machining process is typically limited to one face of the board being cut. When a new product is designed for manufacture by this process the designer must bear this in mind and make the appropriate decisions. The necessity to put the board through further machining operations will increase the cost of the product.

Industrial-scale CNC routers are very expensive indeed. However, a hand-operated **plunge router** with a good selection of accessories will enable most of the industrial processes to be simulated in a workshop. If it is possible to make the prototype with a plunge router then it is very likely that the product will be suitable for mass manufacture using modern production methods.

Forming

Laminating to provide a surface finish

The first main purpose of **laminating** is to apply a tough easy-clean surface to **chipboard** and occasionally to **MDF**.

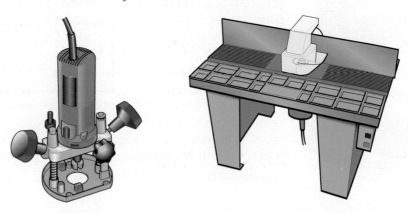

Plastic laminates are available in a staggeringly diverse range of colours and textures as well as the predominant black or white that is often seen in cheap furniture stores. Although plastic laminates fell out of favour a little in the late 1970s and early 1980s, there is a new-found interest in their use. This interest was started again by the Memphis Group of Italian designers who used very brightly coloured and patterned laminates in their post-modern furniture. Interest continues today as products like *Formica*, a **melamine** laminate, increase in technical sophistication. A recent range of *Formica* has a textured 'metallised' finish and is almost indistinguishable from brushed aluminium or stainless steel. Some of these more exotic laminates can be very expensive indeed. Plastic laminates no longer have to be a cheap substitute for solid wood, and are offering designers new and interesting possibilities.

Plastic laminates are applied to manufactured boards using an **adhesive**. When adhesives cure, or set, they contract. This contraction can cause problems when using plastic laminates. As the adhesive cures and contracts, relatively large stresses are set up across the laminated surface of the board. These stresses will eventually bend or warp the board. To overcome this problem all laminated boards should have a second sheet of laminate applied to the reverse. The second sheet will set up opposing stresses which will balance those from the top sheet. This explains why the bottom sheet is often referred to as a **balance sheet**.

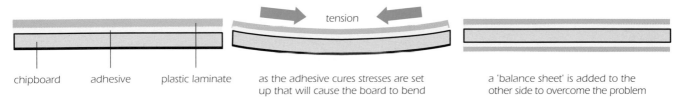

chipboard   adhesive   plastic laminate

as the adhesive cures stresses are set up that will cause the board to bend

a 'balance sheet' is added to the other side to overcome the problem

Laminating as a forming technique

Plywood is made from thin sheets of wood which are glued together with an **adhesive**, which produces a strong board that has a natural wood finish. However, plywood does not have to be flat. The thin plies of wood can be moulded in a **former** as they are glued together. This allows the production of very strong curved forms which are extensively used in the furniture industry. The process has also been used in architecture to form very large, curved, laminated beam sections.

In industry, complex moulds and high-power presses are used, but laminating can be done in the workshop using some simple techniques. It is quite difficult and time-consuming to prepare individual laminas, but thin plywood ranging from 1 to 4 mm can be used instead. For small forms a mould can be made from a single block of wood that has the desired profile cut through it by using a bandsaw. The two pieces then form the male and female moulds.

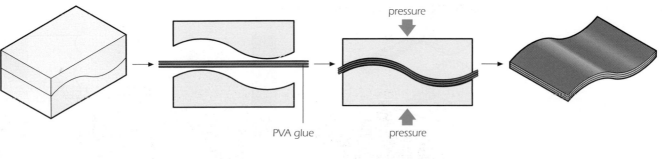

mould made from block of wood, which has profile cut using a bandsaw

the plies are 'laid up' between the moulds with PVA glue on the mating surfaces

PVA glue

pressure

pressure is applied to the mould, e.g. in a vice, and the glue is left to cure

the finished forming

For larger forms, such as furniture, it is obviously not possible to cut the moulds from a single block of wood! In these circumstances a box is made using cheap shuttering ply or similar material.

With larger-scale mouldings it is necessary to make allowances in the mould for the thickness of the plies. It is also useful to 'lay up' the dry lamina in the mould first to check that all is well before reassembling with glue. Cascamite adhesive has a longer initial curing time than PVA and so is more useful for larger-scale laminating processes where extra time is needed to lay up the mould and make adjustments.

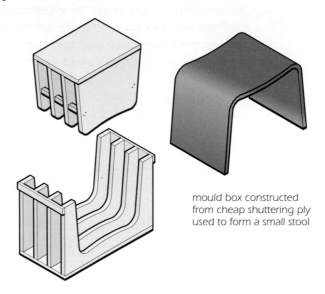

mould box constructed from cheap shuttering ply used to form a small stool

Fabricating

Mechanical fixings

Many of the traditional mechanical fixings that are available, such as nails, screws and hinges, are not suitable for use with manufactured boards. A range of modified or specially developed mechanical fixings are available for use with chipboard and MDF.

sharp corners

rounded corners

conventional wood screw

chipboard screw

- Chipboard screws – These tend to have a larger thread pitch and deeper profile. This allows the screw to cut into the chipboard to give a strong fixing without bursting the board apart.
- Knockdown fixings – These are based on either the rod and screw or the cam lock principles. They are often used when a strong fixing is needed between two boards set at 90° to each other, often in conjunction with dowels or a rebate.

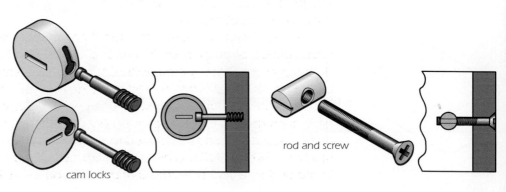

cam locks

rod and screw

Computer-aided manufacture (CAM)

Computer-aided manufacturing (CAM) techniques are now extensively used in industry. CAM uses computer-controlled machines like lathes, mills and routers and, more recently, more innovative machines like water jet and laser cutters. When used along with computer-aided design (CAD) (see page 93) the combination provides a powerful manufacturing process that is very flexible and improves quality control, reduces labour costs, increases levels of production and enables greater predictability of outcome and costings. CAD/CAM processes are often referred to as **computer integrated manufacturing**, or **CIM**, and their use has brought about the possibility of **concurrent engineering** – the process where many individual specialists work on a design simultaneously in a computer-generated, virtual environment.

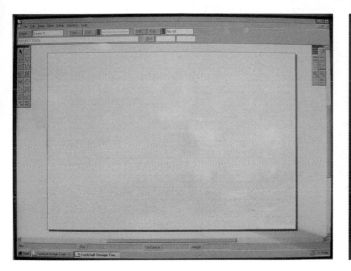

CAD menus on screen

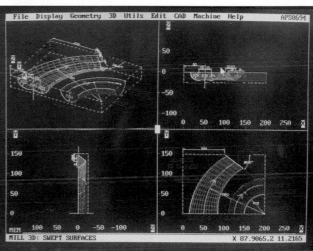

component design using CAD

In a simple linear process the finalised design ideas are input into the computer using a CAD package. Many packages offer the facility to view the product in three dimensions, to render it in realistic colours and textures, and also to animate it. Some packages also allow for mathematical analysis of the product, in terms of structural strength, materials costing, and so on. Some car manufacturers now do most of their vehicle design and testing in a virtual environment. A new car can be designed and performance tested without the need for a prototype to be made. Some advanced systems even allow the virtual car to be crash tested so that any necessary safety modifications can be made. This process drastically reduces the amount of time it takes to get a new car from the initial concept to market.

The CAD file can be output to a **rapid prototyping machine** (see page 46) which gives a physical three-dimensional model to aid in the final stages of the design process. Once complete the CAD file is transferred to a **machining**, or **processor, package** which is used to define the type of machine that will be used and how the machining will be carried out. Once the various parameters have been defined the file is then output in **numeric code (NC)**. This is the general standard code that is used to drive computer numeric control (CNC) machines. When CNC machines were first developed the code had to be typed in line by line, a very time-consuming and laborious activity indeed!

The NC file is then opened in a **post-processor package**. This will be specific to the machine that will perform the cutting operations. The post-processor checks that the NC file is within the operating parameters of the machine and then controls the machine whilst it performs the cutting operations.

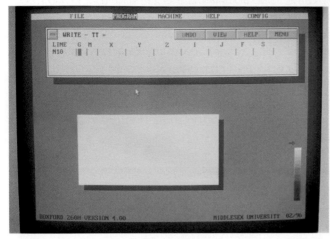

CAD file on screen

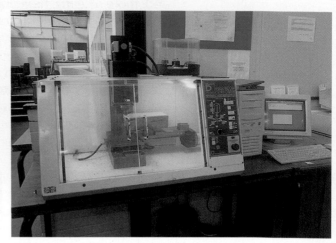

CNC machine

Rapid prototyping

Rapid prototyping is a relatively new process and there are several systems available. Essentially, a rapid prototyping machine is like a 3D printer for CAD files. Instead of printing in ink, the machine uses a solid material to 'grow' a three-dimensional product. Rapid prototyping machines are still very costly to purchase and operate, so many companies rent time on machines or pay external agencies by the job. However, as technology moves on and new systems are developed, it should not be too long before systems are available that are no more expensive than a good quality laser printer – in fact some of the newest wax-based systems (see page 47) are almost there already.

Paper laminate systems

The system splits the CAD file information into layers. The machine then cuts out each layer in paper and sticks the layers together. The final output is like a contour map of the three-dimensional product and has very small ridges where the layers of paper join. This system was one of the first to become available but is still in use today. It is currently one of the cheapest systems to operate.

Resin-based systems

Resin-based systems use a special resin that sets hard when a laser is fired at it. Again, these systems split the CAD file information into layers to build the model. A platform is lowered into a resin bath and then raised out again. This leaves a thin layer of resin on the top of the platform. A controlled laser beam is then fired at the necessary points on that layer to set the resin hard. The platform is then lowered into the resin bath and raised out again. This coats the top surface with resin and the laser then cures the next layer. The process is repeated until the model is finished.

Resin-based systems produce very accurate, well-finished and realistic models. Because the model is built up in very thin layers and defined by a laser, it is also possible to include internal details. Resin-based systems are very expensive to operate but they give such good results that the cost is worthwhile, particularly if the product is going to be mass produced and the manufacturers need to be very sure that the design will perform as necessary. Producing injection-moulding tools is a very costly business. Resin-based rapid prototyping systems enable designers to ensure that everything is correct before the tooling is made.

Wax-based systems

One of the most recently available systems works in a very similar way to a conventional inkjet printer. However, instead of printing in ink the system uses a special wax that air dries. Again the system splits the CAD file information into thin layers. The machine then 'prints' the first layer using the wax that is squirted from a cartridge through a very fine nozzle. The machine bed then moves downwards by a very small amount. The next layer of wax is then 'printed'. This process is repeated until the final model is complete. As the jet of wax is very fine and the layers are very thin, a high level of internal and external detailing can be achieved. Wax-based systems can still only produce small models in comparison with resin-based systems, but they show the most potential for eventually being developed into a low-cost system that anybody might have access to.

Product modelling

Design sketches, rendered presentation drawings, three-dimensional CAD images and animations are all important communication tools that are used in the process of **product development** (see pages 83–94). However, being able to hold, feel and 'operate' a three-dimensional model of the product provides the best form of communication about how a design will actually perform when it is manufactured.

Product models also allow designers to establish the feasibility and appropriateness of their designs before very costly processes like rapid prototyping and toolmaking take place. When new products are undergoing development a whole series of models can be made to aid the design development process.

Sketch models

Sketch models are often made alongside initial design sketches to test and firm up ideas at the start of the design development process. They are normally made from high density polystyrene foam which can be rapidly cut and shaped using conventional saws, files and abrasive papers.

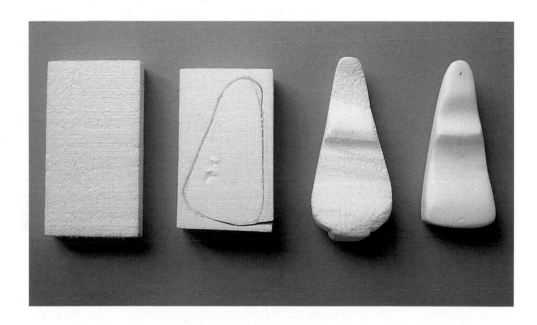

Grey/white models

Grey or white models are often used when the design development is reaching its final stages. They are more highly finished than sketch models and, when professionally produced, are made from resin or *Ureal* (plastic wood). Both of these materials require special handling as the dust is highly toxic. However, very good results can be achieved using **gelutong**. This is a close-grained wood that is very easy to cut and shape. At this stage the models are grey or white so that the designer can concentrate entirely on the form of the product, its anthropometric correctness and ergonomic performance. Colour can often distract the designer from this analysis, as it can give other subtle messages; for example, a yellow product will look larger than a dark-coloured version and will have a 'sporty' feel.

The images in the photograph below show the process of producing a grey model from a block of gelutong.

1 Accurate side, face and end elevations are drawn on the block.
2 The profile of the side and face elevation is then cut round using a bandsaw. The block is reassembled at each stage using masking tape to allow the next profile to be cut easily.
3 The waste material is removed and the model is roughly shaped using surform cutters.
4 The model is then sanded to the final form.
5 Grey spray primer is then applied to finish the model.

Product models

Final product models have all of the detail applied and are correctly coloured. Again, they are professionally produced using resin or *Ureal* (plastic wood) but, with care, professional-looking results can be achieved using gelutong. Good preparation will enable a very high level of finish. The series of images below show how to prepare and paint a gelutong model.

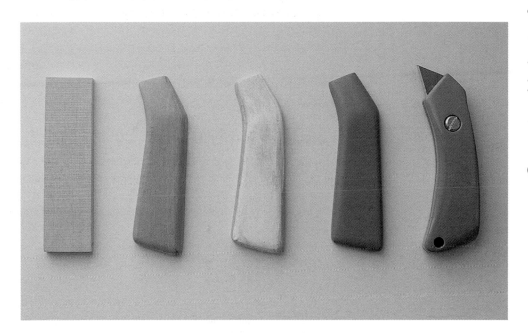

1 The gelutong is shaped into the desired form and sanded smooth.
2 A coating of filler, such as *Polyfilla*, is applied over the whole surface by spreading it on with a finger.
3 The filler is then carefully sanded back to the wood. This will seal any open cells in the surface of the wood.
4 Coats of primer, or filler primer, are then applied. Each coat is left to dry and then rubbed down with very fine grades of wet and dry, then flour paper. The final primer coat is rubbed down lightly using fine wire wool. Three or four coats of primer should be sufficient.
5 The final coloured topcoat is then carefully applied.

Details can be added to product models in a number of ways. If the model contains switches, sockets, lights, and so on, then it is best to include real versions of these. Why spend time modelling a switch that already exists? Letters and logos can be applied using rub down letters (such as *Letraset*), colour printouts from computers or engraved/machined components from CNC machines. A good product model should look as far as possible like the real product and not like a piece of painted wood!

Product prototypes which address the internal workings of a product are also often made at this final design development stage. They use the same components that the final product will use and this is arranged in a similar way to the final product. Product prototypes are often held together on aluminium frameworks or an acrylic chassis. The product prototype and product model make a very powerful combination for a product designer to communicate their design proposals to a manufacturing company.

6 Control

Designing control systems

Designing a control system can be a complex task, as control systems often contain electrical, electronic and mechanical components and need to respond to inputs from a variety of sources. The system may also need to control the operation of a number of different outputs. However, the design process can be made easier by using a design 'tool'. These 'tools' are simply a way of representing how the control system will operate rather than how the actual operations will be achieved. Once the operation of the control system has been decided on, the various ways in which it can be achieved can be considered.

Control statements

At the start of the design process it is useful to write a **control statement**. This can be in the form of a single sentence or a short paragraph and describes in words exactly how the control system will operate. The most useful way to write the statement is to use sentences that use an IF. . .THEN. . . construction; for example:

> If the button is pressed then the door will open.

Now the designer has a clear indication of what has to be achieved and can start to make decisions about how it will be done. Will the system be purely **mechanical**, where the button operates a lever that trips a latch? Will the system be **electrical**, where the button is a switch that operates a **solenoid** which pulls back a bolt? Or will the system be **electronic**, where the button operates a **timer** that operates a solenoid to pull back a bolt which automatically locks again after a set period of time?

Of course, as the operation of the system gets more complicated then more sentences are needed in the statement. However, the statement will often help in deciding exactly what is needed to achieve the desired operation; for example:

- If the greenhouse gets too hot or the 'open' button is pressed then the window will open.
- If the window is fully open then the drive system will stop automatically.
- If the greenhouse is too cold or the 'close' button is pressed then the window will close.
- If the window is fully closed then the drive system will stop automatically.

These statements show that the system will need some form of heat **sensor** that can decide when the greenhouse is too hot or too cold, a **logic** system that can enable the sensor output to be used alongside the manual switches, and some form of **feedback** that can tell the system when the window is fully opened or fully closed.

Control statements are really just a way to help you think clearly when designing a control system and to help in communicating your intentions to others.

Flowcharts

Flowcharts are a method of representing how a control system will operate, but instead of using sentences they use graphic symbols.

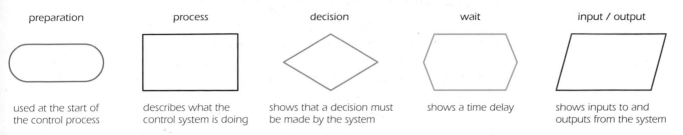

preparation	process	decision	wait	input / output
used at the start of the control process	describes what the control system is doing	shows that a decision must be made by the system	shows a time delay	shows inputs to and outputs from the system

As with control statements they show how a control system will operate without showing how the operations will actually be achieved. Control statements can be converted into flowcharts or they can be used as a starting point in the design process. The example below shows the flowchart for the greenhouse window system described in the control statements above.

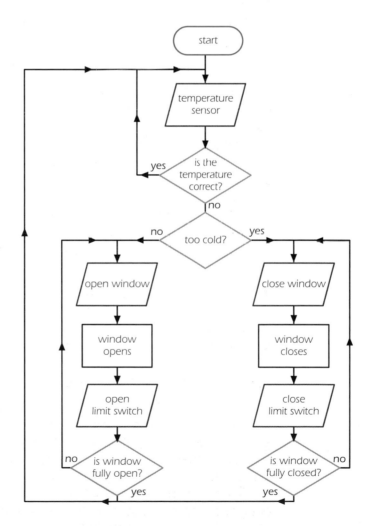

Flowcharts are very useful in setting down clearly how a control system will operate. They allow you to get a visual representation of the control system and make it very easy to communicate your intentions to others. Flowcharts are useful in other applications where the operation of a system, or a sequence of events, needs to be decided and represented, for example in computer software design, in project planning, and so on.

Designing control systems

Block diagrams

Once the operation of the control system has been decided, using control statements and flowcharts, the next stage is to draw a **block diagram**. This form of diagram breaks the control system into blocks, each performing one major function in the control system. Block diagrams allow you to begin thinking about how the operations might be achieved without getting hampered by individual components and how they might be connected.

Block diagrams can be used to represent mechanical, electrical and electronic systems. They are constructed from a series of blocks which have their function written into them. The blocks are then connected with mechanical or electrical/electronic links.

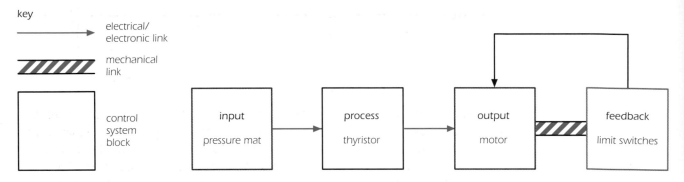

The example shows a block diagram for the greenhouse window system used in the control statements and flowcharts above. Block diagrams are constructed so that they can be read from left to right. Input blocks begin at the left and the system progresses towards the right, to end in the output blocks.

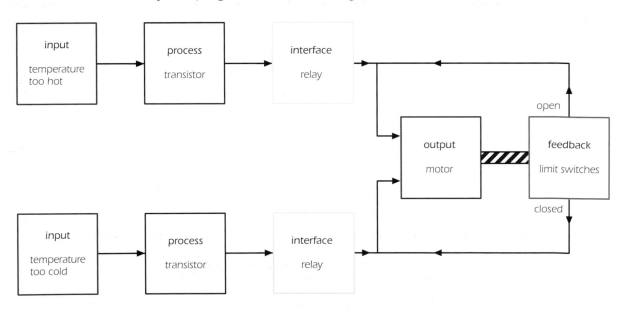

Block diagrams are very useful in deciding how the operations of a control system will be achieved. They form a middle stage between deciding how the system will operate and how the operations will be achieved. Again they are very useful when you want to communicate your intentions to others.

Circuit diagrams

A **circuit diagram** is a way of representing how a control system is constructed, what components are used and how they are connected together. Circuit diagrams use symbols to represent the components and lines to represent the connections. The Data section in this book (page 101) contains the circuit symbols for a wide range of commonly used components. The connecting lines can be drawn in a number of ways, but it is worth noting that some acceptable standards have been developed to avoid confusion.

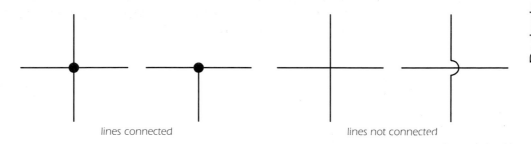

lines connected   lines not connected

Wherever possible, circuit diagrams are constructed so that they can be read from top to bottom and left to right. Positive **power supply rails** are drawn at the top and negative rails at the bottom. Input components are on the left of the diagram and it progresses through to output components on the right. The example shows a possible circuit diagram for the greenhouse window system described above.

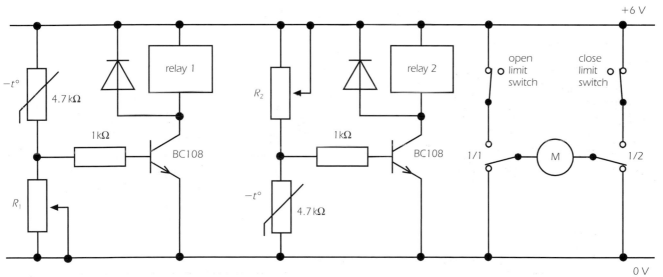

set variable R_1 to energise relay 1 when too hot (e.g. 30°C)
set variable R_2 to energise relay 2 when too cold (e.g. 10°C)

See

- Electronic timer, page 215

Circuit diagrams are the last stage in designing control systems. They allow you to make decisions about what components to use and how they will be connected. They are also very useful in communicating to others how your control system achieves its operation.

Mechanical control

Mechanical control systems or 'mechanisms' are used in systems that move. They can be used to:

- change the **velocity** of movement
- change the **distance** or **direction** of movement
- decrease the **effort** that is required to move a load
- convert one **type of motion** to a different type of motion. There are four different types of motion: **linear**, **reciprocating**, **rotary** and **oscillating**.

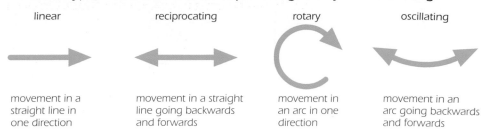

linear	reciprocating	rotary	oscillating
movement in a straight line in one direction	movement in a straight line going backwards and forwards	movement in an arc in one direction	movement in an arc going backwards and forwards

Drive systems

Drive systems are used to connect a **motor** to a rotating **output shaft**.

A drive system can change:

I/P (motor) → drive system (gearbox) → O/P (drive shaft)

- the **direction** of rotation
- the **velocity** of rotation
- the amount of available **torque** or turning force.

The most common type of drive system in contemporary products is the **gearbox**. However, drive systems can be made from **belts** and **pulleys** or from **chains** and **sprockets**.

worm drive gearbox

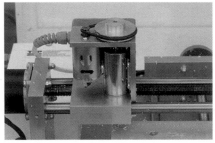
CNC machine belt drive

cycle chain drive

Drive systems are most often used to slow down the rotation of the output shaft in relation to the speed of the motor. This reduction in speed will also increase the available torque. Drive systems are used in almost every product and system that contains a motor or engine, for example toys, hi-fi systems, many domestic appliances, cars, robots, and so on.

Levers

Levers are used to change the **direction**, **distance** or **velocity** of movement or to decrease the **effort** required to move a **load**.

There are three basic types or classes of levers. The class of lever is decided by the position of the **fulcrum** and where the effort and load forces are applied.

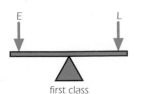
first class

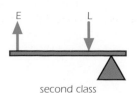
second class

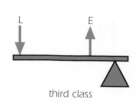
third class

Levers can be used to change the direction of movement. When they are used like this they are often called **linkages**.

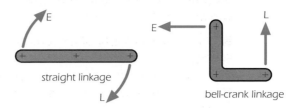

straight linkage

bell-crank linkage

Levers can be used to change the distance moved.

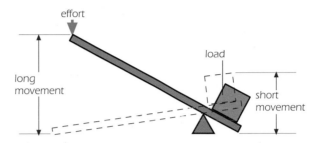

If a lever changes the distance moved then it will also change the velocity of movement. The formula for velocity is:

Velocity = distance moved ÷ time

So if the distance moved changes from the input to the output then the velocity will also change.

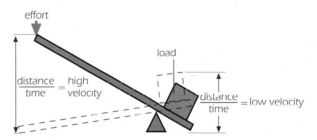

Levers can be used to decrease the effort needed to move a load. To understand how this is achieved you need to know about **moments**.

Moments are a way of calculating what effect a force will have when it is applied to a lever. A moment is calculated by multiplying the size of the force by the distance from the fulcrum.

For a lever to be balanced, the clockwise moments and the anti-clockwise moments must be the same. In this condition the lever is said to be in **equilibrium**. In the lever shown, the effort force and the load force are applied at the same distance from the fulcrum. So if the lever is to be in equilibrium, the effort force required to balance the load force can be calculated:

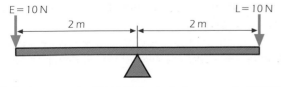

anti-clockwise moment = 2 × 10 N m   clockwise moment = 2 × 10 N m

Clockwise moments = anti-clockwise moments

Effort (E) × distance = load (L) × distance

$$\text{Effort (E)} = \frac{\text{load(L)} \times \text{distance}}{\text{distance}}$$

$$= \frac{10\,\text{N} \times 2\,\text{m}}{2\,\text{m}}$$

$$= 10\,\text{N}$$

So if the effort force and the load force are applied at the *same* distance from the fulcrum, they will be *equal* if the lever is in equilibrium. If the effort force has to move the load force then the effort force needs to be bigger than the load force.

In this example the effort force is applied twice as far away from the fulcrum as the load force.

For the lever to be in equilibrium the clockwise and anti-clockwise moments must be equal, so the effort force required to balance the load force can be calculated:

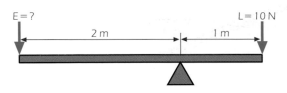

Clockwise moments = anti-clockwise moments

Effort(E) × distance = load(L) × distance

$$\text{Effort(E)} = \frac{\text{load(L)} \times \text{distance}}{\text{distance}}$$

$$= \frac{10\,\text{N} \times 1\,\text{m}}{2\,\text{m}}$$

$$= 5\,\text{N}$$

In this situation an effort force that is bigger than 5 N will move the load force of 10 N.

If a smaller effort force can move a bigger load force, the mechanism is said to have a **mechanical advantage (MA)**. Mechanical advantage is calculated using the formula:

$$\text{MA} = \frac{\text{distance moved by effort}}{\text{distance moved by load}}$$

In our example the effort force will move twice as far as the load force. You can calculate this by using π.

Each side of the lever represents the radius of a circle. If the lever were to make one full revolution, the distances moved by the effort and load would be the circumference of the circles drawn by the two radii.

The circumference of a circle = $2\pi \times$ radius, so

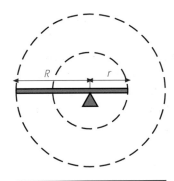

$$\text{MA} = \frac{2\pi R}{2\pi r}$$

In the equation you can see that the 2π above and below the line will cancel, so

$$\text{MA} = \frac{R}{r}$$

In the case of our lever,

$$\text{MA} = \frac{2}{1} = 2$$

See

- Air muscle mechanism, page 210
- Shape memory actuator, page 230

If you know the mechanical advantage for a lever then you can calculate how much effort is required to move a load, as

$$\text{Effort} = \frac{\text{load}}{\text{MA}}$$

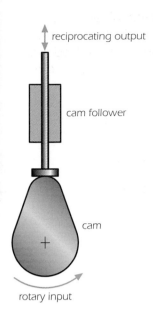

reciprocating output

cam follower

cam

rotary input

Cams

Cams are most often used to convert **rotary** motion to **reciprocating** motion. They are specially shaped pieces of material that are fitted to a rotating shaft. A **cam follower** makes contact with the edge, or profile, of the cam. As the shaft rotates, the cam follower is moved up and down.

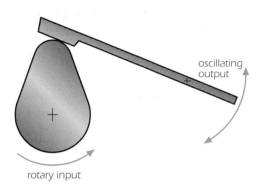

oscillating output

rotary input

Sometimes the cam follower is arranged as a second- or third-class lever (see page 54). This enables the cam to convert rotary motion to oscillating motion.

The profile of the cam will set how far and how fast the follower moves as the cam rotates. Cams can be made in many different shapes to suit them to their application. Here are four common types.

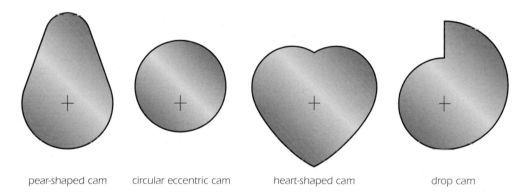

pear-shaped cam   circular eccentric cam   heart-shaped cam   drop cam

- ■ **Pear-shaped cams** – Often used for controlling **valves**, for example in a car engine, or systems that need to stay closed for a time then quickly open and close again. For half the revolution the cam follower is at the bottom of its travel and does not move. This is called the **dwell period** of the cam. For the other half-revolution of the follower rises and then falls.

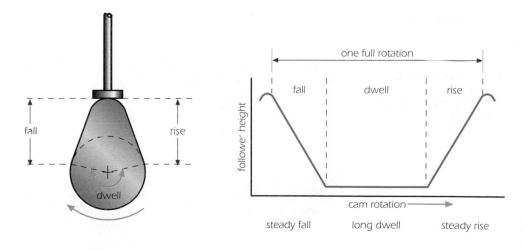

fall   rise   dwell

one full rotation

fall   dwell   rise

follower height

cam rotation

steady fall   long dwell   steady rise

■ **Circular cams** – Sometimes called **eccentric cams** and often used in applications that require a smooth and regular reciprocating motion, such as pumps in kidney dialysis machines. The circular cam produces the most regular form of reciprocating motion, called **simple harmonic motion**.

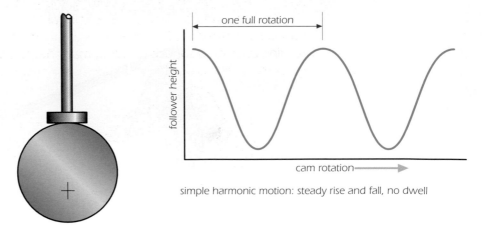

simple harmonic motion: steady rise and fall, no dwell

■ **Heart-shaped cams** – Cause the follower to move up with a uniform (steady) velocity, stop, and then come back down with a uniform velocity. They are used in systems that require this uniform movement, such as the mechanism that winds the tread evenly onto a bobbin or winds wire onto a solenoid coil.

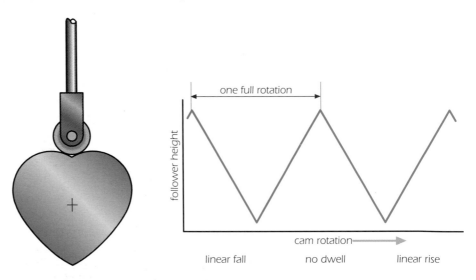

linear fall   no dwell   linear rise

■ **Drop cams** – Used in systems that need the follower to be raised steadily upwards and then fall rapidly down again, such as mechanical hammers, pressing and forming machines.

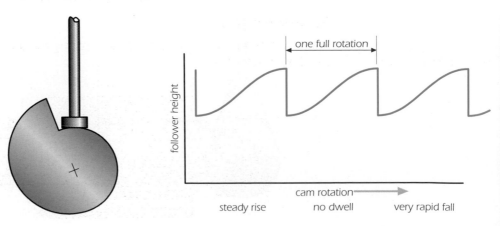

steady rise   no dwell   very rapid fall

Crank and slider

The **crank and slider** is used to convert **rotary** motion to **reciprocating** motion and vice versa.

- Rotary to reciprocating – The input turns the shaft which causes the slider to move forwards and backwards. Examples of the reciprocating motion produced are the drive for a mechanical saw or the movement of the machine table on a surface grinding machine. The slider could be in the form of a piston which is used to pump fluids for hydraulic or pneumatic systems.

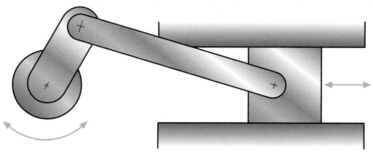

rotary to reciprocating

- Reciprocating to rotary – The input pushes the slider which causes the crank to turn. The crank must be away from bottom dead centre (BDC) if the mechanism is going to start, and this arrangement normally requires a **fly-wheel** to be attached to the shaft. A fly-wheel is a disc that has a relatively large mass. When the slider is pushed the momentum stored in the fly-wheel will cause the mechanism to run on and return to top dead centre (TDC) ready for the slider to be pushed again. The slider is often in the form of a piston, for example in an engine.

See

- Automaton, page 236

bottom dead centre (BDC)   top dead centre (TDC)

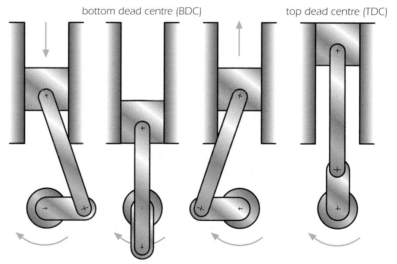

reciprocating to rotary

See

- Air tools, page 213
- Moiré fringe display, page 241

Screw thread

A **screw thread** can be used to convert **rotary** motion to **linear** motion, such as in a **linear actuator**.

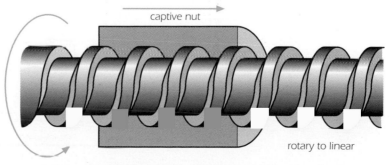

captive nut

rotary to linear

Electrical control

A variety of quite complex control systems can be built using simple electrical or electromechanical components such as **switches, microswitches, relays** and **mechanisms**.

Using switches

A single switch can be used to control one or more output components.

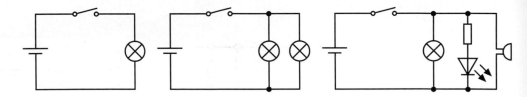

Note that the power supply voltage must always be matched with the voltage rating of the output components, and that connecting the output components in parallel ensures that each component has the full power supply voltage applied to it.

Using more than one switch allows different parts of the circuit to be controlled independently.

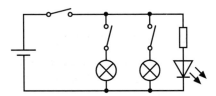

Connecting switches in **series** prevents an output component from operating until all the switches are closed, for example in a safety interlock system for a machine. Switches in series form a simple **AND gate**.

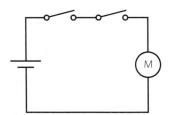

Connecting switches in **parallel** allows an output component to operate when any of the switches is closed, for example in an alarm or warning system. Switches in parallel form a simple **OR gate**.

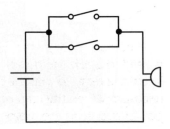

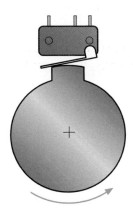

Two-point position control

Switches can be used to control a mechanism that needs to move between two points, such as a barrier, linear actuator, motorised sliding door, and so on.

This simple method uses a **double pole double throw (DPDT)** switch and two microswitches. The DPDT switch controls the direction of the motor. The microswitches cut the power to the motor when the mechanism reaches the desired position. When microswitches are used like this they are called **limit switches**, because they set the limits between which the mechanism can move.

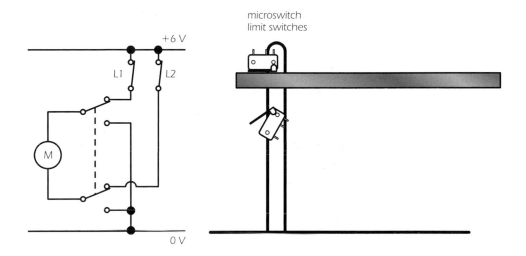

One-shot control

Switches and relays can be used to give a form of **one-shot** control. In one-shot systems the mechanism is driven through one complete cycle and then stops automatically, for example in a dispensing system.

In this system the motor drives a mechanism and somewhere in the mechanism is a **cam** (see page 57) that operates the limit switch. When the cam operates the limit switch the motor stops.

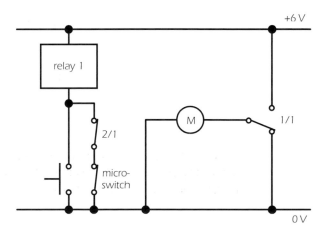

See

- Micro-rover, page 211
- Electronic timer, page 215
- Alarm, page 217
- Membrane panel switch, page 218
- Auto-shutdown product, page 219

When the push switch is pressed the relay will energise. Contact 1 of the relay is used to apply the power supply to the motor, and contact 2 is used to 'self-latch' the relay so that the motor will continue to turn after the push switch is released. When the cam operates the microswitch the relay unlatches and the power supply to the motor is cut.

Electronic control

Three-stage control systems

A very large number of automatic electronic control systems can be made using three simple stages: **input**, **process** and **output**.

The input block

The input block contains a sensor made in the form of a **potential divider** (see Resistors, page 102).

The process block

The process block contains an active electronic component that can respond to the signal provided by the sensor. It will switch the output component on or off depending on the signal from the sensor. The process block could contain the following:

- a **bipolar transistor**
- a **field effect transistor** which will give the system a '**switch**' function. The output will switch on when the input is high and off when the input goes low again. This function is useful in warning systems or automatic control
- a **thyristor** which will give the system a '**latch**' function. The output will switch on when the input is high and stay latched on even if the input goes low again. This function is useful in alarm systems or event-checking systems.

The output block

The output block contains one or more output components, such as a lamp, buzzer, LED, and so on.

To design a three-stage electronic control system you need to select the sensor to detect the necessary change, choose whether to have a 'switch' or a 'latch' function in the process, and then decide what kind of output the system will give. The table shows some of the options.

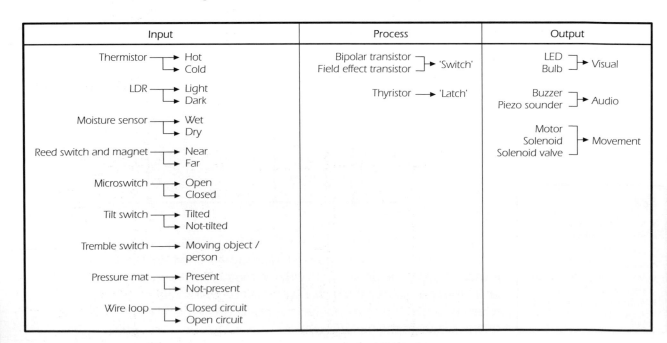

When you have made the selections, you can construct the circuit diagram.
Draw the three stages, then connect them together, as in the diagram.

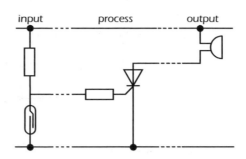

Input sensors

The diagrams show the 17 different input sensors listed in the table.

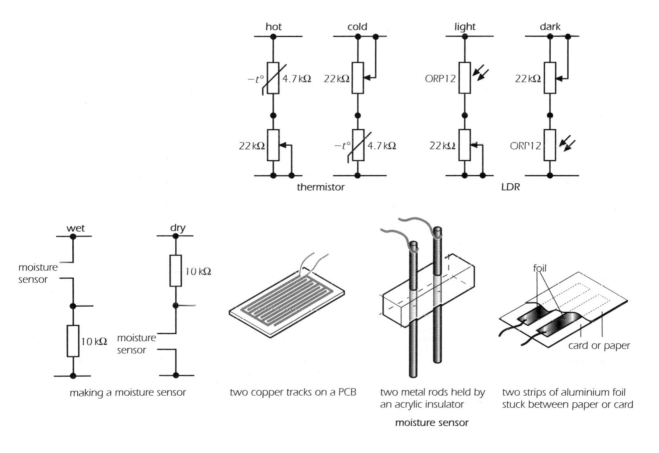

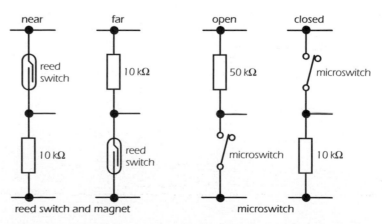

tilted   not tilted

tilt
switch

50 kΩ

10 kΩ

tilt
switch

making a tilt switch

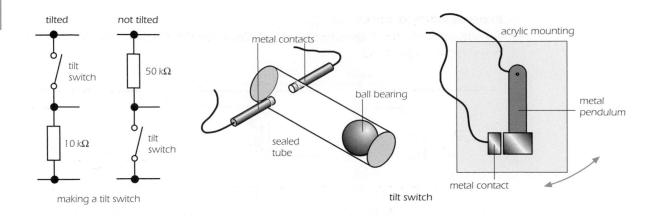

metal contacts

ball bearing

sealed
tube

acrylic mounting

metal
pendulum

metal contact

tilt switch

still/moving

tremble
switch

10 kΩ

making a tremble switch

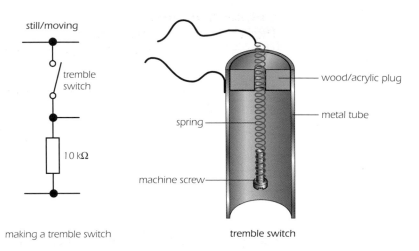

wood/acrylic plug

metal tube

spring

machine screw

tremble switch

person/object present   person/object not present

pressure
mat

10 kΩ

50 kΩ

pressure
mat

making a pressure mat

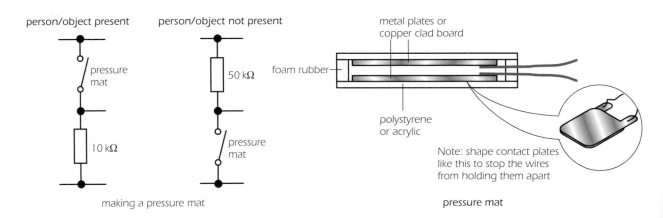

metal plates or
copper clad board

foam rubber

polystyrene
or acrylic

Note: shape contact plates
like this to stop the wires
from holding them apart

pressure mat

open circuit
(loop is broken to activate circuit)

closed circuit
(loop is completed to activate circuit)

50 kΩ

wire
loop

wire
loop

10 kΩ

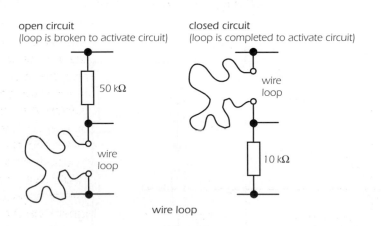

wire loop

Process components

The circuit diagrams show the circuits for the three different process components in the table on page 62.

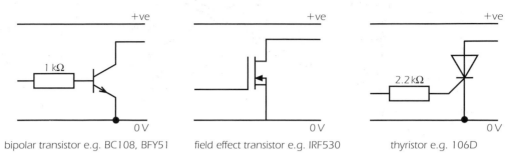

bipolar transistor e.g. BC108, BFY51   field effect transistor e.g. IRF530   thyristor e.g. 106D

Output components

The output components in the table will need extra components connected to them in some cases. Examples are illustrated in the diagrams.

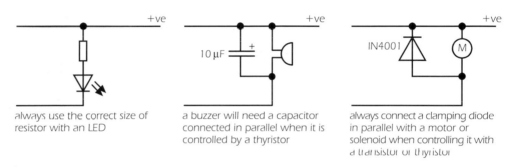

always use the correct size of resistor with an LED

a buzzer will need a capacitor connected in parallel when it is controlled by a thyristor

always connect a clamping diode in parallel with a motor or solenoid when controlling it with a transistor or thyristor

Using more than one input (combinatorial systems)

You can use **logic gates** to build systems that can respond to a combination of one or more inputs. The logic gates form the process block in the system. A **transistor** is used as an **amplifier** to allow the output from the logic gates to control the output component. This stage is called a **buffer**.

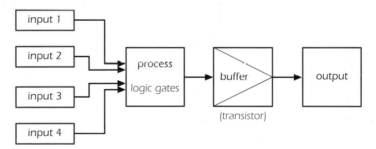

Using operational amplifiers (op amps)

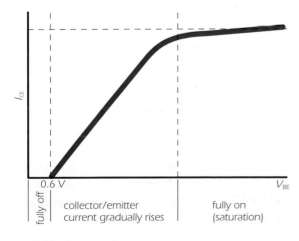

Simple three-stage control systems based on a transistor are useful for many applications. However, they are not accurate enough for all applications. This is because of the way that a transistor works. In a three-stage control system we use the transistor as a switch. A transistor is actually a current amplifier. The graph shows how the voltage across the base emitter affects how much current is allowed to flow through the collector and emitter.

Note that a field effect transmitter (FET) operates in a similar way except that the switch-on point is higher than 0.6 V. An IRF 530 starts to switch on at about 2 V.

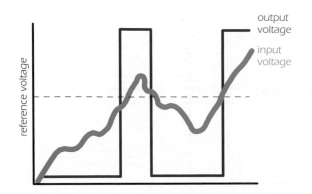

The problem with using a transistor as a switch is that there is a large 'gap' between it being fully switched off and fully switched on. During this 'gap' some current will be flowing through the output component. You can see this in systems that use a lamp as the output. The lamp will begin to glow dimly and then get brighter as the base–emitter voltage rises. Likewise buzzers can sometimes buzz quietly and get louder as the base–emitter voltage rises. This can cause problems in applications where you need a very accurate switching point.

To overcome this problem of inaccuracy you can use an **operational amplifier (op amp)** connected as a voltage comparator (see page 117). The comparator makes a very quick and accurate change from being switched off to being switched on. The graph shows the output from a comparator.

In a working system a transistor is used as an amplifier to allow the output from the comparator to control the output component. This stage is called a **buffer**.

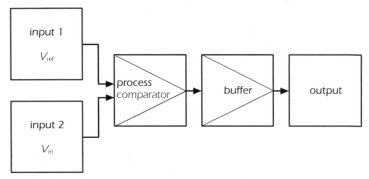

Sequential control systems

Sequential control systems turn a number of output components on and off in the correct sequence, that is, one after the other. Sequential controllers are used in automatic washing machines, industrial production lines, and so on.

You can build a simple electromechanical sequential controller using cams (see page 57) and switches. A motor and gearbox drive the cams round and they operate a series of microswitches. This device is known as a 'cam timer' and was often used in automatic washing machines.

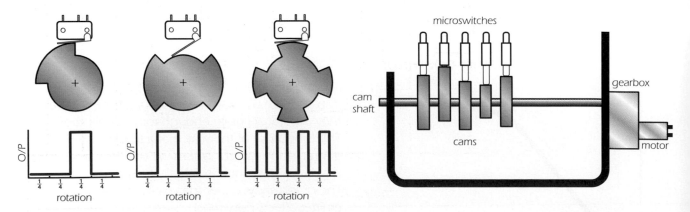

You can make an electronic version of the cam timer using an **integrated circuit (IC)**. The example shown at the top left of page 67 uses a CMOS 4017 decade counter/divider.

A series of pulses are fed into the input pin 14. The output lines labelled with letters switch on and off in the alphabetical sequence of the letters.

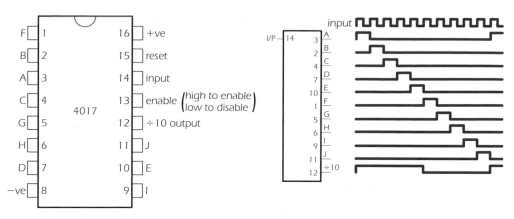

You can use the sequence of pulses created to control output components via transistors. In the example application below the pulses are 'steered' towards an output component using a **diode matrix**. In a diode matrix a diode connected gives an 'on' signal and no diode connected gives an 'off' signal.

	O/P1	O/P2	O/P3	O/P4
I/P1 On	On	Off	On	Off
I/P2 On	Off	On	Off	On
I/P3 On	On	Off	Off	Off
I/P4 On	Off	Off	Off	On

The figure below shows the circuit diagram for the whole cam timer system. The input pulses are created by a **555 timer** connected as an **astable multivibrator**. The 4017 sequences the input pulses to its ten outputs. In the example, output E is connected back to the reset pin. This will cause the 4017 to reset back to A, so the sequence will be A, B, C, D, A, B, C, D, A, and so on. The diode matrix steers the sequence of pulses to the output components. The output components are controlled via FETs.

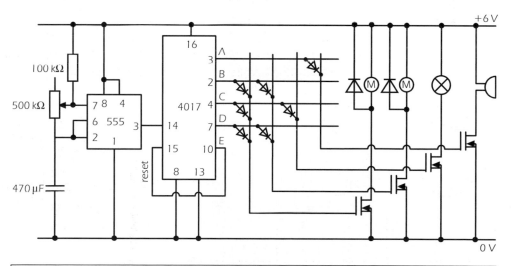

	Motor A	Motor B	Lamp	Buzzer
Pulse 1	Off	Off	Off	On
Pulse 2	On	On	Off	Off
Pulse 3	On	Off	On	Off
Pulse 4	On	On	Off	Off

Programmable control

A **programmable control** system allows the user to set, or program, how the system will operate. Programmable controllers can often react to inputs from one or more sensors and control a number of outputs. They can also be programmed to carry out sequential operations. Programmable controllers were developed in the manufacturing industries to control automated production lines, machinery and robots. Although the industrial applications might seem expensive and complex, there are now many systems available that can be used in school workshops.

The first systems to become available were **computer interface boxes**. There are now many of these but they all do similar things. They allow you to connect input and output components into the interface box so that the computer can act as the process stage in the control system. The computer is programmed using a simple language like control logo. Computer interface boxes are very useful for quickly modelling systems and to learn more about control. However, they are really like construction kits, and your teacher will probably not let you build the computer into your product!

More recently, programmable controllers have become available that you *can* build into your products. They are all based on a special kind of **integrated circuit (IC)** known as a **PIC microcontroller**. PIC stands for programmable instruction circuit. PIC chips are almost like a blank IC. You program them to make them do what you need. The program will stay in the PIC chip until you reprogram it. There is almost no limit to the number of times that you can reprogram a PIC chip. PIC chips are now widely used in industry as they allow complex systems to be constructed, with fewer components and without the need to have special ICs manufactured. There are now a number of different PIC microcontroller systems that you can use in school.

Bit-by-bit controller

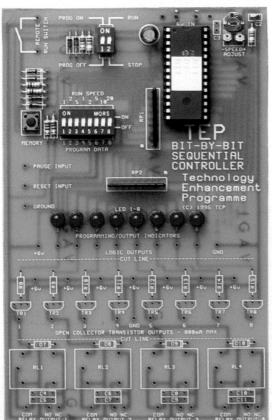

The **bit-by-bit controller** is a self-contained unit that can control up to eight output components. It comes as a 'part populated' **printed circuit board (PCB)**. The PCB has spaces for transistor buffers or for relays. The controller will also respond to two inputs. One input will rest the controller back to the start of its program and the other will pause the program.

The bit-by-bit controller is very easy to program. The output lines are switched on or off using switches on the PCB and then this 'line' of program is stored in the PIC by pressing the program button. The state of the output lines can then be changed and the next line stored in the PIC. Programming the controller is like recording the outputs line by line. When the controller is set to run, the program sequence is played back.

Smartcard system

Smartcards look and feel like plastic credit cards but they have a PIC chip embedded in them. You may already own a smartcard as they are being more widely used for commercial applications. All phone cards now use this technology and many banks are now switching over to it.

PIC chip embedded in plastic card

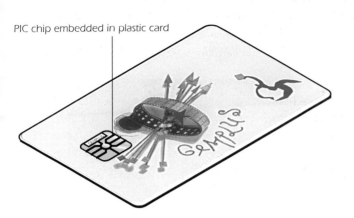

smartcard reader

A system is available that allows you to program a smartcard and use it as a microcontroller. This is useful in applications where you need to have a number of different programs and you need to be able to run them at different times without reprogramming a PIC chip.

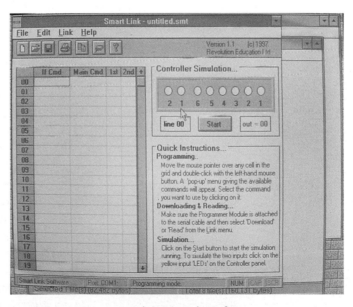

smartcard programming software

The smartcard system comprises a **programmer module** and a **controller board**. The blank card is inserted into the programmer module. The program can be written on the module itself so you can write it on a computer. Using the computer allows you to see more of the program and save it for future use.

The program is stored on the card. When it is inserted into the controller module the program will automatically run. The controller module has six output lines and two input lines. The outputs are all buffered so they can be connected directly to output components like bulbs, buzzers, motors, and so on.

The *Basic Stamp* computer

The *Basic Stamp* is really quite a stunning device. Although it is very small in size, it is actually a fully-functioning computer. The *Stamp* is programmed using a special form of BASIC called PBASIC. This is not too complicated to learn with some practice. The *Stamp* has eight lines that can be used as inputs or outputs. It can respond to inputs from a wide variety of sensors and control outputs such as lamps, buzzers, LEDs, stepper motors, servo motors, LCD displays, and so on. It can store data in its own memory and can undertake mathematical functions with the data. Using the *Stamp* will allow you to build very complex control systems quite easily.

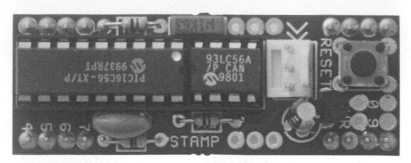

The *Chip Factory*

Until very recently, programming individual PIC chips for use in control systems was a very complicated and highly technical task. They are programmed for industrial applications using a complicated language called assembler. This takes a long time to learn. However, the *Chip Factory* overcomes this problem by allowing you to program individual PIC chips using an easy programming language. The *Chip Factory* can program three different types of PIC chip which have different facilities for inputs and outputs. The big advantage of using the *Chip Factory* is that you can then build your own control board using the programmed chips. This makes using microcontrollers very cheap indeed.

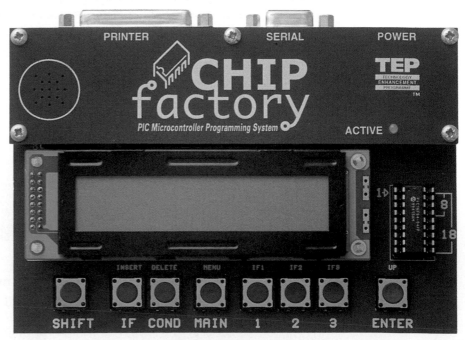

See

- Robotic arm, page 209
- Air tools, page 213
- Paper feeder, page 214
- Smartcard application, page 220
- Decorative lighting, page 221
- Designer chip, page 223
- Moiré fringe display, page 241

More comprehensive information and application notes for the bit-by-bit, smartcard system, *Stamp* computer and *Chip Factory* can be obtained from: Teaching Resources, Middlesex University, Trent Park, Bramley Road, London N14 4YZ.

7 Structures

A **structure** is something that supports a **load**. An obvious example might be a bridge. The bridge spans a gap and supports the load of the cars driving over it. However, structures are very widespread. The desk and chair that you might be using now are both examples of structures. When you sit on the chair it supports the load applied by your body. Anything that is designed to support a load could be described as a structure. Designing effective structures is easier when you understand the basic principles.

Types of forces

The load acting on a structure will apply a **force** to it. Forces can be **static** or **dynamic**. A static force does not move, but a dynamic force does. Dynamic forces will be larger than static forces if they are applied by the same object. To illustrate this, think about a hammer driving a nail into some wood. If the hammer rests on top of the nail, the force will be static. Unless the hammer is very large indeed, the nail will not go into the wood! If the hammer is swung then the force will be dynamic. The faster the hammer moves the greater the force will be.

static force

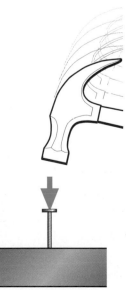

dynamic force

Force is measured in **newtons** (N) and has two components. The first component is the **mass** (kg) of the object that is applying the force. As the mass of the object increases the amount of force that it applies increases. The second component is the **acceleration** of the object ($m\,s^{-2}$). As the acceleration of the object increases, the force that it applies increases. The general formula to calculate force in newtons is:

$$Force = mass \times acceleration$$

Note that a static force appears to have no acceleration as it is not moving. However, **gravity** will be constantly trying to move the load. Gravity will accelerate any mass by approximately $10\ m\,s^{-2}$.

There are five basic types of forces: **compression**, **tension**, **bending**, **torsion** and **shear**.

Compression

Compression forces will try to *squash* the structure. The parts of structures that resist compression forces are called **struts**.

The legs of a stool are under compression. When somebody sits on the stool the compression increases.

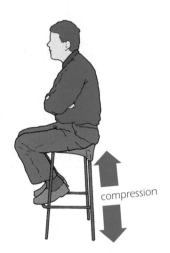

compression

Tension

Tension forces will try to *stretch* the structure. The parts of a structure that resist compression forces are called **ties** (see Tensile strength, page 22).

The cables in a suspension bridge are under tension.

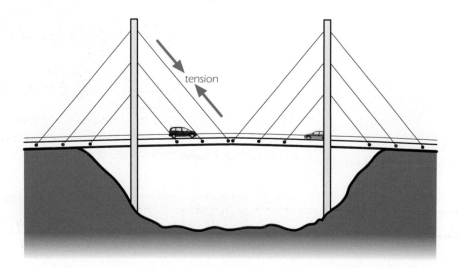

tension

Bending

Bending forces will try to *bend* the structure. When a person sits on this simple bench the seat will bend.

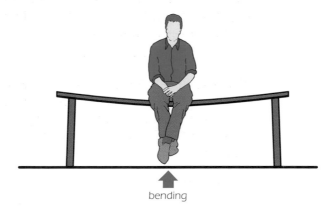

bending

Torsion

Torsion forces will try to *twist* the structure. The joints in this gate are under torsion. If they cannot resist the torsion forces then the gate will sag.

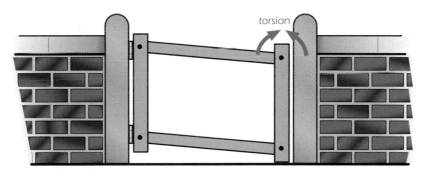

torsion

Shear

Shear forces will try to *cut* the structure in two. Shear forces normally happen where two parts of a structure are joined. A bolt holding two metal plates together will be under a shear force when the plates are pulled apart. Shear forces act like the blades of a pair of scissors.

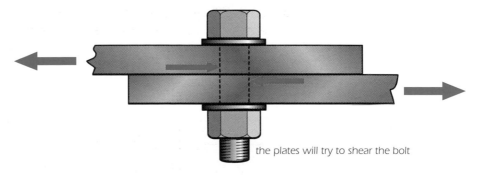

the plates will try to shear the bolt

Arrows are often used to show forces. They can sometimes be confusing unless you understand that the arrows show how the material *resists* the force rather than indicating the direction of the force, as shown in the following diagrams.

compression

tension

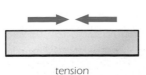

bending

torsion

Using structures to convert forces

Of the five types of forces, two are 'good' and three are 'bad' in structures:

■ tension and compression – good forces
■ bending, torsion and shear – bad forces.

This is because structural materials are very resistant to good forces but not very resistant to bad forces. Successful structures convert the bad forces into good forces so that they can resist them and support the load.

Converting bending forces in beams

The amount that a structural member, or **beam**, will bend depends upon the **material** it is made from and its **cross-sectional area** and **shape**. By changing the cross-sectional area and shape you can increase the beam's resistance to bending forces (see Properties of materials, page 19). Resistance to bending forces is known as **stiffness**.

You can demonstrate this principle by using a standard ruler. If you lay the ruler flat between two supports it will bend easily. However, if you stand the ruler on its edge it will be far more resistant to bending.

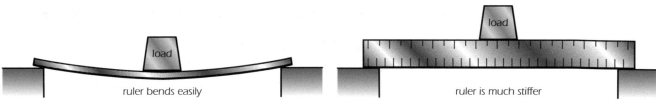

ruler bends easily

load

ruler is much stiffer

The reason why the ruler is stiffer when it is on its edge is that the bending forces are converted into compression and tension forces. Imagine a line running through the centre of the ruler. This is known as the **neutral axis**. The amount of material on each side of the neutral axis affects how stiff the ruler will be. More material will make it stiffer.

neutral axis

bends easily

neutral axis

very stiff

When the ruler is subjected to bending forces, the material that is above the neutral axis is forced together, so it will be under compression. The material below the neutral axis will be pulled apart, so it will be under tension. You can demonstrate this with a strip of foam rubber. If you draw lines on the foam and then bend it, you will see that they get closer together below the neutral axis and further apart above the neutral axis.

foam rubber strip with lines drawn on it

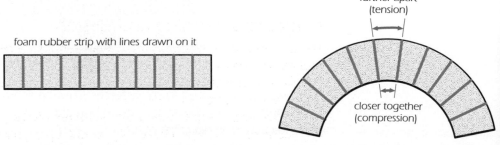

further apart
(tension)

closer together
(compression)

So, if there is only a small amount of material on each side of the neutral axis then the load force will bend the beam. As the amount of material increases the load forces will be converted from bending forces into compression and tension forces. However, it is not a simple matter of just making the beam thicker in the horizontal plane.

Consider the ruler again. If you continue to increase the load on the ruler, it will begin to bend in the vertical plane. This is because there is still only a small amount of material on each side of the neutral axis in this plane.

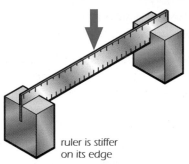

ruler is stiffer
on its edge

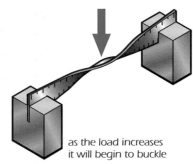

as the load increases
it will begin to buckle

To prevent the ruler, or beam, from bending, the same principles also need to be applied in the vertical plane – that is, by having more material on each side of the neutral axis. You could achieve this by using a solid block of material, but this would be heavy. Structures need to support themselves as well as the load, so extra weight is a disadvantage! The most resistant member to bending forces is one with an I-shaped cross-section. The central section makes it stiff in the horizontal plane to prevent bending, and the top and bottom plates make it stiff in the vertical plane to prevent buckling. (See Stiffness of sections, page 23.)

Converting torsion forces in beams

Torsion forces will act in very similar ways to bending forces in beams. If you hold a ruler at its ends you can apply a torsion force by twisting it.

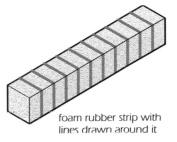

foam rubber strip with
lines drawn around it

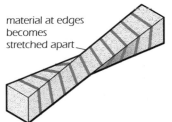

material at edges
becomes
stretched apart

Again, the ability of the beam to resist torsion forces depends upon how much material is around the neutral axis. When a beam is twisted the material on each side of the neutral axis is pulled apart, so it is under tension. You can see this by using the same strip of foam rubber but this time with lines drawn all round it.

You may need to look carefully, but you will see that the lines become distorted into curves and the material at the edges becomes stretched apart. Beams that are most resistant to torsion forces are those which have a symmetrical cross-section, where the material is evenly distributed around the neutral axis and is concentrated at the furthest points from the neutral axis.

Comparing bending and torsion

The table on page 24 shows the relative stiffness of beam sections for bending and torsion forces. Notice how the I-beam is the most resistant to bending forces but the least resistant to torsion forces. Using the table can help you to select the best cross-section for an application.

For example, the best quality bicycle frames are very stiff. They need to resist both bending and torsion forces. If you look up a thick-walled round section tube you will see that it is very resistant to torsion forces but not very resistant to bending forces. Making the tube with thinner walls but with a bigger diameter makes it more resistant to both bending and torsion forces. The bicycle frame will still be the same weight but it will be much stiffer and so will perform much better. This is why many of the more expensive cycle frames use 'over-size' tubing.

Converting torsion and avoiding shear in frames

In a simple square or rectangular frame a load will exert a bending force on the top beam and compression forces on the two upright beams. The frame will be stable and resist the forces. However, if the direction that the force acts in moves slightly away from the vertical then torsion forces will be concentrated at the joints. Unless the joints are very strong indeed, the frame will begin to twist into a parallelogram. Also, as the frame begins to twist under the torsion forces at the joints, any fixing bolts will be subjected to shear forces which could damage them.

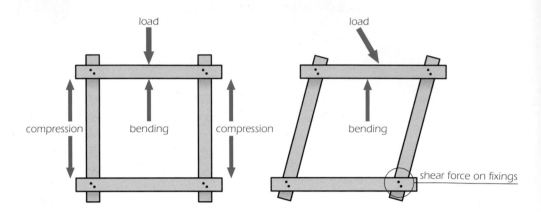

To overcome this problem the torsion forces must be converted into compression or tension forces. This is done by adding struts or ties. A strut resists compression and a tie resists tension.

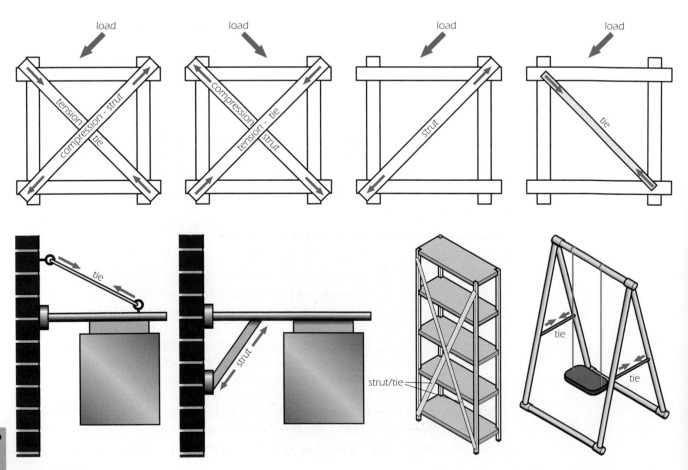

Why structures fail

From the above you can see that by using materials carefully we can build strong structures that can support loads. In effective structures we can prevent:

■ bending and torsion by carefully choosing the cross-sectional shape of beams, and
■ torsion and shear by using struts and ties in frames.

Both of these strategies are used to make structures that are rigid enough to support their loads. However, there are still some other things to consider when designing effective structures.

Stability

Newton's third law of motion states that for every action there is an equal and opposite reaction.

This means that whenever a force is applied to a structure by a load the structure will resist the force by a force of an equal amount. The resisting force is known as the **reaction** force. The reaction forces are applied wherever the structure is supported or where it touches the ground.

The diagram below shows a decorator standing on a plank supported between trestles. When he stands at the end of the plank the whole load is applied to trestle A. If he moves to the centre of the plank then the load is shared equally between trestle A and trestle B.

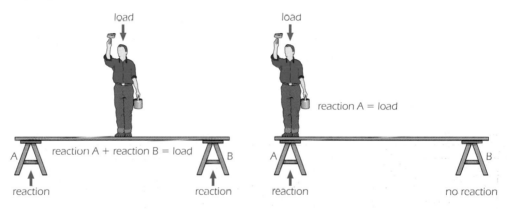

You can prove this mathematically by using **moments**. The turning effect or moment of a force is measured by multiplying the force by the *perpendicular* distance from the pivot. It is measured in newton metres (N m).

In this example it is assumed that the load applied by the decorator is 700 N and the trestles are 4 m apart.

Situation 1: Decorator in centre of plank

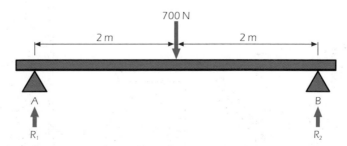

The reaction force R_2 can be calculated by imagining that trestle B has been removed. The plank will now have a clockwise moment of

$$700\,N \times 2\,m = 1400\,N\,m$$

R_2 will have to oppose this moment, so the anti-clockwise moment must equal the clockwise moment of 1400 N m:

$$1400 \text{ N m} = R_2 \times 4 \text{ m}$$
$$1400 \text{ N m} \div 4 \text{ m} = R_2$$
$$350 \text{ N} = R_2$$

which is half the load force. You can calculate R_1 in the same way and your answer will again be 350 N.

Situation 2: Decorator above trestle A

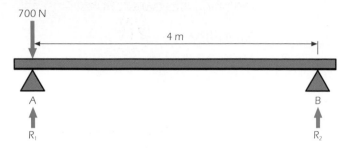

This time calculate the anti-clockwise moment by removing trestle A. The plank will now have an anti-clockwise moment of

$$700 \text{ N} \times 4 \text{ m} = 2800 \text{ N m}$$

R_1 will have to oppose this moment, so the clockwise moment must equal the anti-clockwise moment of 2800 N m:

$$2800 \text{ N m} = R_1 \times 4 \text{ m}$$
$$2800 \text{ N m} \div 4 \text{ m} = R_1$$
$$700 \text{ N} = R_1$$

So in this situation trestle A supports the whole load. As the load moves around, the reaction forces will change.

Consider now a table. The four legs will set up the reaction forces. The reaction forces will change as the load moves around.

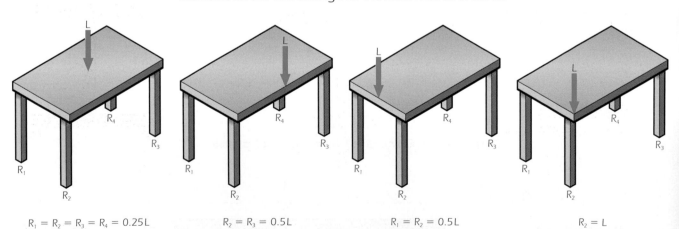

$R_1 = R_2 = R_3 = R_4 = 0.25L$ $R_2 = R_3 = 0.5L$ $R_1 = R_2 = 0.5L$ $R_2 = L$

When structures are designed it is important to consider where the load will be applied. If it is static and in the centre then each support will share the load. However, if the load moves around the supports must be stronger as the reaction forces will change.

In these examples the structures will remain stable and not fail as long as the supports are strong enough. However, there is a second reason for their stability. This relates to where the load is applied in relation to the reaction points. In the situation with the decorator's trestle, no matter where he moves, the load will always be applied between the reaction points. If the trestles are repositioned we can make the structure very dangerous indeed.

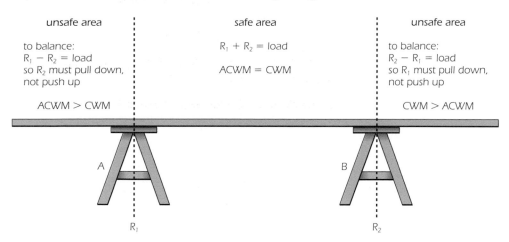

unsafe area

to balance:
$R_1 - R_2$ = load
so R_2 must pull down, not push up

ACWM > CWM

safe area

$R_1 + R_2$ = load

ACWM = CWM

unsafe area

to balance:
$R_2 - R_1$ = load
so R_1 must pull down, not push up

CWM > ACWM

A

B

R_1

R_2

Now the plank is overhanging the trestles. If the decorator steps to the left of trestle A the structure will become unstable. For the structure to be balanced the anti-clockwise moments (ACWM) must equal the clockwise moments (CWM). For this to happen R_2 must now operate in the opposite direction (pull down and not push up). As the plank and the trestle are not fixed, they cannot do this, so the plank will rotate around trestle A and the decorator will fall.

In any structure the **clockwise moments** must always equal the **anti-clockwise moments**. This is achieved by making sure that the reaction forces can balance the load forces. If this is achieved then the structure is in **equilibrium** and will be safe. If a structure loses its equilibrium then it will fail.

The simplest way to achieve equilibrium is to make sure that the load force is always applied between the reaction points. This is practical for many applications but sometimes alternative solutions are needed.

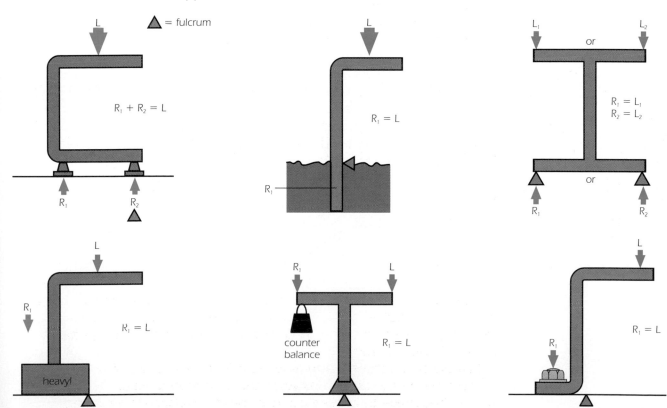

L

▲ = fulcrum

$R_1 + R_2$ = L

R_1

R_2

▲

L

R_1 = L

R_1

L_1 or L_2

$R_1 = L_1$
$R_2 = L_2$

or

R_1

R_2

L

R_1

R_1 = L

heavy!

▲

R_1 L

counter balance

R_1 = L

▲

L

R_1 = L

R_1

▲

Stress points and elastic limits

Stress is a measure of how much force is applied to a particular area of material. So,

Stress = force ÷ area

All materials will have a maximum stress that they can withstand. The tensile strength table on page 22 gives figures for the maximum safe stress of various materials. If the maximum stress is exceeded then the material will break and the structure will fail. Increasing the cross-sectional area of a structural member will decrease the amount of stress that it is under.

Examples

1 A 10 mm × 10 mm strut is loaded with 100 N. What is the stress?

Stress = force ÷ area
= 100 N ÷ (10 mm × 10 mm) = 1 N mm^{-2}

2 How much is the stress reduced by if the strut is increased in size to 20 mm × 20 mm?

Stress = force ÷ area
= 100 N ÷ (20 mm × 20 mm) = 0.25 N mm^{-2}

The area has increased by four, so the stress has been quartered.

3 Using figures from tables helps you decide how large a structural member needs to be. From a look-up table you would find that oak has a maximum compression stress of 6. So a 40 mm × 40 mm oak strut can support a maximum load as follows.

Stress = force ÷ area, so force = stress × area

Maximum stress = 6 N mm^{-2}

Area = 40 mm × 40 mm = 1600 mm^2

Force = 6 N mm^{-2} × 1600 mm^2 = 9600 N

Unfortunately this is only part of the stress consideration in structures. The shape of materials can concentrate stress at particular points. Stress is concentrated at fixing points and where there are sharp corners. You can demonstrate this using a strip of polystyrene. If you bend the plain, undamaged strip it will bend quite freely and not snap. However, if you score a line across it, it will snap easily at the line when you try to bend it. This is because the stress is concentrated at the sharp corners of the score line.

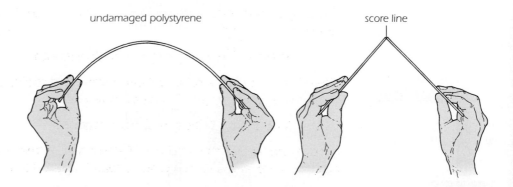

undamaged polystyrene　　　　　　　　　　　　　　score line

Structural members must be free from sharp corners and holes that are not round. The picture shows how stress concentration points are avoided in an I-beam.

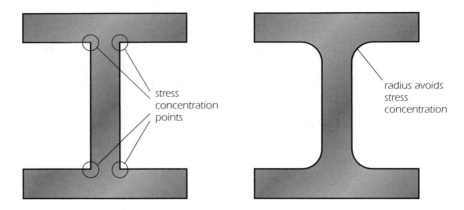

stress concentration points

radius avoids stress concentration

Stress at fixing points can be reduced by increasing the number of fixings and by supporting the joint with a gusset plate.

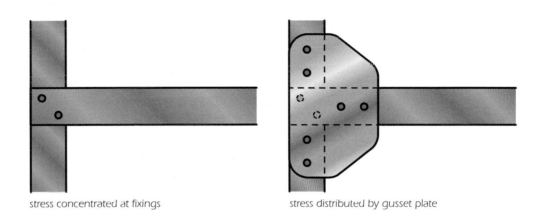

stress concentrated at fixings

stress distributed by gusset plate

Elasticity

When a load is applied to a material it will stretch. The extent to which a material stretches is determined by:

■ the type of material, for example rubber will stretch much further than steel
■ the amount of stress (force ÷ area). More force will stretch the material further. A larger cross-sectional area will reduce the stretch.

The proportional extent to which a material stretches is called the **strain**, and is given by the formula

Strain = change in length ÷ original length

There is a useful relationship between stress and strain. It is known as **Young's modulus of elasticity (E)**. This is calculated by

Modulus of elasticity = stress ÷ strain

If a designer knows the modulus of elasticity then they can predict how far a piece of material will stretch when a load is applied to it.

Example

A steel cable is 50 m long and 20 mm in diameter and supports a load of 5000 N. How far will the cable stretch?

1 Calculate the stress:

$$\text{Radius} = r = 20 \div 2 = 10 \text{ mm}$$
$$\text{Area} = \pi r^2$$
$$= \pi \times 10 \text{ mm} \times 10 \text{ mm} = 3.14 \times 100 \text{ mm}^2 = 314 \text{ mm}^2$$

$$\text{Stress} = \text{force} \div \text{area}$$
$$= 5000 \text{ N} \div 314 \text{ mm}^2 = 15.9 \text{ N mm}^{-2}$$

2 The modulus of elasticity (E) for steel:

$$E = 210 \text{ kN mm}^{-2} \text{ or } 210\,000 \text{ N mm}^{-2}$$

3 Calculate the strain:

$$E = \text{stress} \div \text{strain, so strain} = \text{stress} \div E$$
$$\text{Strain} = 15.9 \text{ N mm}^{-2} \div 210\,000 \text{ N mm}^{-2} = 0.000\,08$$

4 Find the change in length:

$$\text{Strain} = \text{change in length} \div \text{original length}$$
$$\text{Change in length} = \text{strain} \times \text{original length}$$
$$= 0.000\,08 \times 50 \text{ m} = 0.004 \text{ m}$$
$$= 4 \text{ mm}$$

Materials stretch by a predictable length up to a maximum point. This is known as the **elastic limit**. As long as the stress stays below this limit, the material will return to its original length once the stress is removed. The relationship between stress and strain can be seen from a **stress/strain curve** for the material.

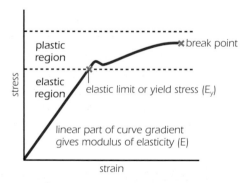

Structural members must never be taken beyond their elastic limit, otherwise the structure will be permanently deformed.

Summary of important points for designing structures

- Types of forces: compression, tension, bending, torsion and shear.
- Good forces: compression and tension.
- Bad forces: bending, torsion and shear.
- Avoid bending and torsion in beams by choosing the most appropriate cross-section.
- Avoid torsion and shear in frames by using struts and ties.
- Always make sure that the structure is in equilibrium (clockwise moment = anti-clockwise moment). Apply the load between reaction points that can move, or fix or counter balance the reaction points.
- Avoid stress concentrations by using rounded corners and round holes.
- Be aware of elasticity and elastic limits.

See

- Space frame, page 224
- Space frame display system, page 225
- Hanging shelf system, page 226
- Packaging for survival, page 227
- Kite, page 228

8 Graphics

Introduction

Drawings and diagrams are the most important way of describing in detail products and systems. Engineers and designers must be able both to read and make drawings. It is important that you learn the language of drawings so you can communicate fluently with other people. Finding a solution to a design problem or brief is often a challenging task. In every situation, there are many things to consider if the final solution is to satisfy and meet the need you have identified. When you are designing, you need to use a wide range of techniques and tools to help you analyse, record, develop and solve problems. It is impossible to keep all your ideas in your head, so you must be able to use drawings to communicate with yourself and with others.

Different types of drawings have different purposes. There are three main reasons for using drawings.

Developing ideas – sketches

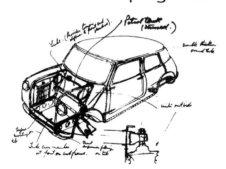

Sketches are used for getting ideas down on paper and are often very personal. To begin with, they can be fairly rough as only you have to understand them. As your ideas develop, your sketches need to become more detailed and refined so you can discuss your ideas with others.

Communicating ideas – pictorial views and diagrams

As your idea begins to take shape, you need to draw it in more detail. This may be to give you a better idea of what it will look like or to check out the idea with the client or potential user. There are a range of drawing systems you can use to produce a pictorial view – **isometric**, **axonometric** or **perspective**, for example. If you want to show how various parts fit together, you might do an **exploded drawing** or a **cutaway** view. Sometimes, a diagram is needed to show how a system will work or how a circuit will be laid out.

Production drawings – orthographic projection and detailed diagrams

When you have found the best solution, you need to establish the precise size of all the parts you have to make. The best way of doing this is to produce **orthographic** drawings. If the solution consists of several parts, each component has to be drawn separately so every detail can be shown and dimensioned. In addition there needs to be a **general arrangement (GA)** drawing to show the relationship of the various parts. Orthographic projection is a precise language used by everyone to communicate the exact details of a product.

As a designer, you have to select which type of drawing is suitable for a particular task. Always ask yourself:

- What will the drawing be used for?
- Who will use the drawing?
- Will they be able to understand the drawing?
- Is it the best method of communication?

Freehand sketches

Freehand sketching is not easy but you can improve your technique by practising.

Writing is a form of sketching which you practised until you had perfected it. Writing is made up of letters; once you learned how to make the shapes, you could write. Sketching is very similar. Objects are formed from shapes which consist of lines. Practise sketching lines and shapes and you will soon be able to sketch objects.

Most of the things you design can be broken down into geometric forms. If you can sketch these forms, you will be able to put them together to sketch the products you have designed. It's just like putting words together to write a sentence or story.

There are also a number of exercises you can do to improve the quality of your sketching.

Curves

Start by sketching a circle or ellipse inside a square or rectangle. If it helps, mark the points where the curve should touch the sides of the square or rectangle you have drawn. Let your pencil go round several times to define the shape.

The shape of an object

When you sketch the shape of an object, you show only two dimensions such as the height and length.

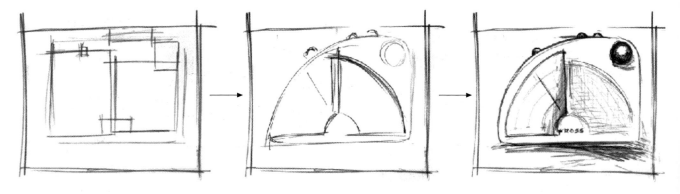

- Start by drawing a rectangle into which the object will fit. It is important to get the proportions right.
- Next, divide the original rectangle into which the various parts fit.
- Now draw the shape of each of the parts and you have a hi-fi system.
- Add shading or texture to make the sketch look more three-dimensional.

Geometric forms

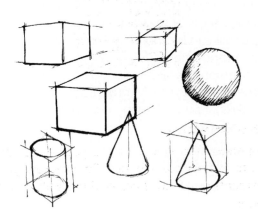

Being able to sketch boxes, cylinders, cones and spheres is important.

- Try drawing boxes in perspective like the one shown.
- When you're sketching cylinders and cones, start by sketching the box in which they will fit.
- A sphere is a circle with shading.

The form of an object

This type of sketch will show all three dimensions of an object.

- Start by sketching the box into which it will fit. This is often called 'crating' the object.
- Divide the faces into the shapes which make up the object.
- Draw in the detail.
- Add shading or texture to make the sketch look more realistic.

Using sketches to record ideas

However many ideas you have, you will never think of all the possibilities. Looking at other people's designs and recording their ideas is not cheating. Most designs bring together ideas which already exist but in a different arrangement. Keep a sketch book and, whenever you see a clever idea or novel solution, record it using a sketch – you never know when it might be useful.

Using sketches to generate ideas

Sketching is a means of thinking on paper as the design sheet shows. Ideas will blossom and develop from your initial sketches. Your eyes will also be opened to other possibilities and ideas.

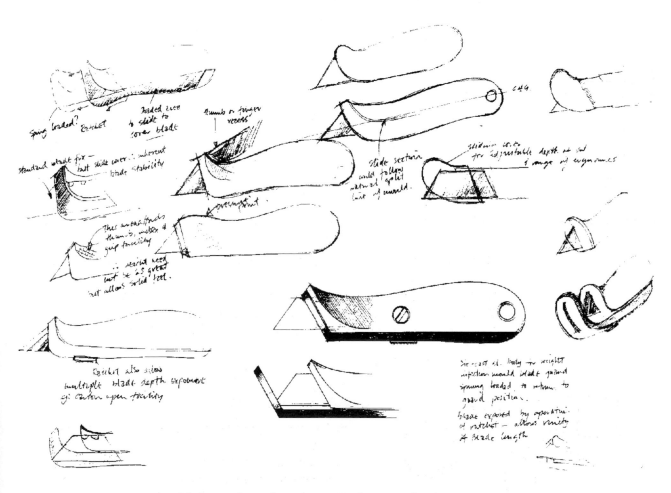

Using sketches to explore solutions

Once you have reached conclusions about the basic principles you will adopt to solve a problem, sketches allow you to explore many things. For example, you can investigate the possible arrangements of various parts or the possible ways in which components might be made.

Communicating ideas – pictorial views

If you want to produce a more precise view of an object, you need to use a drawing system. These can be divided into two categories:

■ **Paraline** drawings – these are made up of **parallel** lines to a set of rules.
■ **Perspective** drawings – these take account of **foreshortening** and, although there are rules, they can be modified.

Paraline drawings – isometric projection

Rules:

■ Lines which are vertical on the object are vertical in the drawing.
■ Lines which are horizontal on the object are at least 30 degrees to the horizontal on the drawing.
■ All measurements are true and must be made on the parallel lines.

The three stages in drawing a torch in **isometric** projection are shown here.

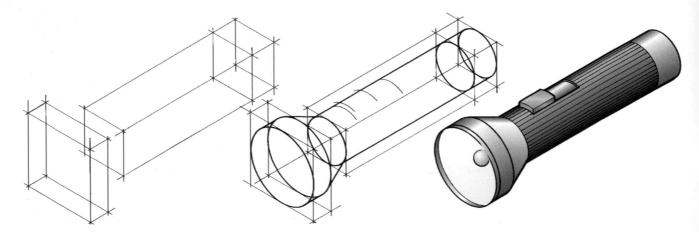

Paraline drawings – planometric or axonometric projection

Rules:

■ The plan is true and drawn at an angle to the horizontal, usually 45 degrees.
■ All measurements are true and must be made on the parallel lines.
■ Circles which are horizontal appear as circles, while all others appear as ellipses.

The three stages in drawing a PET bottle used for containing soft drinks are shown in **planometric** or **axonometric** projection.

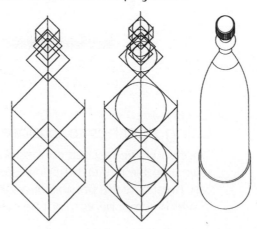

Perspective drawings – one-point perspective

Rules:

- All parallel lines converge towards one of the two vanishing points where they disappear.
- Equal lengths foreshorten the further they are away from the viewing point.
- The surface closest to the viewing point is the only true one and all measurements must be made on it.

The four stages in drawing a tape measure in one-point perspective are shown here.

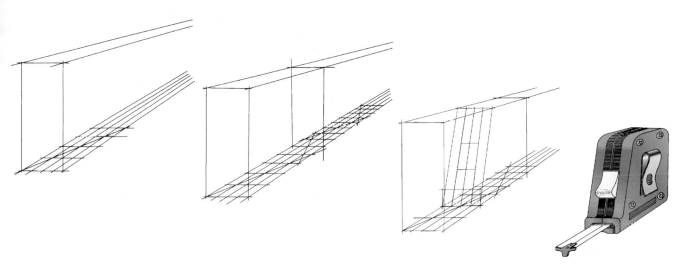

Perspective drawings – two-point perspective

Rules:

- The vertical edge closest to the viewing point is the only true one and all heights must be measured on it.
- The vanishing points are positioned on the horizon line which is always horizontal.
- Equal lengths foreshorten the further they are away from the viewing point.
- The vertical edge closest to the viewing point is the only true one and all measurements must be taken on it.

The four stages in drawing a personal stereo in two-point perspective are shown here.

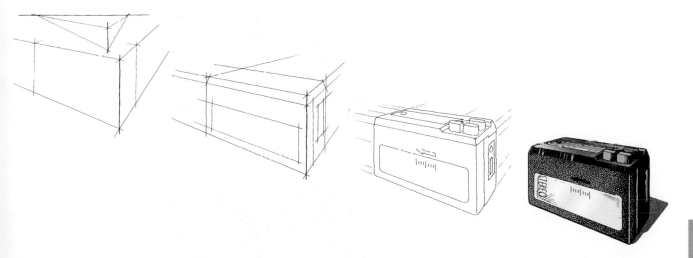

Exploded views

This type of view stretches the space between the various parts of an object. The different parts are positioned to show the relationship between them. These drawings illustrate the technique.

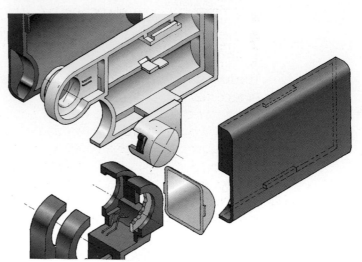

This type of pictorial view might be used in a manual or instruction book to show how things fit together or how they can be taken apart. Because the drawings are complicated, they are usually produced using the paraline system.

Cutaway drawings

This type of drawing cuts away part of the outer casing or shell of an object to show how the components fit together. It can be used to reveal the interior of anything from a gearbox to an aircraft. All the parts are shown in their actual position. This type of drawing is very good at explaining how something works as the relationship of the components is extremely clear. Because the drawings are complicated, they are usually produced using the paraline system. Sometimes, when an object is extremely complex, exploded and cutaway drawings are both used.

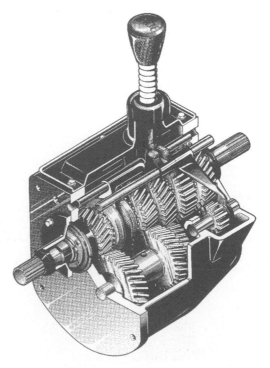

Presentation techniques – using markers

The illustration below shows the six stages involved.

1 Every visual starts with an accurate drawing of the product. It may be three-dimensional, normally perspective, axonometric or isometric, or a two-dimensional orthographic view, as in the case of the power drill shown.

2 The body of the drill is loosely streaked with a marker.

3 The surface relief is shown either using a darker marker or by several applications of the same marker. The detail is reinforced, especially in the recessed surface features.

4 The chuck is rendered to give the appearance of polished metal. This is done using black and grey markers and a blue coloured pencil.

5 A black marker is used to define very clearly the surface detail, such as the trigger and screws which hold the mouldings together. Sometimes a white coloured pencil, pastel or white paint is used to show the highlights, where light catches an edge or the surface of a spherical or curved object.

6 Finally, the drawing is cut out using a scalpel, and remounted.

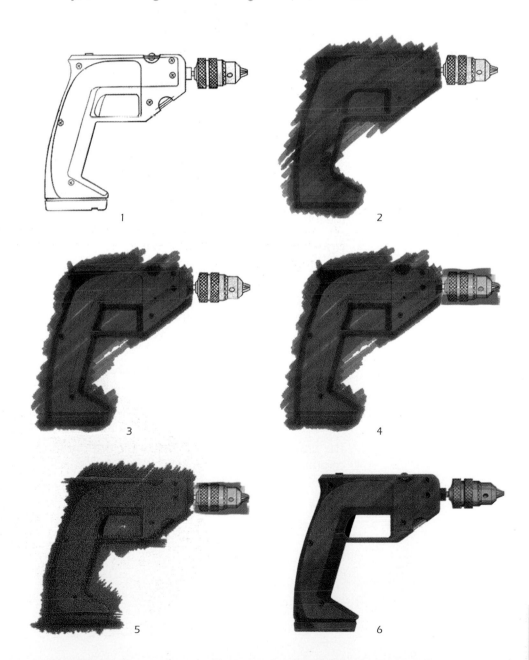

1

2

3

4

5

6

Production drawings

Orthographic projections

Production drawings or working drawings have to show every detail of an object so that it can be made exactly to the designer's specifications. All designers use the same language to communicate size, shape, form and accuracy – **orthographic projection**. This is a system of drawing that allows you to make very detailed drawings. Orthographic projection consists of producing a number of interrelated views of the same object; normally these views are drawn at right angles to each other.

There are two forms of orthographic projection in use throughout the world – **first angle** projection and **third angle** projection. Both systems are approved internationally and have equal status.

All orthographic drawings are made in relation to two **planes** – the **horizontal** plane and the **vertical** plane. The line where they intersect is called the **XY line**. These planes divide space into four **quadrants**. In a first angle orthographic projection, the object is imagined to be in the first quadrant. In a third angle orthographic projection, the object is imagined to be in the third quadrant. This determines the relationship of the views. When you draw the view from the top, it is called the **plan**. The particular orthographic projection system that has been used should always be indicated using the appropriate symbol.

The rules or guidelines for these types of drawings are laid down by an organisation called the British Standards Institution (BSI). BSI is principally concerned with ensuring quality and consistency. There are a number of British Standards which control the language of drawing. The one which will be of most use to you is **BS 308 Engineering Drawing Practice**.

If you produce working drawings to this standard, anyone will be able to manufacture what you have designed; standardisation is essential in any manufacturing industry. An abbreviated version, PD 7308, provides you with all the information you need to produce working drawings to British Standards.

First angle

In **first angle** orthographic projection:

- The elevations are above the XY line.
- The plan view is below the XY line.
- The front elevation is the most important elevation; the plan is always projected from it.
- The left-hand end of the object is seen in the end elevation to the right of the front elevation.
- The right-hand end of the object is seen in the end elevation to the left of the front elevation.

The drawings here show, in first angle orthographic projection, three views of a ceramic water valve.

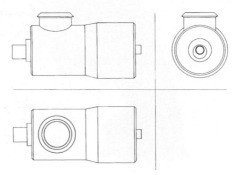

Third angle

These drawings show, in third angle orthographic projection, three views of a ceramic water valve.

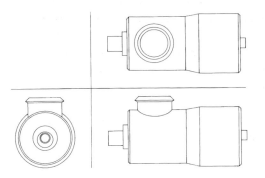

In third angle orthographic projection:

- The elevations lie in a horizontal line and are below the XY line.
- The plan view is above the XY line.
- The front elevation is the most important elevation; the plan is always drawn from it.
- The left-hand end of the object is seen in the end elevation to the left of the front elevation.
- The right-hand end of the object is seen in the end elevation to the right of the front elevation.

How to show more information

There are two important ways in which more information can be shown on an orthographic drawing.

Hidden detail

Internal edges which cannot be seen from the outside of an object can be shown using **dotted lines**. The valve has been drawn with dotted lines showing the hidden detail. The dotted lines provide a lot more information about the interior of the valve, but they are often quite difficult to interpret.

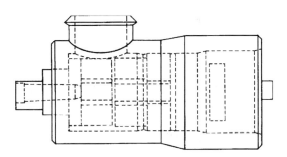

Sectioned views

An object can be drawn as if it has been cut in half; this is called **sectioning** the drawing. In some sectioned views, only a quarter of the object is cut away. The front elevation of the valve has been sectioned; now you can see clearly the internal workings of the valve.

There are some important rules to follow when drawing a sectioned view:
- **Cross-hatch** the cut surface at 45 degrees.
- Each part should be cross-hatched in a different direction or with different spacing between the cross-hatched lines.
- Show the plan of the section on an adjacent view.

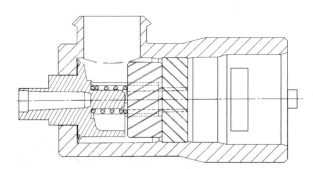

How to show dimensions

- **Dimension lines** should be drawn as continuous thin lines. They should be lighter than the outline of the component to avoid confusion.
- Try to put all dimension lines outside the component.
- Always leave a small gap between the dimension leader and the outside of the component.
- The dimension (the size) should be placed near the middle and slightly above the dimension line.
- Larger dimensions should be placed outside smaller dimensions.

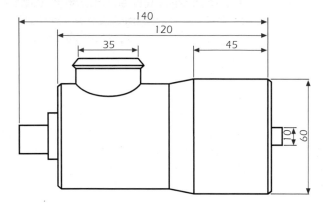

You can see how these rules have been applied to the drawing of the valve.

Using conventions

Some engineering components are too complicated to be drawn realistically. Conventions are used to show components such as screw threads. These are detailed in BS 308. All electrical components are shown by symbols on a circuit diagram: these are shown in BS 3939. Symbols for fluid power systems are given in BS 2917. BSI has published a compendium of standards for design and technology in schools – PD 7302. This is an extremely useful document as it covers many topics.

What other information should there be on a drawing?

It is traditional to put a border around an orthographic drawing. There should also be a title block which should include the following information:

- Descriptive title of the part or assembly.
- The projection symbol – first or third angle.
- The unit of measure.
- The scale of the drawing.
- The material of which the component is made.
- Name of the draughtsperson and the date.
- Sheet number and number in series, for example 3 of 10.
- If the product is made up of a number of components, a parts list.

Computer-aided design

Although you will learn how to draft working drawings to British Standards using traditional instruments, you should also have the opportunity to make drawings using computer-aided techniques. There are many different programs available, some more complex than others. They can, however, be divided into two main categories:

- drawing programs, and
- paint programs.

In a **drawing** program, elements such as a line or a circle can be manipulated as an independent object simply by selecting the object and moving it. In a **paint** program, moving a selected area of pixels requires repairing a 'hole' left by the moved area. This type of program lends itself better to freehand drawing.

Computer-aided drawings offer many advantages:

- They give constant drawing quality. Lines, dimensions, details, and so on, are independent of the individual draughtsperson.
- Commonly used symbols in electronics, pneumatics and hydraulics, and frequently used components, can be cut and pasted from a library of symbols.
- The drawings can be easily revised and edited, and time and effort saved on repetitive parts of drawings.

Most drawing programs use the same basic tools. These tools allow different shapes and lines to be drawn. An example of a **tool** 'palette' or 'box' is shown in the diagram on the left.

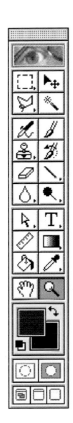

Computer models

Some drawing packages allow you to create computer-generated three-dimensional models from your two-dimensional orthographic drawings.

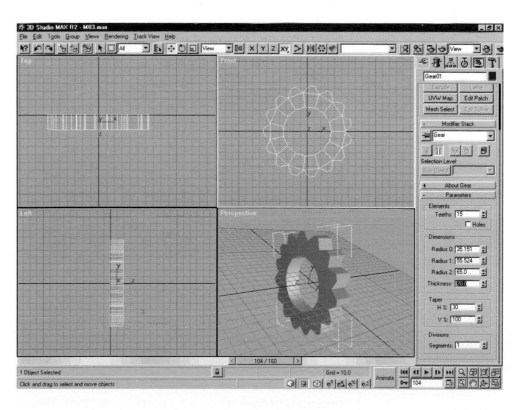

There are three types of computer modelling: wireframe, surface and solid.

Wireframe modelling

The image looks as if the object is made up of thin wires connected to all the edges and faces of the component.

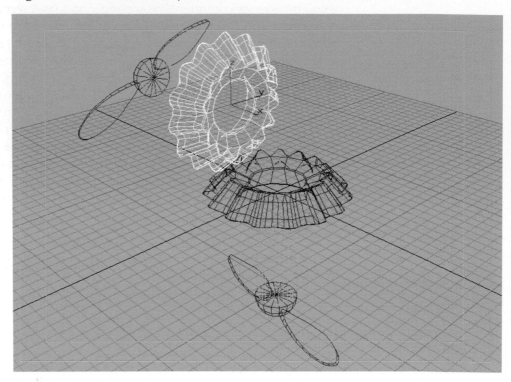

Surface modelling

The generated image is made up of the outer surface or shell of the object and therefore gives a good impression of the design. It is particularly useful for displaying complex curved shapes.

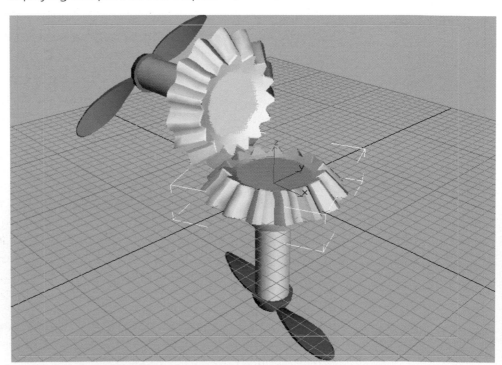

Solid modelling

This is similar to surface modelling but it also has information about the volume and mass of the object, not just the outer shell. This means that sectional views can be obtained readily.

See

- Membrane panel switch, page 218
- Radio, page 222
- Thermochromic indicator/display, page 233
- Personal organiser, page 234
- Torch, page 238
- Kaleidoscope, page 240

(See also Manufacturing, page 29.)

9 Ergonomics

Any engineer designing a product or a system will require exact information about materials, structures, tolerances, power and the capacities of various components, and how to combine them when trying to meet a specification. However, in the past, designers relied on common sense when considering the needs of the people who would use and operate the products and systems they designed. The study of people in order to design products and systems which are better adapted to human capabilities is known as **ergonomics**; it is a relatively new science.

Ergonomists are employed to improve efficiency, reliability and safety. They aim to improve the design of things, such as control panels, to make them easier for people to use. An ergonomist would carry out detailed experiments to ensure, for example, that information is presented in the most appropriate way, that controls are placed within easy reach, and that the force required to operate the controls is in relation to the accuracy required. Ergonomists are also concerned with the environment – the level of lighting, temperature and noise – as these are all important factors in creating good working conditions.

As well as trying to improve the design of new products and systems, ergonomics is also used to improve the efficiency of existing ones. It is very important to ensure that people who spend a long time in the same position do not develop painful and crippling problems such as repetitive strain injury (RSI). Computer operators, for example, sit for long periods repeating very simple movements. One way of solving the problem might be to design a better chair. Most chairs are like the ones you sit on at school: they cannot be adjusted. We have to adjust ourselves to fit the chair; this results in fidgeting, discomfort and loss of attention. Ergonomic designers believe that adjustable chairs would be better. If the operator were more comfortable, efficiency would be improved and there would be less chance of injury. To meet this need, engineers have produced fully-adjustable chairs that have up to 150 moving parts and come with a user's manual for the owner!

The challenge for designers and engineers is to design things which can be used by the majority of the population. Because we are all different this often means providing a limited form of adjustment. The driver's seat in a car has a number of adjustments which allow it to be customised by each driver. It is only Formula One drivers who have cockpits tailor-made to their own measurements!

Knowing the measurements of the person or persons for whom you are designing is the key to successful design. **Anthropometrics** is the scientific study of the measurements of the human body. Henry Dreyfus, an American industrial designer, pioneered the gathering of this information; he called it **human engineering**. He was concerned about extreme dimensions as well as the average ones, as people come in all shapes and sizes. In addition to producing charts of the average anatomical size of every conceivable part of the body, he also gathered information on every conceivable aspect, such as the amount of pressure the average foot can comfortably exert on a pedal, how hard a hand can effectively squeeze, the reach of an arm, and so on. All this information provides a very detailed picture of the average man and woman. Dreyfus called these average adults Joe and Josephine. In addition he created Joe and Josephine junior, average six-year-olds.

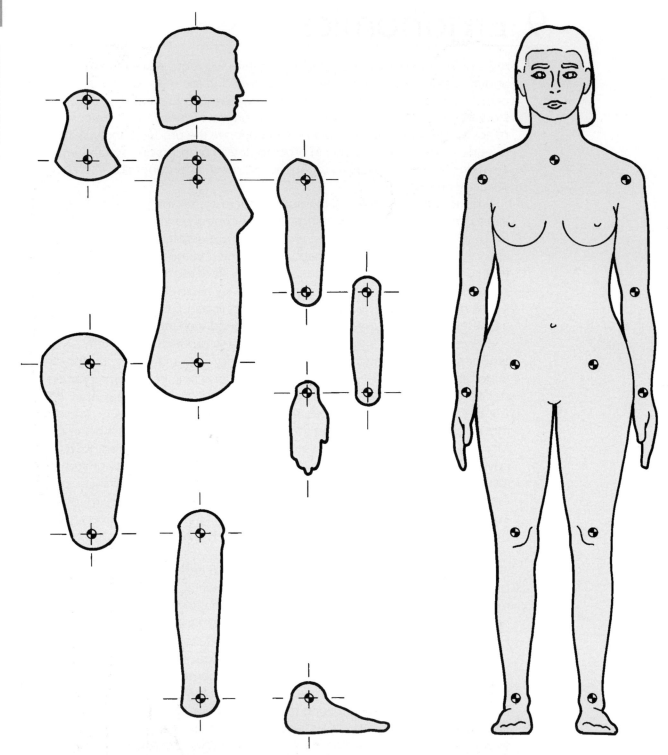

However, ergonomic data differ between races, and change with time. For example, some Asian races were traditionally smaller than western races. British manufacturers exporting beds to Japan had to make smaller beds than those they sold in Europe. However, with improved diet, mainly by increased protein intake, these races are quickly catching up. In most races succeeding generations are gradually getting bigger because of both better diet and better health care. Look at the doorways in old houses: nowadays many people have to bend down to get through them. In Britain, the average height of a man is 1753 mm and that of a woman is 1626 mm; 400 years ago the average height was at least 250 mm less.

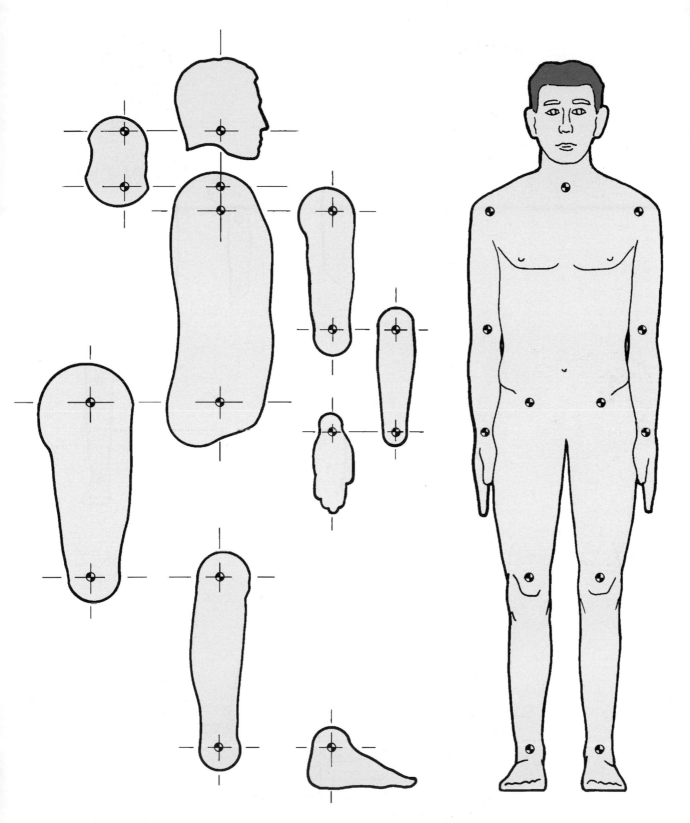

Ergonomic information can come in the form of charts, line drawings or models with pin joints, known as **ergonomes**. If you copy the line drawings on pages 96–98 onto card you can make an ergonome. Paper fasteners or eyelets can be used to make rotating joints or, alternatively, use drawing pins and a board.

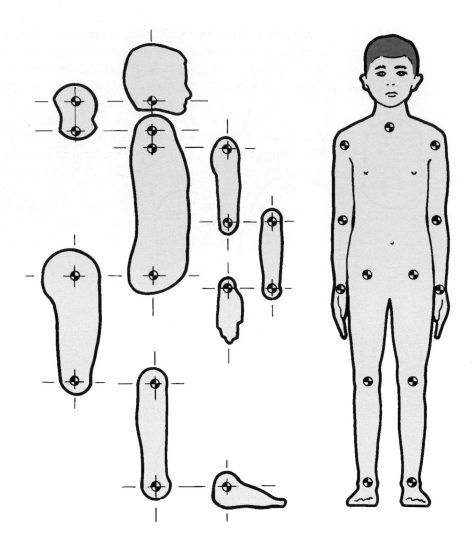

An ergonome can be used to investigate the size and layout of things you are designing, like the drawings of the console/desk. If you do this you must make sure that the drawings and ergonome are to the same scale.

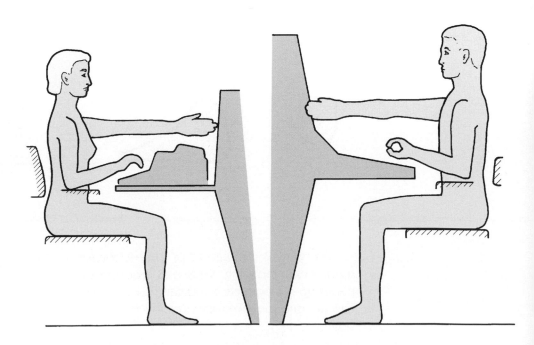

Models, both scale and full-size, could be used to investigate the layout of a working environment. A kitchen is a working environment and the position of the sink, cooker, fridge and work surfaces relative to one another will affect efficiency. In industry people's movements are recorded using such techniques as time-lapse photography, lights attached to limbs to record movement, and electronic probes fitted to prototypes. In a commercial kitchen good organisation and layout are even more important. Look at what goes on behind the counter next time you buy a hamburger. Ergonomists have evolved a highly efficient layout so that your order is produced in the shortest possible time and is of consistent quality.

The British Standards Institution provides ergonomic information in relation to a wide variety of things. It produces a compendium for design and technology (PD 7302) which contains much useful data. A few examples are as follows:

- dimensions in designing for the elderly
- design of housing for disabled people
- play equipment for outdoor installation
- educational furniture
- office furniture.

See

- Ergonomic handle, page 229

SECTION 2

data

1 Electronic devices

Resistors

What they look like

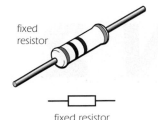

fixed resistor

fixed resistor

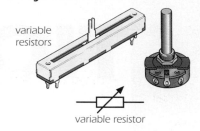

variable resistors

variable resistor

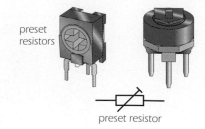

preset resistors

preset resistor

What they are used for

Resistors are very common components in electronic circuits. At first sight they do not appear to do much at all, but without them it would not be possible to control the operation of most electronic circuits. This is because resistors are used to limit the amount of current flowing in a circuit or to set the voltage level in a particular part of a circuit.

What they are made of

Most materials can be classified as either **conductors** or **insulators**. A conductor, such as copper, will allow a current to flow through it easily. An insulator, such as acrylic, will not allow a current to flow through it easily. However, this is a very simple method of classification, as some conductors conduct better than others and some insulators insulate better than others.

It would be more accurate to think of a scale, or range, of materials where at one end there would be the best insulator and at the other end the best conductor. The ability or inability of a material to conduct an electric current is known as its **resistance**. All materials have some resistance to the flow of electric current. Resistance is measured in **ohms** and this quantity is given the symbol Ω.

The most common type of resistor is made from a composite (mixture) of a conducting material (carbon) and an insulating material (ceramic). By changing the proportions of these two materials it is possible to attain different values of resistance, since

> More carbon and less ceramic = low resistance
> Less carbon and more ceramic = high resistance

These resistors are known as **carbon composition** resistors.
Resistors are also made from the following materials.

■ A thin layer of carbon around a ceramic rod. The thickness of the layer of carbon sets the resistance, since a thicker film gives a lower resistance. These are known as **carbon film** resistors.

■ A metal alloy wire wound around a ceramic tube. The resistance is set by a number of factors but mainly by the length of the wire. A longer wire gives a higher resistance. These are known as **wire-wound** resistors and are most often used in high power applications.

■ A mixture of ceramic and metal oxide. This composite is known as **cermet** and the resistance is set in a similar way to carbon composition resistors. Cermet is used to make **variable** resistors. The material is arranged as a track that a slider can move along. Moving the slider changes the length of the track that the current has to flow through and, hence, the total value of resistance.

How they work

If one volt is applied across a resistor and it allows one amp to flow through it, then its resistance is one ohm.

So the resistance (R) of a resistor can be calculated by dividing the voltage (V) applied across it by the current (I) flowing through it:

$$R = V \div I$$

This equation is known as **Ohm's Law**.

How you use them

Resistors can be used to **limit the current** flowing in part of a circuit or to **set the voltage** at a particular point in a circuit.

Current limiting

Some electronic components such as an LED (light-emitting diode) (see page 128) or the base/emitter junction of a transistor (see page 110) have a very low resistance. You use a resistor to limit the amount of current that flows through them so that they can operate correctly and not be damaged.

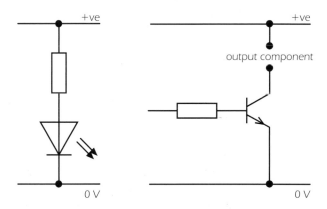

Setting voltage (potential divider)

Two resistors connected in series will work as a potential (voltage) divider.

If a voltmeter is placed across the supply shown in the figure it will read 9 V. If it is placed between the junction of the two resistors and the 0 V rail it will read 4.5 V. The supply voltage will have been divided exactly in half.

If the value of the resistors is changed then the voltage at the junction of the two resistors will also change. The voltage at the junction is set by the ratio of the two resistor values. This can be calculated by using the formula:

$$V = \text{supply voltage} \times \frac{R_2}{R_1 + R_2}$$

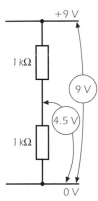

For example, if R_1 is kept at 1 kΩ but R_2 is made 2 kΩ,

$$V = 9\,V \times \frac{2000\,\Omega}{3000\,\Omega}$$

$$= 9\,V \times \frac{2}{3}$$

$$= 6\,V$$

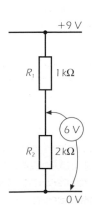

Resistor values

Colour code

Resistors are painted with bands of **colour**. These coloured bands are a code which is used to give their value. This might seem like a complicated way to do things, but remember that many resistors are quite small so printing their value in numbers would be difficult and expensive, and they would be difficult to read.

To find the value of the resistor, it should be placed so that the three bands of colour that are close together are on the left, and the single band of colour is on the right. The colour bands are then read from left to right to give the resistance in ohms (Ω). The first two bands state the first two digits of the value and the third band gives the number of zeros to be added.

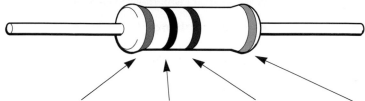

Colours	Band 1	Band 2	Band 3	Tolerance
Black	0	0	×1	
Brown	1	1	×10	
Red	2	2	×100	
Orange	3	3	×1000	
Yellow	4	4	×10 000	
Green	5	5	×100 000	
Blue	6	6	×1 000 000	
Violet	7	7		
Grey	8	8		
White	9	9		
Silver				±10%
Gold				±5%

Colours	Brown	Black	Red
Meaning	1	0	+2 zeros
	1	0	00
Resistance	1000 Ω		

Colours	Yellow	Violet	Brown
Meaning	4	7	+1 zero
	4	7	0
Resistance	470 Ω		

The final band of colour gives the resistor **tolerance**. The stated value of a resistor can never be exact. Instead, manufacturers give an indication of a range of values that the resistor will be within.

- Gold band = ±5%
- Silver band = ±10%

For example, brown, black, red and gold bands would indicate a 1 kΩ resistor with a ±5% tolerance. This means that the actual resistor value could be anywhere between 950 Ω and 1050 Ω, which is 5% more or 5% less than the given value.

Written values

Values of resistance can use the normal prefixes that other units use, for example:

- kilo = 1000 (abbreviated to k)
- mega = 1 000 000 (abbreviated to M)

So,

- 1 kilohm (kΩ) = 1000 Ω
- 1 megohm (MΩ) = 1 000 000 Ω

and, for example,

- 4700 Ω = 4.7 kΩ
- 2 200 000 Ω = 2.2 MΩ

This avoids confusion for larger values of resistance where counting lots of zeros could lead to mistakes.

Printed code

An alternative method to colour codes is used with variable resistors. This method is also sometimes used in circuit diagrams.

This code uses **letters and numbers** to give the value of the resistor.

- R stands for 1
- K stands for 1000
- M stands for 1 000 000

The position of the letters gives the decimal point, for example:

- 10R – 10 Ω
- 2K2 = 2.2 kΩ or 2200 Ω
- 4M7 = 4.7 MΩ or 4 700 000 Ω

Sometimes letters are added at the end of the code to give the manufacturer's tolerance for the resistor:

- J = ±5%
- K = ±10%

For example, 6K8K = 6.8 kΩ ± 10%.

Note that K can be used for two different things. In the middle of the code it refers to the value, but at the end of the code it refers to the tolerance.

Preferred values

Although it is technically possible to produce every value of resistor from less than one ohm to many millions of ohms, it would not be economical to do so. Instead manufacturers produce a range of resistors in a series of **preferred values**.

The E12 and E24 series of preferred values start as shown in the table.

E12	E24	E12	E24
10R	10R	330R	330R
	11R		360R
12R	12R	390R	390R
	13R		430R
15R	15R	470R	470R
	16R		510R
18R	18R	560R	560R
	20R		620R
22R	22R	680R	680R
	24R		750R
27R	27R	820R	820R
	30R		910R
33R	33R	1K	1K
	36R		1K1
39R	39R	1K2	1K2
	43R		1K3
47R	47R	1K5	1K5
	51R		1K6
56R	56R	1K8	1K8
	62R		2K0
68R	68R	2K2	2K2
	75R		2K4
82R	82R	2K7	2K7
	91R		3K0
100R	100R	3K3	3K3
	110R		3K6
120R	120R	3K9	3K9
	130R		4K3
150R	150R	4K7	4K7
	160R		5K1
180R	180R	5K6	5K6
	200R		6K2
220R	220R	6K8	6K8
	240R		7K5
270R	270R	8K2	8K2
	300R		9K1
		etc	etc

Resistors in series and parallel

Resistors can be connected together in **series** or **parallel** networks to obtain different total values of resistance or to divide voltage and current. The diagrams show how this is done.

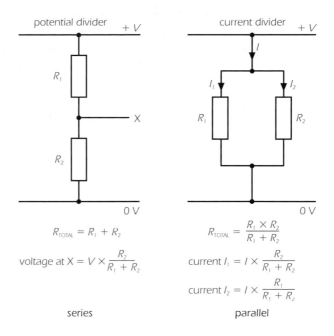

potential divider	current divider

$$R_{TOTAL} = R_1 + R_2$$

$$\text{voltage at } X = V \times \frac{R_2}{R_1 + R_2}$$

$$R_{TOTAL} = \frac{R_1 \times R_2}{R_1 + R_2}$$

$$\text{current } I_1 = I \times \frac{R_2}{R_1 + R_2}$$

$$\text{current } I_2 = I \times \frac{R_1}{R_1 + R_2}$$

series   parallel

Power rating

When a current flows through a resistor it will heat up. If resistors get too hot, they burn out. Higher power resistors are physically larger and can dissipate (get rid of) more heat.

Power (P) is measured in **watts** (W) and can be calculated using either

$$P = IV \quad \text{or} \quad P = I^2R$$

The typical size of resistor used in electronics has a power rating of 0.25 W.

See

- Electronic timer, page 215

■ Light-dependent resistors (LDRs)

What they look like

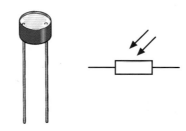

What they are used for

Light-dependent resistors (LDRs) are special resistors that change their value of resistance depending on how much light is shining on them. The example shown in the diagram above is an ORP 12. This is the most common type used. In the dark its resistance is about 10 MΩ and in bright sunlight this will fall to about 150 Ω. LDRs are used in electronic control circuits that need to respond to a change in light levels, for example in automatic lighting systems.

What they are made of

LDRs are made from a **semiconductor** material. Semiconductors are used in diodes, transistors and integrated circuits (ICs). All semiconductors will respond to light energy. Their resistance falls when more light falls on them. However, diodes, transistors and ICs are made from silicon and, although this material is sensitive to light energy, its response is not sensitive enough to make an LDR.

LDRs are made from cadmium sulphide. This material is often called by its chemical symbol CdS. So LDRs are also known as CdS cells.

If you look through the transparent plastic window of an LDR you will see the brownish coloured track of CdS which forms the LDR.

How they work

The resistance of an LDR falls as the light level rises and rises as the light level falls. However, this simple change in resistance cannot be used to control an electronic circuit. LDRs are used in potential divider circuits (see below) which can convert this change in resistance to a change in voltage. This change in voltage can be used to control electronic circuits.

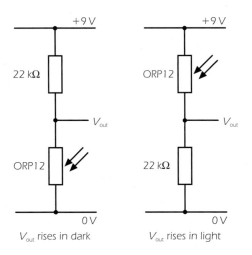

V_{out} rises in dark V_{out} rises in light

How you use them

When the LDR is connected into a potential divider circuit it can be used as a sensor. From the diagrams below you can see that the LDR can be used as a light sensor or a dark sensor. The output voltage from the sensor can be used to control a transistor or to trigger an integrated circuit (IC).

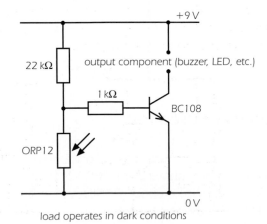

load operates in dark conditions

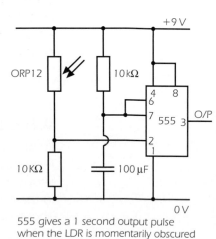

555 gives a 1 second output pulse when the LDR is momentarily obscured

■ Thermistors

What they look like

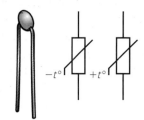

What they are used for

Thermistors are special resistors that change their value of resistance depending on their **temperature**. Thermistors can operate in one of two ways. The diagram shows the two different circuit symbols. One type has a **positive** symbol next to it and the other has a **negative** symbol next to it. The symbol tells you how the thermistor responds to a change in temperature. A positive symbol indicates that resistance increases as it gets hotter, and a negative symbol indicates that resistance decreases as it gets hotter. This concept is known as the **temperature coefficient**. The most common type has a negative symbol.

Thermistors are available in a variety of values (1 kΩ, 4.7 kΩ, 100 kΩ, and so on). The resistance stated is normally the resistance of the device at 20 °C.

Thermistors are used in electronic control circuits that need to respond to a change in temperature, as in overheat alarms, frost warning systems, and so on.

What they are made of

There are several different types of thermistor available. The most common types are made from a composite material which contains carbon and ceramic.

How they work

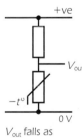

V_{out} rises as
temperature rises

V_{out} falls as
temperature rises

The resistance of a thermistor with a negative temperature coefficient falls as it gets hotter and rises as it gets cooler. However, this simple change in resistance cannot be used to control an electronic circuit. Thermistors are used in potential divider circuits (see left) which can convert this change in resistance to a change in voltage. This change in voltage can be used to control electronic circuits.

How you use them

When the thermistor is connected into a potential divider circuit it can be used as a **sensor**. From the diagram you can see that the thermistor can be used as a heat sensor or a cold sensor. The output voltage from the sensor can be used to control a transistor or to trigger a thyristor.

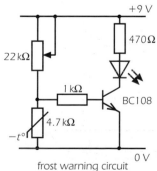

frost warning circuit

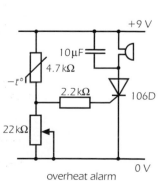

overheat alarm

Bipolar transistors

What they look like

underside view

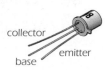

collector

base

emitter

collector

base

emitter

What they are used for

- As a current **amplifier** (making the current bigger). Depending on the device chosen, they can amplify current from 20 to 1000 times.
- As a high-speed electronic **switch**. The typical switching speed for a bipolar transistor is 5 ns. (1 nanosecond is 1/1 000 000 000 of a second.)

Bipolar transistors are available as discrete components (see figure above). They can also be part of an integrated circuit (IC).

What they are made of

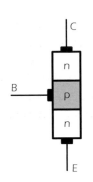

Bipolar transistors are made from **silicon** which is a semiconductor material. The silicon has either boron or phosphorus diffused into it. Silicon with boron is known as a **p-type** semiconductor and silicon with phosphorus is known as an **n-type** semiconductor. A bipolar transistor is made from a sandwich of n-type and p-type semiconductors. The **base**, **emitter** and **collector** connections are made to each layer.

The silicon is enclosed in either a metal or plastic case or 'can'. Note that if a transistor has a metal case or metal heat-sink tag, this normally has an internal connection to the collector of the transistor. Take care that you do not short the metal case to the 0 V rail.

How they work

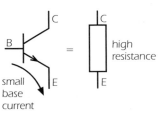

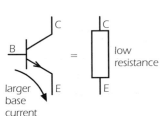

The word 'transistor' is a shortened form of 'transfer-resistor'. This gives an indication of how the device works. The transistor is controlled from the base connection.

Applying a voltage of more than 0.6 V across the base emitter will cause a small current to flow into the base and out of the emitter. This base current causes the resistance between the collector and emitter to fall. Up to a certain limit, the more current that is pushed through the base emitter of the transistor the more the resistance between the collector and emitter will fall.

The control of the resistance between the collector and emitter by the current flowing into the base is used to amplify signals and in electronic switching.

How you use them

You need to connect the device to be switched on and off in the collector circuit of the transistor. The device is switched on and off by changing the current that flows into the base. This arrangement is often used in the process stage of simple transistor switching circuits or to interface a fairly high current-consumption output component (such as a buzzer or lamp) to the output of an integrated circuit (IC).

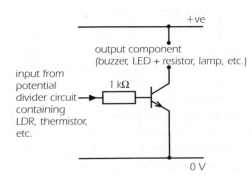

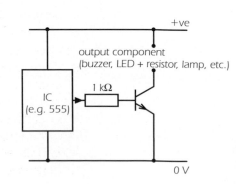

Phototransistors

What they look like

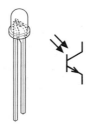

What they are used for

Phototransistors are special transistors that change the resistance between their collector and emitter depending on how much **light** is shining on them. The example shown in the diagram above is a silicon n-p-n type. This is a readily available and useful type. They are used in similar applications to light-dependent resistors (LDRs), but they offer two main advantages. They allow less leakage current to flow in the potential divider input circuit (see page 112) and they are generally more sensitive with a faster response time.

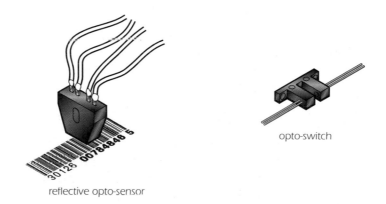

reflective opto-sensor

opto-switch

In the dark the resistance between the collector and emitter will be very high indeed. In a typical application this would allow only a few nanoamps to flow through the potential divider part of the circuit. (1 nanoamp = 1/1 000 000 000 of an amp.) In bright light the resistance between the collector and emitter falls, which will allow currents of up 500 µA to flow. Phototransistors are used as input devices to electronic control circuits that need to respond to a change in light levels. Because they have a low leakage current and a fast response time, they are often used in **counting** objects or as part of an **opto sensor/switch**.

What they are made of

Phototransistors are made in almost the same way and from the same materials as conventional bipolar transistors. They are made from **silicon** which is a semiconductor material. The silicon has either boron or phosphorus diffused into it. Silicon with boron is known as a **p-type** semiconductor and silicon with phosphorus is known as an **n-type** semiconductor. A phototransistor is made from a sandwich of n-type and p-type semiconductors.

In a phototransistor the junction between the base and emitter is generally larger than for a bipolar transistor and is arranged so that the junction can be exposed to light. Light enters the transistor via a transparent plastic window in the metal case, or sometimes the whole transistor case is made from solid transparent plastic.

How they work

Phototransistors are used in similar ways to light-dependent resistors. In most applications only their collector and emitter connections are used and the base is left disconnected.

When light falls on the base/emitter junction a small base current is generated at the junction. This is achieved by the same process as in a solar cell. The base current generated by the light has the same effect as it would in a conventional transistor, that is, the resistance between the collector and emitter falls.

Phototransistors are often used in potential divider circuits (see below), which can convert this change in resistance to a change in voltage. The change in voltage can be used to control electronic circuits.

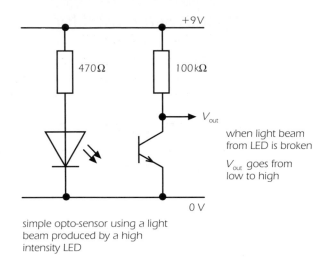

when light beam from LED is broken

V_{out} goes from low to high

simple opto-sensor using a light beam produced by a high intensity LED

How you use them

When the phototransistor is connected into a potential divider circuit it can be used as a **sensor**. The output voltage from the sensor can be used to control a transistor or to trigger an integrated circuit (IC).

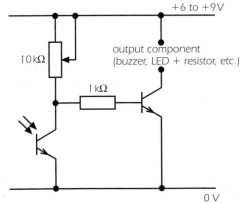

using a phototransistor instead of an LDR to reduce the current in the potential divider which will increase battery life

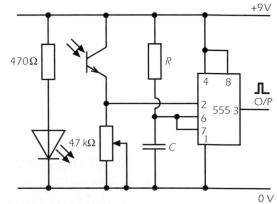

555 gives clean pulse output when light beam is broken. Choose values of R and C to get the pulse duration that you need

Field effect transistors (FETs)

What they look like

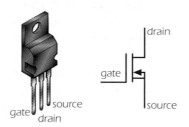

What they are used for

Field effect transistors (FETs) are used in similar applications to bipolar transistors (see page 110). However, FETs are often used to control high currents or to switch high-current devices, like motors, on and off.

What they are made of

A FET is made from a combination of **n-type** and **p-type** semiconductors (see page 126) with metal contacts.

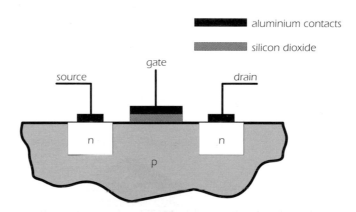

How they work

A voltage of more than 2 V applied to the **gate** will cause the resistance between the **drain** and **source** to fall. As the voltage applied to the gate rises, the resistance between the drain and source continues to fall.

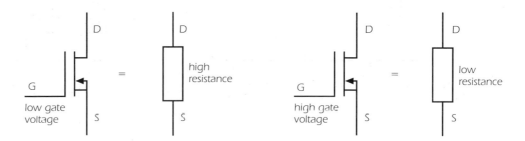

The control of the resistance between the drain and source by the voltage applied to the gate is used to **amplify** signals and in electronic **switching** in high-current applications.

See

• Dispensing system, page 206
• Auto-shutdown product, page 219

How you use them

Connect the device to be switched on and off in the drain circuit of the FET. The device is switched on and off by changing the voltage that is applied to the base. This arrangement is often used in the process stage of simple transistor switching circuits or to interface a high-current-consumption output component to the output of an integrated circuit (IC).

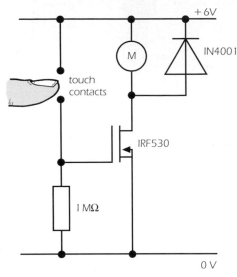

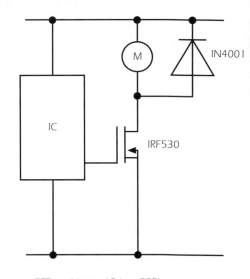

a 'touch sensitive' switch (motor runs when touch contacts are bridged by a finger)

a FET enables an IC (e.g. 555) to control a high current load like a motor

■ Integrated circuits: The 555 timer

What they look like

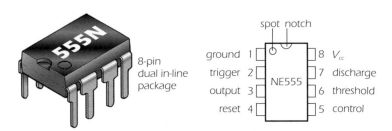

8-pin dual in-line package

ground	1	8	V_{cc}
trigger	2	7	discharge
output	3	6	threshold
reset	4	5	control

NE555

spot notch

What they are used for

The **555** is used as the main component in one of two **multivibrator** circuits.

■ Monostable multivibrator – Used to switch something **on or off** for a certain amount of time.
■ Astable multivibrator – Used as a **pulse generator**, for example to provide a series of clock pulses for a counter, to turn something on and off continually, or to generate audible tones.

What they are made of

The 555 is an **integrated circuit (IC)** which consists of a **silicon chip** inside a plastic **8-pin DIL package**. The circuit contains two **comparators**, a **bistable**, **resistors** and **transistors**. It is also available in a dual package which has two individual 555s on one chip, called a **556**.

How they work

Monostable mode

The output from the 555 is at 0 V until the circuit is triggered. The trigger can come from a switch or from an electronic signal. When the circuit is triggered the output switches on, and stays on for a set amount of time. This time period is set by one resistor and one capacitor which are connected to the 555. When this time period is complete the output switches off again. The output will stay switched off until the circuit is triggered again.

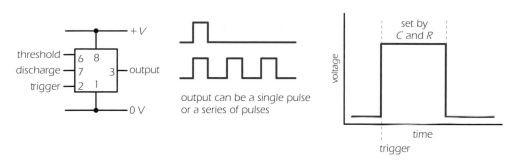

output can be a single pulse or a series of pulses

Astable mode

The output switches on and off continually to form a series of pulses. The number of pulses per second (the frequency) is set by two resistors and one capacitor which are connected to the 555.

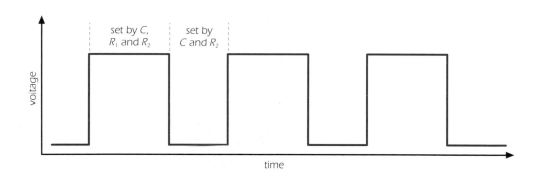

How you use them

Monostable mode

The time that the monostable switches on for (T) after being triggered is set by the values of C_1 and R_1.

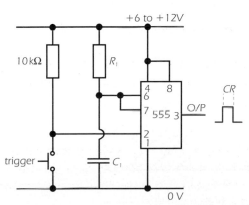

This time period can be calculated by using the formula

$$T = 1.1 \times CR \quad \text{(where 1.1 is a constant)}$$

For example:

$$C_1 = 100 \text{ k}\Omega$$
$$R_1 = 10 \text{ }\mu\text{F}$$
$$T = 1.1 \times CR$$
$$= 1.1 \times (100\,000 \times 0.000\,01)$$
$$= 1.1 \times 1$$
$$= 1.1 \text{ s}$$

Astable mode

The number of pulses in one second (the frequency) is set by the values of C_1, R_1 and R_2. The output frequency can be calculated using the formula

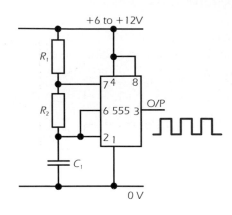

$$f = \frac{1.44}{(R_1 + 2R_2)\, C_1}$$

For example:

$$R_1 = 10\ \text{k}\Omega$$
$$R_2 = 100\ \text{k}\Omega$$
$$C_1 = 1\ \mu\text{F}$$

$$f = \frac{1.44}{(10\ 000 + 200\ 000)\ 0.000\ 001}$$

$$= \frac{1.44}{210\ 000 \times 0.000\ 001}$$

$$= \frac{1.44}{0.21}$$

$$= 6.9\ \text{Hz}$$

Note that the length of time for which the output is switched on (the **mark**) is set by R_1 and R_2 in series. The length of time it is switched off (the **space**) is set by R_2 only. Because of this, the output can never be a symmetrical waveform, that is, the mark to space ratio can never be 1 : 1.

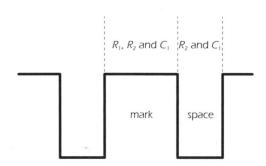

To get a reasonably symmetrical output, always make R_1 at least ten times smaller than R_2.

A quicker method of finding the output frequency is to look it up on a series chart (see below).

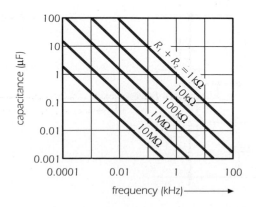

Integrated circuits: The 741 operational amplifier (op-amp)

What they look like

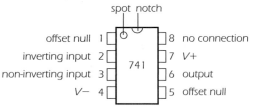

spot notch

offset null 1 | | 8 no connection
inverting input 2 | 741 | 7 V+
non-inverting input 3 | | 6 output
V— 4 | | 5 offset null

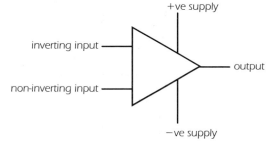

+ve supply

inverting input

non-inverting input

output

−ve supply

What they are used for

Op-amps have many uses, depending upon the components that are connected to them. The main uses are:

- As an **amplifier**. The gain of the amplifier can be easily set using resistors.
- As a **voltage comparator** in control circuits (see below).

What they are made of

The **741 op-amp** is an **integrated circuit (IC)** which consists of a silicon chip in a plastic **8-pin DIL package**. The circuit contains 20 transistors, 11 resistors and a capacitor.

The 741 op-amp has a maximum gain of 100 000 (10^5).

How they work

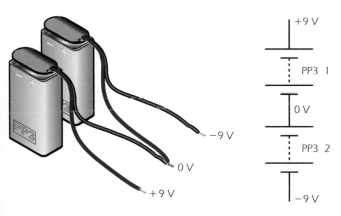

+9 V

PP3 1

0 V

−9 V

PP3 2

−9 V

Most 741 op-amp circuits require a **dual polarity** power supply. This is different from many other circuits. The dual polarity supply can be made from two 9 V PP3 batteries.

The 741 op-amp has two inputs and one output. It works as a **differential amplifier**. This means that the 741 amplifies the difference between the two inputs.

If both inputs are at the same voltage then the output will be at 0 V. The output becomes more positive as the non-inverting input (see below) rises, and more negative as the inverting input rises.

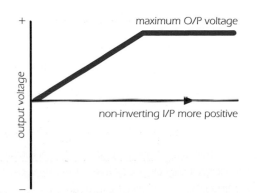

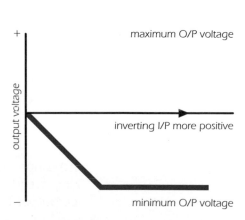

How you use them

With any amplifier circuit the voltage gain (A_v) is calculated using the formula:

$$A_v = \frac{\text{output voltage}}{\text{input voltage}} = \frac{V_{out}}{V_{in}}$$

For example, if $V_{in} = 0.5$ V and $V_{out} = 7$ V then

$$A_v = \frac{7}{0.5}$$

$$= 14$$

Inverting amplifier

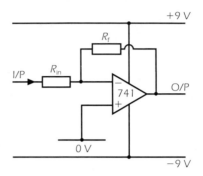

The gain is set by R_f (feedback resistor) and R_{in} (input resistor). A_v can be calculated using the formula:

$$A_v = -\frac{R_f}{R_{in}}$$

The minus sign means that the output is positive when the input is negative and vice versa. The output will always be inverted with respect to the input.

Non-inverting amplifier

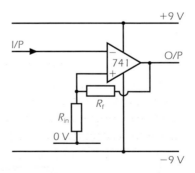

The gain is set by R_f (feedback resistor) and R_{in} (input resistor). A_v can be calculated using the formula:

$$A_v = 1 + \frac{R_f}{R_{in}}$$

If the input goes positive then the output will go positive, and if the input goes negative then the output will go negative. With a non-inverting amplifier the output will be an amplified version of the input.

Summing amplifier

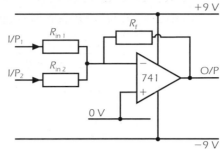

In a simple summing amplifier the output will be the sum of the two inputs. For this circuit to work the gain of the amplifier must be 1, or unity.

$$R_{in1} = R_{in2} = R_f$$

Voltage comparator

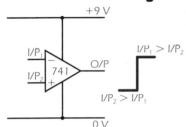

A comparator circuit can use a dual polarity supply in the same way as the op amp circuits on pages 118–19, but it is more often used with a single supply as shown in this diagram.

The comparator circuit has no feedback resistor (R_f). This will cause the op-amp to be working at its maximum gain of 100 000.

The comparator compares two input voltages and amplifies the difference between them. Any slight difference between the two voltages causes the output to swing to either maximum positive or maximum negative. In practice the output can reach only to approximately 2 V within the supply voltage, so in the case of a single supply comparator circuit with a 9 V supply, the output will always be at either 2 V or 7 V.

Practical comparator circuit (non-inverting)

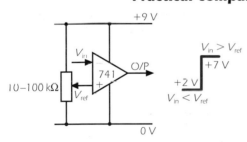

In a practical comparator circuit the inverting input is kept at a constant voltage set by either a potential divider or a potentiometer. This is known as the **reference voltage**. The input voltage is then fed to the non-inverting input.

- If $V_{in} < V_{ref}$ then $V_{out} = 2$ V
- If $V_{in} > V_{ref}$ then $V_{out} = 7$ V

Note that the 741 can source a current of only about 10 mA. Outputs requiring a greater current will need to be interfaced with a transistor. However, the threshold voltage of a bipolar transistor is 0.6 V so it would always be switched on with a single supply comparator. This difficulty can be overcome by using a potential divider (see below) at the output of the comparator circuit.

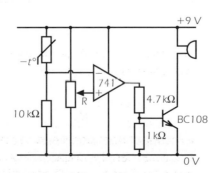

Integrated circuits: Logic gates

What they look like

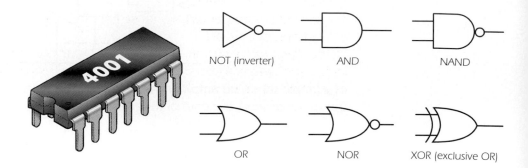

NOT (inverter) AND NAND

OR NOR XOR (exclusive OR)

What they are used for

Logic gates are used in control circuits to:

■ enable control systems to respond to a number of inputs
■ control the flow of data through a system.

Logic gates are circuits which have a logical function such as AND, OR, NAND, NOR, NOT; for example a central heating system will switch on if the time clock is on AND the thermostat is on, OR the manual override switch is on.

What they are made of

Logic gates can be made from discrete components but they most commonly come in the form of an **integrated circuit (IC)**. The IC will normally have a number of individual logic gates of the same type within it.

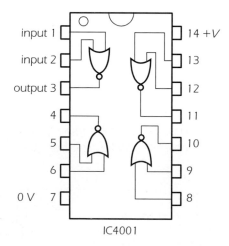

IC4001

The diagram above shows the internal circuit of a 4001 IC. This is a quad, two-input NOR gate. There are four individual NOR gates each with two inputs. The power supply fed to pins 7 and 14 is internally connected to all of the individual gates.

How they work

Logic gates are **digital** devices so their inputs and outputs can only ever be at **logic** 0 or **logic** 1.

■ Logic 0 = 0 V.
■ Logic 1 = supply voltage.

The state of the output will always be controlled by the state of the inputs and the function of the gate.

The diagram (below left) shows an AND gate. So if input A AND input B are at logic 1 then the output will be at logic 1. Any other combination of inputs will cause the output to be at logic 0.

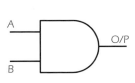

A	B	O/P
0	0	0
0	1	0
1	0	0
1	1	1

The function of logic gates is often expressed as a **truth table** (above right) which lists the possible combinations of inputs and the resulting outputs.

The large table below shows a number of different types of logic gates, their circuit symbols, their truth tables and their type numbers.

Logic gate	Symbol	Truth table			CMOS IC type number
		Inputs A B		Output X	
NOT (Inverter)		0 1		1 0	4049
AND		0 0 0 1 1 0 1 1		0 0 0 1	4081
NAND		0 0 0 1 1 0 1 1		1 1 1 0	4011
OR		0 0 0 1 1 0 1 1		0 1 1 1	4071
NOR		0 0 0 1 1 0 1 1		1 0 0 0	4001
XOR (Exclusive OR)		0 0 0 1 1 0 1 1		0 1 1 0	4070

How you use them

Logic gates can be used individually:

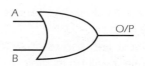

output switches on when input A OR input B switches on

A	B	O/P
0	0	0
0	1	1
1	0	1
1	1	1

or they can be used in combination:

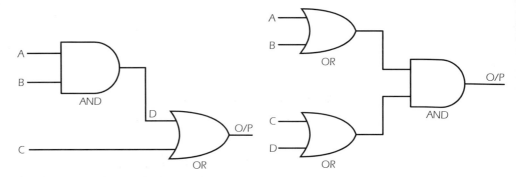

output switches on if input A AND input B OR input C switches on

output switches on if input A OR input B AND input C OR input D switches on

Most logic gates can source a current of only approximately 20 mA, so output devices that require more current than this will need to be interfaced with a transistor.

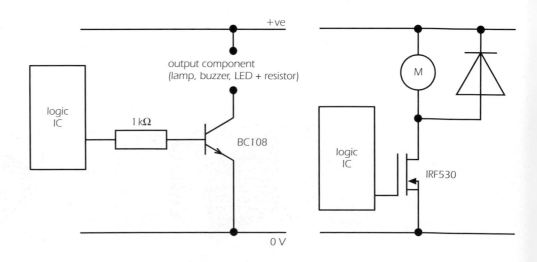

■ Capacitors

What they look like

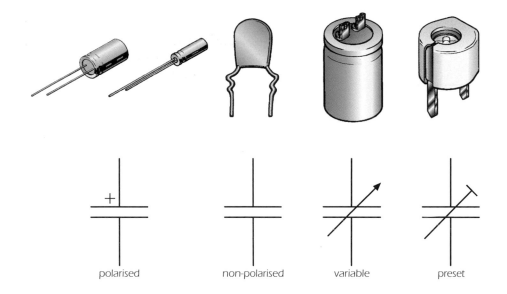

polarised	non-polarised	variable	preset

What they are used for

Capacitors can be used in many different applications. In control electronics they are most often used to:

■ control the delay in a timing circuit
■ control the frequency of an oscillator or multivibrator circuit
■ smooth the input from a power supply.

What they are made of

A capacitor is made from two metal **plates** that are separated by an insulating material which is known as a **dielectric**.

Fixed value capacitors come in two types – **polarised** and **non-polarised**. The metal plates are made from aluminium or tantalum. Various materials are used for the dielectric. These include polyester, mica, ceramic and air.

Variable capacitors are moving metal plates separated by a dielectric of air or sheets of thin metal foil with a mica dielectric.

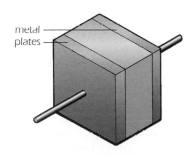

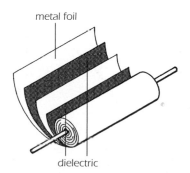

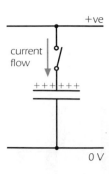

current
flow

+ve

+ + + + + +

0 V

How they work

Capacitors can store **electrical charge**. When they are connected to a power supply, current flows into them and they charge up.

The capacitor will store the charge even if the power supply is disconnected. In theory the capacitor can keep its charge forever. However, in reality the charge will gradually leak away through the dielectric. This leaking of the charge is known as an **internal leakage** current.

When a capacitor charges it takes a certain amount of time to reach its full charge. The capacitor is fully charged when the voltage across it reaches the power supply voltage. The amount of time that the capacitor takes to charge will depend on two things:

- the size of the capacitor – the bigger the capacitor, the longer it takes
- the amount of resistance that the charging current is flowing through.

Capacitance is measured in farads (F). 1 farad is a very large amount of capacitance, so capacitors are available only in fractions of a farad. These are typically microfarads (µF, millionths of a farad) in control electronics.

The amount of time that a capacitor takes to charge through a resistor is known as the **CR time**. This can be calculated using the formula:

$$\text{CR time (in seconds)} = C \text{ (in farads)} \times R \text{ (in ohms)}$$

In the example shown in the diagram (left),

$$\text{CR time} = 0.0001 \text{ F} \times 10\ 000\ \Omega$$
$$= 1\ \text{s}$$

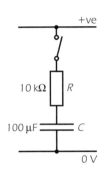

+ve

10 kΩ   R

100 µF   C

0 V

However, after one CR time the capacitor would not be fully charged. In fact it would only charge to about 0.6 of its full charge. This is because capacitors charge in a way that follows an *exponential* function. Basically this means that over each CR time the capacitor charges to about 0.6 of the remaining charge.

A good general rule states that the capacitor will be fully charged after five CR times.

Capacitors discharge in the same way that they charge. The amount of time that they take to discharge again depends upon the size of the capacitor and the size of the resistor. Larger values of either make the discharge time longer. Capacitors discharge following the same exponential function. They lose about 0.6 of the charge that they contain over each CR time.

See

- Dispensing system, page 206
- Electronic timer, page 215
- Auto-shutdown product, page 219

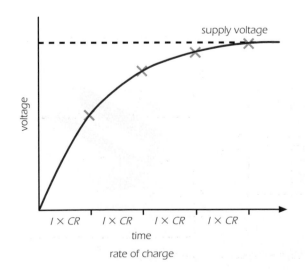

rate of charge

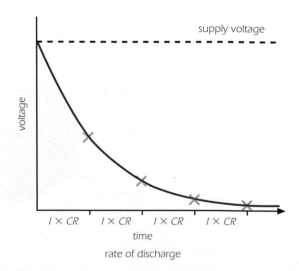

rate of discharge

How you use them

Three examples are shown in the diagrams.

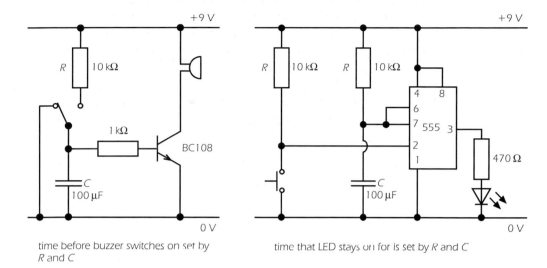

time before buzzer switches on set by R and C

time that LED stays on for is set by R and C

1 to control the delay in a timing circuit

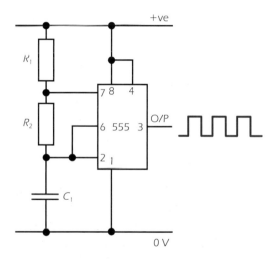

2 to control the frequency of an oscillator or multivibrator circuit

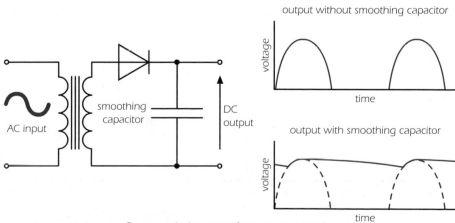

output without smoothing capacitor

output with smoothing capacitor

3 to smooth the output from a power supply

125

Diodes

What they look like

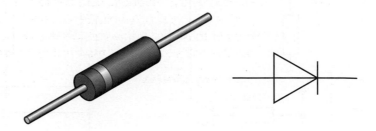

What they are used for

Diodes can be used to:

- suppress electrical noise and back e.m.f.s (see page 127) to protect transistors in control switching circuits – **clamping** diodes
- steer electronic signals to the correct place at junction points in a circuit – **steering** diodes
- **convert ac to dc** in a rectifier circuit.

What they are made of

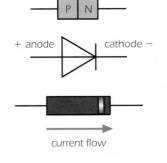

current flow

Diodes are made from **silicon** which is a **semiconductor** material. The silicon has either boron or phosphorus diffused into it. Silicon with boron is known as a **p-type** semiconductor, and silicon with phosphorus is known as an **n-type** semiconductor. A diode is created at the junction of n-type and p-type semiconductors.

The connection to the p-type semiconductor is the **anode**, and the connection to the n-type semiconductor is the **cathode**.

The convention for identifying the connections to a diode is that the cathode is indicated by a band on the diode body.

How they work

A diode is like a one-way street to electric current. Current can flow through it only **from anode to cathode**. A current will flow through the diode when the anode is more positive than the cathode. In this state the diode is said to be **forward biased**.

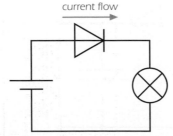

diode is forward biased so the lamp lights up

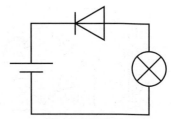

diode is reverse biased so the lamp is off

If the cathode is more positive than the anode then no current can flow through the diode. In this state the diode is said to be **reverse biased**.

How you use them

Back e.m.f. suppression – clamping diode

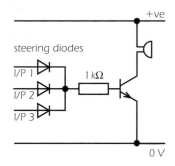

In normal conditions the diode is reverse biased so no current flows through it. When the relay or solenoid de-energises (see page 138) a large back e.m.f. is created by the magnetic field collapsing. The back e.m.f. will be opposite in polarity to the supply voltage. As soon as the back e.m.f. rises to a level that is greater than the supply voltage, the diode will be forward biased. This will short out the coil and prevent the back e.m.f. from rising any further.

Steering diodes

An input signal 1, 2 or 3 can be fed to the base of the transistor but cannot feed back from one input circuit to another.

Half-wave rectifier

On the positive half-cycle the diode is forward biased and the positive voltage is fed to the output (see below left).

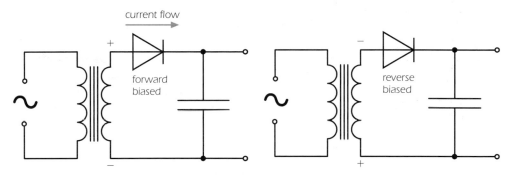

On the negative half-cycle the diode is reverse biased so the negative voltage is blocked from the output (see above right).

Full-wave bridge rectifier

On the first half-cycle the top of the transformer secondary goes positive and the bottom goes negative. Diodes B and D are forward biased so the voltage charges the smoothing capacitor in the correct polarity.

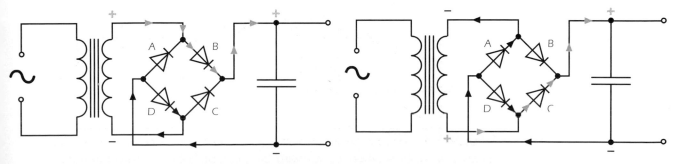

On the second half-cycle the top of the transformer secondary goes negative and the bottom goes positive. Diodes A and C are forward biased so the voltage again charges the smoothing capacitor in the correct polarity.

Light-emitting diodes (LEDs)

What they look like

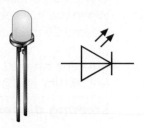

What they are used for

Light-emitting diodes are used as **indicator lamps** in electronic devices. They do not have a wire filament that can burn out like a normal lamp and they use much less energy. If used correctly an LED will last almost indefinitely.

LEDs come in a variety of colours: red, green, yellow and even, very recently, blue.

Multi-coloured LEDs are also available. They have two or more LEDs in the same package.

Flashing LEDs are special devices that have an integrated circuit inside them that causes them to flash automatically when they are connected.

High-intensity LEDs can now be obtained. These produce a much brighter source of light than standard LEDs. They are often used in lightweight warning lights, such as on a cycle.

What they are made of

LEDs are very similar to conventional diodes. They are made from a junction of **n-type** and **p-type** semiconductor material. The p-type material forms the **anode** and the n-type material forms the **cathode**. Current can flow only **from anode to cathode**. In this state the LED is said to be **forward biased**.

In an LED the p-type material has either gallium arsenide phosphide or gallium phosphide diffused into it. These compounds are naturally **fluorescent** materials.

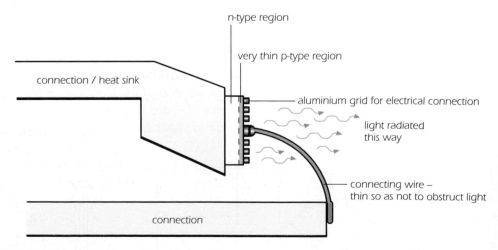

How they work

An LED will light up when it is forward biased. Current flows through the LED from anode to cathode. The flow of current through the LED causes the gallium arsenide phosphide or gallium phosphide in the p-type material to fluoresce (give off light).

A standard bulb gives off light when the filament becomes white hot. This is known as **incandescence**. All the colours of the spectrum are given off so the light appears to be white. However, fluorescence is very different from incandescence. When a material fluoresces it gives off light of only one colour. This is why LEDs are coloured.

How you use them

When they are forward biased, LEDs have only a tiny resistance. If you were to connect an LED to a power supply then a very large current would flow through it. This would burn out the LED. Because of this low forward resistance, you must always limit the amount of current flowing through the LED with a series resistor. The current should be limited to an amount that will cause the LED to light up to the desired brilliance, but not so much that it will damage it. The safe working current for a typical LED is 20 mA.

The size of the resistor will depend upon the supply voltage that is connected to the LED. You can calculate the value of the resistor using Ohm's Law.

Example

Using a 9 V supply with a typical LED requiring 20 mA operating current,

$$V = IR$$

$$R = 9\,V \div 0.02\,A$$
$$= 450\,\Omega$$

Note that the closest resistor in the range of preferred values will be 470 Ω.

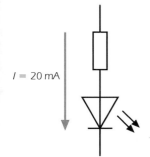

I = 20 mA

■ Thyristors

What they look like

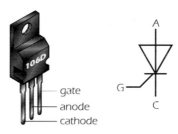

106D

gate
anode
cathode

A
G
C

What they are used for

The thyristor can be used to switch large current devices on and off electronically in a similar way to a FET (see page 113). However, unlike a transistor, the thyristor will **latch** (stay switched on) once it is **triggered**. To reset the thyristor the power supply has to be interrupted or switched off. The latching action of the thyristor is very useful in control systems that must give a continuous output after only a momentary trigger, such as alarms.

What they are made of

The thyristor is made in a very similar way to a diode, from **silicon** which is a **semiconductor** material. The silicon has either boron or phosphorus diffused into it. Silicon with boron is known as a **p-type** semiconductor, and silicon with phosphorus is known as an **n-type** semiconductor. A thyristor is made from a piece of silicon with some p-type material joined to some n-type material.

The **anode** is formed by the p-type material and the **cathode** is formed by the n-type material. In a thyristor the gate connection is made to the side of the n-type material.

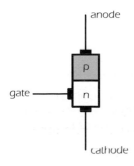

anode

p

gate

n

cathode

How they work

A trigger voltage of more than 2 V at the gate controls the flow of current between the anode and the cathode. Before the trigger voltage is applied, the resistance between the anode and cathode is very high. The trigger voltage causes the resistance between the anode and cathode to fall, which allows a current to flow. The resistance between the anode and cathode stays low even after the trigger voltage has been removed.

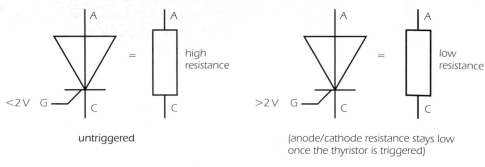

untriggered

(anode/cathode resistance stays low once the thyristor is triggered)

triggered

The control of the resistance between the anode and cathode, by the trigger voltage applied to the gate, is used in control systems that need to give a continuous output when the input is only a momentary trigger, such as alarms.

How you use them

Connect the device to be switched on and off in the anode circuit of the thyristor. The device is switched on and off by applying a trigger voltage of more than 2 V to the gate. This arrangement is often used in the process stage of simple alarm and warning circuits.

See

- Alarm, page 217

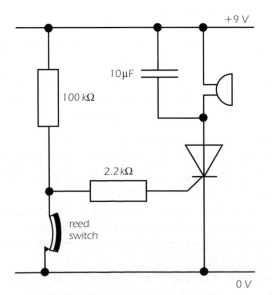

simple alarm circuit triggered by a reed switch

Note: some electronic buzzers will need to have a capacitor in parallel with them to keep the thyristor latched

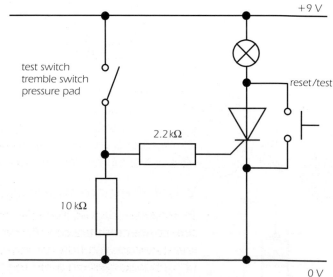

lamp will light continuously after switch closes momentarily

Note: alternative method of resetting thyristor is to momentarily bypass the thyristor with a switch

2 Mechanical devices

DC motors

What they look like

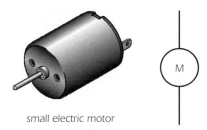

small electric motor

What they are used for

Small DC (direct current) motors are used to convert electrical energy into the mechanical energy of movement. They have many applications, but you can find them in products such as toys, personal stereos, cassette decks, CD players, video recorders, cordless power-tools, and so on.

What they are made of

DC motors are made from a variety of materials which include:

- steel for the case
- sintered ferrite compound for the magnets
- copper wire for the rotor windings
- brass/bronze for the bearings
- nylon for insulators and the back of the case.

How they work

The three main components in a DC motor are as follows.

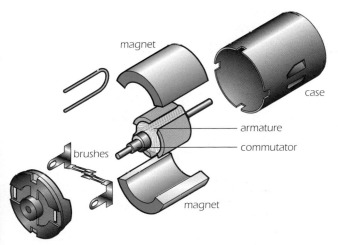

- **Stator** – This is made from one or more permanent **magnets**.
- **Rotor** – This is the **motor shaft** that runs in brass or bronze bearings. It carries a **coil** of copper wire that forms an **electromagnet**.
- **Commutator** – This is attached to the end of the rotor. It makes the electrical connection to the rotor coil by rotating between two **brushes**.

Current passes through the brushes and the commutator and flows around the rotor coil. This causes the coil to become an electromagnet. In the same way as a permanent magnet, an electromagnet will have a **north** and a **south pole**. In an electromagnet the poles are decided by the direction of the current flowing through the coils. The diagram on page 132 shows how the poles of the stator and rotor are arranged at the start of the cycle.

If you take two magnets and put both north or both south poles together, they will repel or push each other away. With the motor in the position shown in the diagram above, the poles of the rotor and stator will repel each other. This will cause the motor to turn. As the motor turns, the poles of the rotor and stator will attract, as shown in the diagram at the top of page 132.

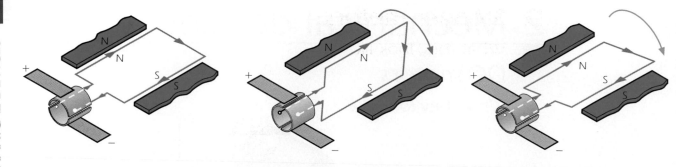

Without the commutator the rotor could make only a half-turn, because the poles of the rotor and stator would simply align north to south and the motor would stop. However, as the rotor turns, the commutator switches the direction of the current flowing through the rotor coil. This reverses the polarity of the magnetic field so the cycle of repulsion followed by attraction can continue.

How you use them

DC motors require quite large currents to drive them compared with many other electronic components. Typical small DC motors operate between 200 mA and 500 mA. However, as the load on the motor increases it will draw more current, sometimes as much as 1 A or more. Some typical characteristics for a DC motor are shown in the table below. You can normally get this sort of information from a supplier's catalogue.

Nominal	No load		At maximum efficiency					
Constant (volts)	Speed (r.p.m.)	Current (amps)	Speed (r.p.m.)	Current (amps)	Torque (g cm)	Output (W)	Efficiency (%)	Stall torque (g cm)
3.0	1800	0.022	1430	0.085	8.4	0.123	48.3	41
6.0	3700	0.028	3060	0.134	14.5	0.455	56.4	84

Because DC motors require quite large currents, they are normally interfaced to a controlling circuit using either a transistor or a relay. This also allows for the motor to be driven by a different power supply from the control circuit, if required.

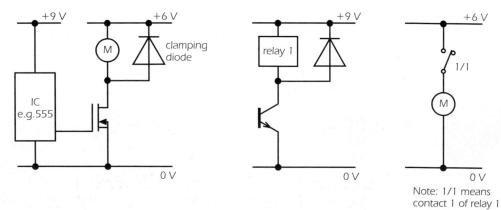

Note: 1/1 means contact 1 of relay 1

See

- Dispensing system, page 206
- Ball launcher, page 207
- Tumbler unit, page 208
- Smartcard application, page 220

Note that the switching action of the commutator in a DC motor can cause large voltage spikes to be produced across the motor when it is operating. These spikes are often known as electrical **noise**. This noise can either interfere with the correct operation of sensitive control circuits or damage switching transistors. The noise can be suppressed by using a clamping diode.

■ Stepper motors

What they look like

stepper motor

What they are used for

Stepper motors are special DC motors that can be driven in either direction in a series of small, accurate steps. This makes them very useful in applications that require precise positional control. They are generally larger and more expensive than standard DC motors, but the precision control that they offer makes them indispensable in products such as computer printers, photocopiers and fax machines.

Stepper motors are also used extensively in industrial applications such as CNC machinery and industrial robots.

What they are made of

The construction of a stepper motor is similar to that of a standard DC motor except that a stepper motor has a permanent **magnet rotor** revolving within fixed **stator coils**. The rotor is driven round by switching the coils on and off in the correct sequence using an electronic **driver circuit**. So a stepper motor does not have a commutator to control it like a standard DC motor.

Stepper motors are made from a variety of materials which include:

■ steel for the case
■ sintered ferrite compound for the magnets
■ copper wire for the rotor windings
■ brass/bronze for the bearings
■ nylon for insulators.

How they work

A stepper motor consists of a permanent magnet rotor placed between a number of stator coils. When these are energised (switched on) in the correct sequence the magnetic field set up in the coils causes the rotor to move around step by step. You can demonstrate this principle by using a cheap magnetic compass which has two fine insulated copper wire coils wound round it. The compass needle is the equivalent of a very simple stepper motor rotor which has just one north and one south pole.

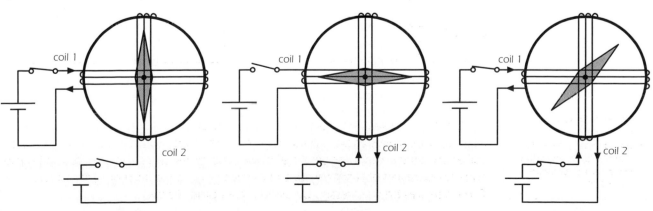

If coil 1 is energised and coil 2 is de-energised, then the magnetic field set up by coil 1 will cause the magnetic compass needle to line up at right angles to it.

If coil 1 is now de-energised and coil 2 is energised, then the magnetic compass needle will swing around through 90° to line up at right angles to coil 2.

If both coils are energised together, then the magnetic compass needle will line up at 45° to the two coils. In stepper motor terminology this is called **half-stepping**.

From the basic principles of how stepper motors work you can see that they are not as complicated as they first appear. The critical things to know are how the leads are connected to the stator coils and what the sequence of energising the coils needs to be.

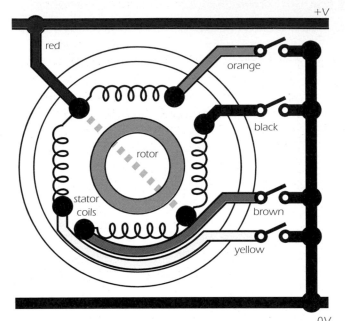

A number of different types of stepper motor are available, but a common and easy to use type is the **unipolar** stepper motor. It is called a unipolar motor because of the way that the coils are arranged and connected. A typical unipolar motor has four stator coils arranged as two pairs. The ends of each pair are connected together to form a **centre-tap**. This centre-tap connection from both pairs of coils is connected to the power supply lead which is fed out of the motor case, along with wires that connect to the other ends of the stator coils. The internal connections of a unipolar stepper motor are shown in the diagram on the left, which uses manual switches to demonstrate how the coils could be energised individually.

The colours of the connecting wires and the sequence of energising the coils depend on the type of unipolar stepper motor that you use. A very good general purpose stepper motor that is readily available is the SM42.

The SM42 will take whole steps of 7.5° (48 steps per revolution). To make the motor turn, the sequence of energising the coils is as shown in the table.

Each time the combination of energised coils changes, the motor will take one whole 7.5° step. Once stage 4 has been reached then the sequence repeats itself from stage 1 again.

To get the motor to go in the opposite direction, the sequence is simply reversed and again the four stages are repeated to get the motor to run continuously.

So, by stepping up or down the four stages, the stepper motor can be made to take a precise series of steps and can be stopped in an accurate and predetermined position.

motor coils

	yellow	orange	black	brown
1	on	off	off	on
2	on	off	on	off
3	off	on	on	off
4	off	on	off	on

How you use them

It is often thought that the control circuit for a stepper motor is complicated, making it suitable only for commercial or industrial applications. However, this is simply not true, as there are a number of ways in which the desired stepping sequence can be achieved. You can use a dedicated **stepper motor driver integrated circuit (IC)** or a standard **decade counter IC** connected as a stepper motor driver to achieve direct control of a stepper motor. You can achieve programmable control of the motor by using one of the readily available microcontroller systems such as the TEP **bit-by-bit** controller, a programmed PIC chip from the TEP *Chip Factory* or the *Stamp* microcontroller (see Programmable control, page 68). Using one of these systems will allow you to achieve complex control functions that can also respond to a variety of input signals.

All the following circuits and systems use the SM42 unipolar stepper motor.

SAA 1027 stepper driver IC

The SAA 1027 is a dedicated stepper motor driver chip. It enables you to control one unipolar stepper motor. There are two inputs to the chip:

- Direction – When this pin is pulled low (0 V) the motor turns in one direction, and when high (+12 V) it turns in the opposite direction.
- Step input – When a positive pulse is fed to this pin the stepper motor will take one step. The direction of the step is set by the state of the direction pin as above.

Note that the reset pin is normally connected to the positive supply. However, if a reset function is required it can be connected via a switch to ground and a pull-up resistor of 10 kΩ to the supply.

The step input can be fed from any control circuit that produces a regular positive pulse. This would typically be generated by an **astable multivibrator** circuit, for example a 555 timer.

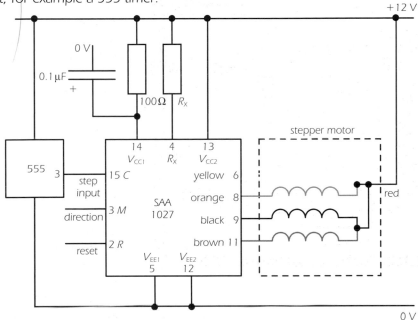

4017 decade counter

An alternative method to using the SAA 1027 is to build a driver board based on a decade counter IC such as the CMOS 4017. When this device is connected to a clock, such as a 555 timer connected as an astable, then each of its ten outputs goes to logic 1 in turn while the other nine remain at logic 0. If you connected LEDs to each of the outputs, you would see the first LED light up, then the next, and so on.

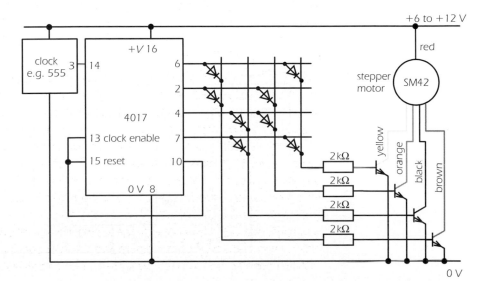

To produce the sequence of steps necessary to drive a unipolar stepper motor, the first four outputs are connected via diode links to four output transistors. A diode link represents an 'on' signal, and one missing represents an 'off' signal. Each output (with diodes) represents one stage in the four-stage sequence.

Note that output 5 of the 4017 is connected back to the reset pin, so that only the first four outputs loop in sequence when a clock signal is applied.

Programmable microcontrollers

Programmable microcontrollers are now becoming readily available in systems that are easy to operate, for example TEP bit-by-bit controller, TEP smartcard system, TEP *Chip Factory*, the *Basic Stamp*, and so on. These controllers can readily be used to provide the necessary signals to drive a stepper motor.

Using one of these programmable systems will enable you to achieve complex control functions and to build systems that can also enable the stepper motor to respond to inputs from a variety of sources.

They can be used individually by dedicating four of their output lines to control the stepper motor. Some systems contain the necessary output transistors to provide sufficient current to drive the motor, whilst others will need these to be added.

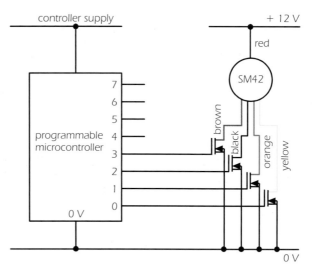

Alternatively they can be used in conjunction with an SAA 1027. This allows only two output lines to control the direction and step of the motor.

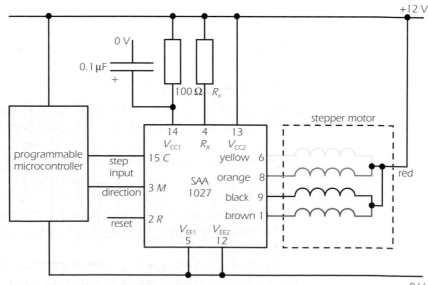

■ Relays

What they look like

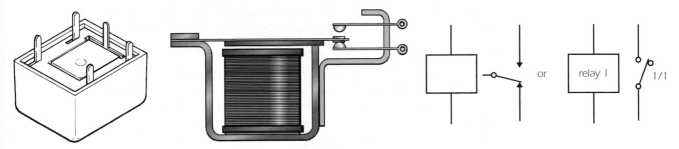

What they are used for

Relays are most often used as an **interface** component. They allow a low current control circuit to switch output components that require much greater currents than the control circuit can supply, for example a small switch on the steering column of a car turns on the headlights through a relay (see below left).

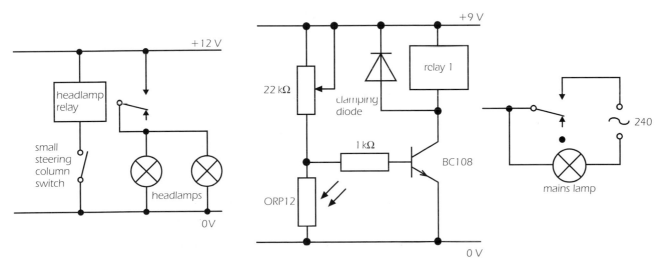

They also allow a control circuit to switch output components that require a different supply voltage, for example an electronic control circuit switching a mains-operated lamp (see above).

> **Warning! Mains voltage is lethal. Only trained and qualified people should build or service mains-operated circuits.**

What they are made of

A relay has three main parts: the **coil**, the **armature** and the **contacts** (switches).

The **coil** is made from very thin, insulated copper wire which is wound around a soft iron **core**. When a current flows through the coil it becomes an **electromagnet**. The core of the coil concentrates the magnetic field at the poles of the magnet. Soft iron is used for the core as it is attracted to a magnet but cannot become a magnet. This allows the electromagnet to be switched on and off. When the magnet is on it is said to be **energised**.

The **armature** is also made from soft iron. It moves the contacts when the coil is energised.

The **contacts** are made from thin strips of beryllium copper (or an equivalent spring material) which have a switch contact at the end.

How they work

When the relay coil has no current flowing through it, it is de-energised. The armature is spring-loaded into a position away from the end of the coil. The armature keeps the contacts in their **normally closed (NC)** position.

When a current is passed through the relay coil it is energised and becomes magnetic. The armature is pulled towards the end of the coil. This causes the contacts to switch across to their **normally open (NO)** position.

How you use them

Relays come in different types and sizes. They are described under several headings:

■ type of case
■ resistance of coil, e.g. 150 Ω
■ number of contacts, e.g. SPST, DPDT
■ expected number of switching operations, e.g. 10 000 000.

One of the main considerations when choosing a relay is the number of contacts.

■ **SPST** means single pole, single throw.
■ **DPDT** means double pole, double throw.

The **poles** are the contacts that the switch moves between and the **throw** is the number of individual switches in the relay.

Note that in the alternative circuit symbols 1/1 means contact 1 of relay 1, 2/1 means contact 2 of relay 1, and so on. These symbols are preferred in more complex circuit diagrams. This is because the contacts can be drawn where it is most convenient, as they do not have to be beside the relay coil to be identified.

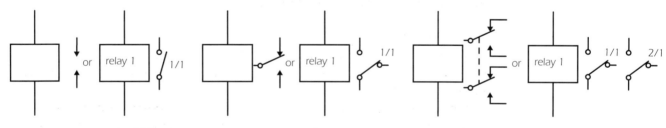

single pole, single throw (SPST) relay   double pole, single throw (DPST) relay   double pole, double throw (DPDT) relay

The type of relay that you choose will depend upon how many output devices you want to control and how you want them to operate.

When a relay coil de-energises, the magnetic field around it collapses. This causes a large voltage spike to be induced back into the relay coil. This is called a **back e.m.f.** (see page 127). The back e.m.f. produced by a de-energising relay coil can damage a switching transistor. It can be suppressed using a **clamping diode** (see page 127).

See
• Alarm, page 217

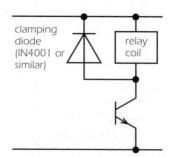

clamping
diode
(IN4001 or
similar)

relay
coil

■ Solenoids

What they look like

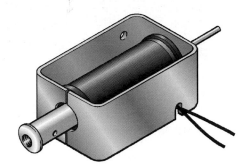

What they are used for

When the **coil** of a solenoid is energised (switched on) the **plunger** will be pulled into the coil. When it is de-energised (switched off) the plunger is pulled out again by a spring. This linear movement produced by a current is used to operate mechanical devices from an electronic control circuit. Solenoids are used to operate valves in washing machines or pneumatic systems, in electronic locks, in dispensing machines, and so on.

What they are made of

The solenoid coil is made from very thin, insulated copper wire wound round a tube, or bobbin, which is normally made from plastic. A typical solenoid coil has many hundreds of turns of wire.

The plunger is normally made from steel.

How they work

When a current flows through the solenoid coil it becomes energised and a strong magnetic field is created around it. The steel core is pulled into the coil by the magnetic field.

When the current is switched off the solenoid coil de-energises and the magnetic field collapses. The spring pulls the plunger back out of the coil again.

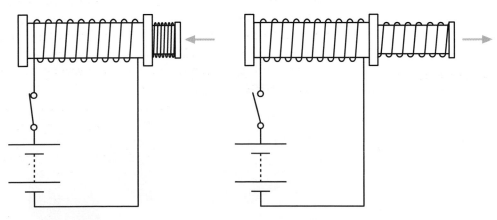

solenoid energised
plunger pulled into coil

solenoid de-energised
spring pulls plunger out of coil

How you use them

To select a solenoid you would probably want to know:

- the operating voltage
- the resistance of the coil
- the pulling force in newtons
- the maximum movement of the plunger.

This kind of information, and more, is normally available from suppliers' catalogues.

Solenoids generally require a high operating current or voltage so they are normally controlled via a transistor or relay in electronic control circuits.

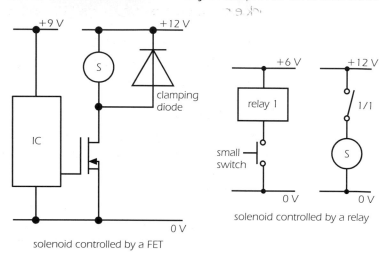

solenoid controlled by a FET

solenoid controlled by a relay

When a solenoid coil de-energises, the magnetic field around it collapses. This causes a large voltage spike to be induced back into the solenoid coil. This is called a **back e.m.f.** (see page 127). The back e.m.f. produced by a de-energising solenoid coil can damage a switching transistor. It can be suppressed using a **clamping diode** (see page 127).

■ Solenoid valves

What they look like

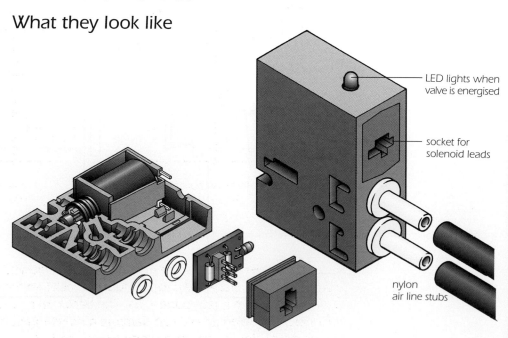

LED lights when valve is energised

socket for solenoid leads

nylon air line stubs

What they are used for

Solenoid valves are used to enable electronic control systems to control the flow of **fluids** in either **hydraulic** or **pneumatic** systems.

Solenoid valves can also be found in domestic appliances such as washing machines, dishwashers, gas cookers and central heating systems, and also in industrial pneumatic and hydraulic systems such as robotics.

A very useful and easy to use solenoid valve for low-pressure pneumatics work is produced by Mead Fluid Dynamics and is called the ISONIC valve. This solenoid valve contains the necessary buffer circuitry to enable it to operate from a low-current 5 V control circuit. This overcomes the need for interface components like transistors and relays. The valve also contains the necessary back e.m.f. protection (see page 127) and an LED to indicate its position.

What they are made of

Solenoid valves consist of a solenoid (see page 139) which is used to open and close a mechanical valve.

How they work

When the solenoid is energised (switched on) the valve opens. The valve can be designed to control the flow of either liquids or gases.

How you use them

Solenoid valves are rated in a similar way to solenoids (page 139) – by operating voltage, coil resistance, and so on. They are also given ratings for the valve, such as maximum fluid pressure and so on. Suppliers' catalogues should give you this essential information and more.

Solenoid valves generally require a high operating current or voltage, so they are normally controlled via a transistor or relay in electronic control circuits.

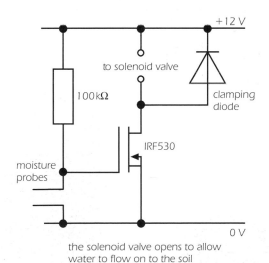

the solenoid valve opens to allow water to flow on to the soil

basic automatic watering system

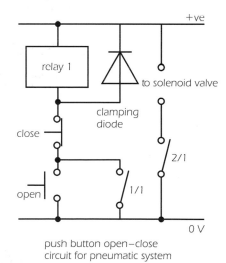

push button open–close circuit for pneumatic system

When a solenoid coil de-energises, the magnetic field around it collapses. This causes a large voltage spike to be induced back into the solenoid coil. This is called a **back e.m.f.** (see page 127). The back e.m.f. produced by a de-energising solenoid coil can damage a switching transistor. It can be suppressed using a **clamping diode** (see page 127).

■ Printed circuit boards (PCBs)

What they look like

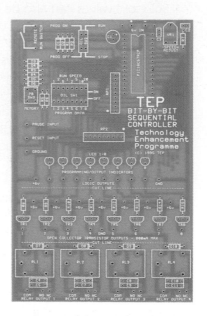

What they are used for

Printed circuit boards (PCBs) are used to build almost all electronic circuits. The PCB has a network of conducting **tracks** and **pads** on its surface. The electronic components are soldered onto the pads, and the tracks make the circuit connections. PCBs allow electronic components to be assembled and soldered together in a small space. They also make the final circuit quite robust and minimise the danger of components and wires shorting out.

What they are made of

A PCB is made from **copper-clad board**. This is a fibreglass board that has very thin copper foil bonded to it. The network of tracks and pads is produced by chemically etching away some of the copper foil.

A second type of board is available which is known as **photo-etch board**. This is the same as copper-clad but it has a light-sensitive coating over the copper. This coating is used in the photo-etching process.

How they are made
Using plain copper-clad board

1 The copper side of the board must be cleaned using fine abrasive paper or wire wool.
2 The outlines of the network of tracks and pads are drawn on the copper surface of the board using a pencil. This allows you to check the layout before going on to the next stage.
3 The pencil outlines are filled in using an **etch-resist** pen. It is important to make sure that the ink completely covers the areas of the copper that you want to retain and that there are no fine gaps or very thin areas.
4 When the ink is dry the board is placed in a warm ferric chloride bath for about 5–10 min. The ferric chloride dissolves the copper that is not covered by the etch-resist ink.
5 The board is then washed and the etch-resist is removed using fine abrasive paper or wire wool.

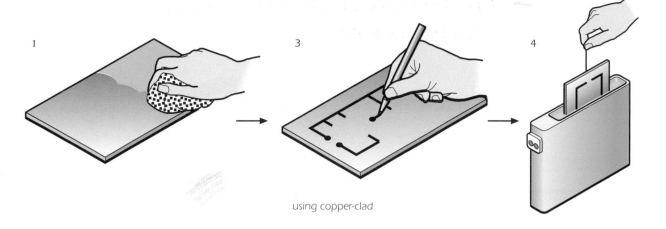

using copper-clad

An alternative method of applying the etch-resist is to use **rub-down transfers**. These transfers can be quite difficult to use and care must be taken to avoid wrinkles and hair-line cracks. However, they are very good for PCBs which require the pads to be accurately spaced, such as when using ICs.

Using photo-etch board

Photo-etch board is similar to copper-clad board except that it has a light-sensitive coating over the copper foil. This coating acts as an etch-resist. The coating has a protective film over it to prevent it getting exposed to light during storage. The network of tracks and pads is produced by photographing them onto the light-sensitive coating.

1 The layout of tracks and pads is produced on a transparent acetate sheet. This can be done either by using rub-down transfers or more often by printing it from a computer or photocopier.
2 The protective film is peeled off the board and the acetate sheet is placed on top of the light-sensitive coating.
3 The board is exposed to ultraviolet light in a special light box. Exposure times can vary depending on the type of board and the power of the light box, but are normally about 5–6 min.
4 The 'image' is then developed by putting the board into a weak solution of caustic soda (sodium hydroxide). The network of tracks and pads will be fixed into place and the exposed coating will be dissolved away.
5 The board is now etched in a ferric chloride bath in the same way as before.

Although it can take longer, photo-etching allows one acetate to produce many PCBs and also allows computers to be used to design the PCB layout.

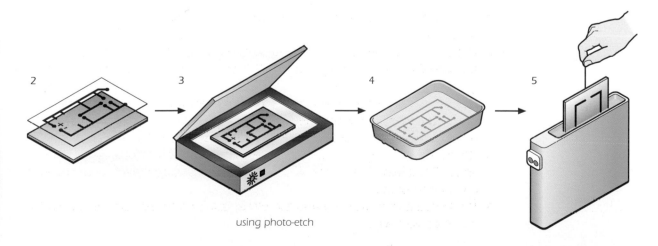

using photo-etch

Air muscles

What they look like

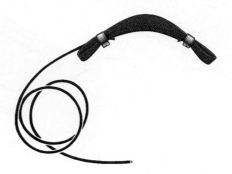

What they are used for

The air muscle is a **pneumatic actuator** (see below) that works in a similar way to a biological muscle. It is used to provide controlled **linear** movement (in a straight line). If it is connected to an appropriate mechanism like a pivoted lever then it can also provide **rotary** movement. The air muscle is often used in **animatronics** (high-tech puppets) and other models and props in film and video production.

Because air muscles are clean, have no moving parts and do not need regular servicing, they are starting to be used in industry in small-scale computer-controlled robots.

What they are made of

The muscle is made from a rubber tube which is sealed at one end. A nylon air line is bonded into the open end. The whole muscle is then surrounded by a polyester mesh or braid. This has loops formed at each end which allow the muscle to be attached to the mechanism that it will operate.

How they work

When the air muscle is relaxed it is at its longest length. To flex or actuate the muscle, compressed air is fed down the air line. The internal rubber tube expands, which causes the polyester braid to pull the two ends of the muscle together. This makes the overall length of the muscle shorter and actuates the mechanism. This process is very similar to human muscles.

The force that the air muscle exerts depends upon the air pressure supplied. This should normally be between 2 and 3 bar.

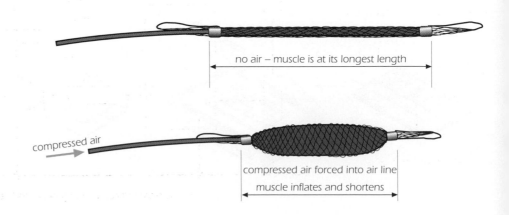

no air – muscle is at its longest length

compressed air

compressed air forced into air line
muscle inflates and shortens

How you use them

Single-acting air muscles have to be stretched to their relaxed length using elastic bands or springs. The diagrams below show how you can use an air muscle in the same arrangement as a human biceps (the rubber bands act as the triceps).

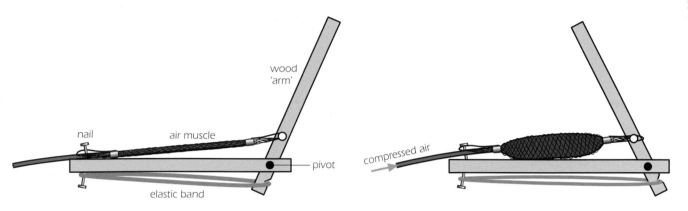

Alternatively you can use two air muscles together in the same arrangement as a human biceps and triceps.

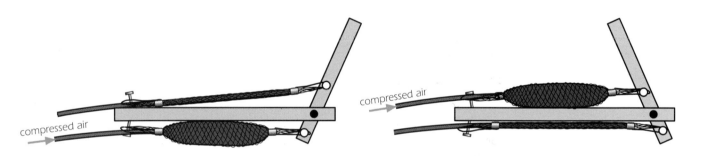

See

- Air muscle mechanism, page 210

This arrangement could be controlled using solenoid valves and a switch, or from an electronic control circuit via a relay.

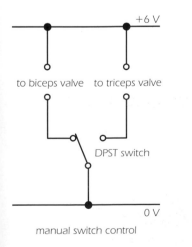

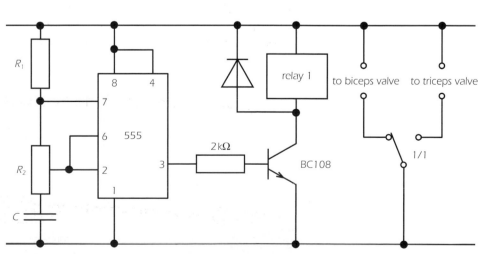

555 astable will continuously bend and flex the 'arm'

Shape memory alloy (smart wire)

What it looks like

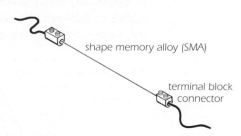

shape memory alloy (SMA)

terminal block connector

What it is used for

Shape memory alloy (SMA) is a relatively new material and new ideas for practical applications are still emerging. It can be used for mechanical actuation (moving things) in robotic devices, valves, locks, and so on. It is also finding applications in the medical field where wire structures can be made to change shape within the body. 'Smart' materials, such as SMA, can respond to changes in conditions in a predictable and useful way.

What it is made of

There are a number of metal alloys that exhibit shape memory properties. The most common alloy used is nickel and titanium. This is often called **nitinol** for short. Nitinol is one of a growing number of 'smart' materials.

SMA can be made in any shape or section. It is commonly available in the form of wire, in diameters of 50 microns, 100 microns, 150 microns, and so on (1 micron (μm) = 0.001 mm or one thousandth of a millimetre).

How it works

SMA can be made to 'remember' a shape by means of heat treatment and will always return to this shape when it is heated to the correct temperature. For example, a length of wire is made to 'remember' that it is straight and is then bent into a different shape at room temperature. It retains this new shape until it is heated and then it goes straight again. The temperature at which the SMA returns to its 'remembered' condition is called the **transition temperature**.

SMA wire can be made to remember its length. If stretched between two points at room temperature it relaxes to a longer length. If it is then heated to the transition temperature it remembers its original length and gets shorter, typically by about as much as 5% (5 mm for a 10 cm length). The shrinking wire pulls with a force that is useful for actuating mechanisms of different types.

When the wire cools down again it relaxes back to its longer length. This cycle can be repeated endlessly.

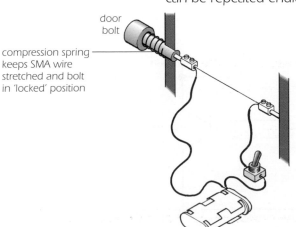

door bolt

compression spring keeps SMA wire stretched and bolt in 'locked' position

SMA wire has a resistance so it can be heated up by passing an electric current through it. The diagram shows a simple means of moving a cupboard locking bolt with SMA wire. The wire shortens when current flows and pulls the bolt open. When the current is switched off the wire relaxes and the bolt closes again under the pressure of the return spring.

How you use it

SMA wire cannot be soldered so you must make connections to it using mechanical fixings. The connectors from terminal blocks are very useful for this.

The table below gives useful information for 100 micron nitinol wire (Flexinol 100).

Properties of muscle wires	Flexinol 100
Bias force	0.3 N*
Pulling force	1.5 N‡
Resistance	150 Ω m^{-1}
Max. current	180 mA
Max. power	5 W m^{-1}
Shortening time	0.1 s
Relaxation time	1 s
Recommended extension	5%
Minimum bend radius	5 mm
Transition temperature	70 °C
Pulling starts at	68 °C
Pulling finishes at	78 °C
Relaxation starts at	52 °C
Relaxation finishes at	42 °C

* Equivalent to a mass of approx. 30 g
‡ Equivalent to a mass of approx. 150 g

To calculate the voltage needed to heat the length of wire that you are using, you need to follow these steps, based on using a 10 cm length of wire.

Step 1

Find the resistance of the length that you are using.

The table shows that 100 micron nitinol wire has a resistance of 150 Ω per metre.

There are 100 cm in a metre, so 100 cm has a resistance of 150 Ω.

Therefore 1 cm has a resistance of

$$150 \div 100 = 1.5 \ \Omega$$

and so 10 cm has a resistance of

$$1.5 \times 10 = 15 \ \Omega$$

Step 2

Look up the maximum current for the wire in the table:

$$\text{Maximum current} = 180 \text{ mA or } 0.18 \text{ A}$$

Step 3

Use Ohm's Law to find the correct voltage:

$$V = IR$$
$$= 0.18 \text{ A} \times 15 \ \Omega$$
$$= 2.7 \text{ V}$$

In practice it is acceptable to use the closest voltage that you can get by combining AA cells in series. In this case it would be two AA cells to give 3 V.

See

- Shape memory actuator, page 230
- Moiré fringe display, page 241

■ Gearboxes

What they look like

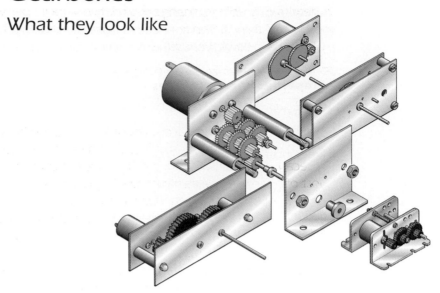

What they are used for

A gearbox is a type of **drive system**. Drive systems are used to connect a motor to a rotating output shaft (see page 54).

A drive system can change:

■ the **direction** of rotation
■ the **velocity** of rotation
■ the amount of available **torque** or turning force.

Gearboxes are most often used to slow down the rotation of the output shaft in relation to the speed of the motor. This reduction in speed will also increase the available torque.

Gearboxes are used in almost every product and system that contains a motor or engine, for example toys, hi-fi systems, many domestic appliances, cars, robots, and so on.

What they are made of

A gearbox is made from a number of **gears** that are mounted on **shafts**. The gears **mesh** together and transmit the rotating force to each other along the **gear train**.

Common types of gears include the **pinion** gear, **spur** gear, **compound** gear, **worm** gear and **bevel** gear. These gears are put together in different ways to form gear trains.

spur gears

compound gear train

worm gear and wormwheel

bevel gears

How they work

A gear train is able to change the relative velocity between two rotating shafts because of the difference in size between two gears. The size of a gear is usually specified in one of three ways:

- the diameter or radius of the gear
- the circumference of the gear
- the number of teeth on the gear.

Of course all three quantities are related. A gear with a larger radius will have a larger circumference and will, hence, have a larger number of teeth!

Because the number of teeth is the easiest quantity to find, it is the one that is most often used in calculations relating to gears.

In this example one gear has ten teeth and the other gear has 20 teeth. The smaller gear is connected to the motor and the larger gear drives the output shaft. Hence, the smaller gear is known as the **driver gear** and the larger gear is known as the **driven gear**.

If the driver gear is moved through one rotation then its ten teeth will mesh with ten of the 20 teeth on the driven gear and move it through half a rotation. So to move the driven gear through one whole rotation, the driver gear would have to be moved through two whole rotations. This shows the relationship between the two gears with regard to distance moved: during constant rotation the driver gear moves twice as far as the driven gear.

Velocity is calculated by dividing the distance that an object moves by the time it takes to complete the movement:

$$\text{Velocity} = \text{distance} \div \text{time}$$

So velocity is expressed as miles per hour (m.p.h.), metres per second (m s^{-1}), and so on. In the case of gear trains a useful measure of velocity is the number of rotations in one minute, that is revolutions per minute, or r.p.m.

In the case of our example the driver gear travels twice as far as the driven gear in the same amount of time. The driver gear completes two revolutions for every one revolution of the driven gear. This means that the driver gear is travelling twice as fast as the driven gear.

This leads to one of the most useful concepts when using gear trains – velocity ratio or VR. The velocity ratio is simply the ratio between the velocity of the two gears. It can be calculated using the simple formula:

$$VR = \frac{\text{number of teeth on driven gear}}{\text{number of teeth on driver gear}}$$

In the case of our example:

$$VR = \frac{20}{10} = \frac{2}{1} \text{ or 2:1 or 2}$$

The velocity ratio is very useful when designing a gearbox for a specific application. If you know the velocity of the motor (input) and the velocity that you want the output shaft to rotate at (output) then you can use the equation to calculate what velocity ratio you will need:

$$VR = \frac{\text{input velocity}}{\text{output velocity}}$$

Gear trains can also give a **mechanical advantage (MA)** (see page 56). Any mechanism that gives a mechanical advantage allows a larger load force to be moved with a smaller effort force. This is possible because the effort force moves further than the load force, the same as for a first-class lever (see pages 54–56).

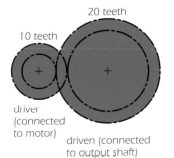

20 teeth

10 teeth

driver (connected to motor)

driven (connected to output shaft)

The general equation for mechanical advantage is:

$$MA = \frac{\text{distance moved by effort}}{\text{distance moved by load}}$$

In our example the effort force is applied by the driver gear and the load force is applied to the driven gear. The driver gear will move twice as far as the driven gear, so:

$$MA = \frac{2}{1} = 2$$

The mechanical advantage for a gear train is the same as the velocity ratio. This is true for all gear trains, so:

$$MA = VR$$

Gears are used to transmit rotating forces and we refer to these forces as **torque**. Torque is a turning force and is expressed as newton metres or N m. The relationship between torque and velocity ratio is shown by the equation

$$\text{Input torque} \times VR = \text{output torque}$$

From this equation you can see that the larger the velocity ratio, the greater the available torque at the output.

Gearboxes with large velocity ratios

In theory it is possible to gain any velocity ratio using a simple gear train. However, in practice the physical size of the gears limits the possibilities. To overcome this problem of size and achieve larger values of velocity ratio, different gear trains are used. One example is a **compound gear train**.

compound gear train

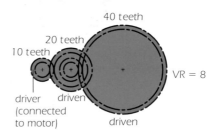

40 teeth

20 teeth
10 teeth

VR = 8

driver   driven
(connected
to motor)   driven

To calculate the velocity ratio of a compound gear train, you must first identify which gears are the drivers and which gears are the driven. In a compound train this starts with the driver and then alternates between the two.

You can calculate the velocity ratio by **multiplying together** the individual velocity ratios for each driven/driver pair of gears, for example

$$VR = \frac{20}{10} \times \frac{40}{10} = \frac{2}{1} \times \frac{4}{1} = \frac{8}{1} \text{ or } 8$$

Higher values of velocity ratio can be achieved by adding further compound gears to the train, for example

$$VR = \frac{20}{10} \times \frac{20}{10} \times \frac{40}{10} = \frac{2}{1} \times \frac{2}{1} \times \frac{4}{1} = \frac{16}{1} \text{ or } 16$$

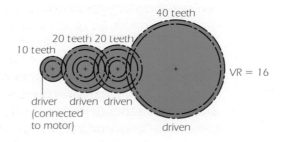

40 teeth

20 teeth 20 teeth
10 teeth

VR = 16

driver   driven driven
(connected
to motor)   driven

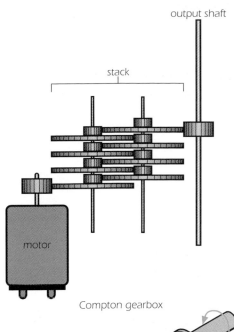

output shaft

stack

motor

Compton gearbox

1 tooth (driver)

40 teeth
(driven)

worm gear and wormwheel

Of course, as more gears are added the train will become longer and take up more space. A different way to arrange the compound gears that takes up less space is the Compton gearbox.

In this arrangement the compound gears are arranged as a **stack**. Each gear in the stack can rotate freely on the shaft. The input drive **pinion gear** is applied to the bottom left gear in the stack and the output pinion gear is meshed with the top right gear in the stack.

Each gear in the stack rotates more slowly than the one beneath it. The Compton gearbox has a secondary advantage because the output gear can be slid up and down the stack. This enables the gearbox to change gear!

Another example of an arrangement of gears that can achieve a high value of velocity ratio is the **worm and wheel**. In this arrangement the driver gear is the worm. This gear looks quite like a screw thread and has one helical (spiral-shaped) tooth. The worm gear meshes with the wheel, which is a standard spur gear.

The velocity ratio is calculated in the normal way, but remember that the worm (driver) has only one tooth. For a driven gear with 40 teeth,

$$VR = \frac{\text{number of teeth on driven gear}}{\text{number of teeth on driver gear}}$$

$$= \frac{40}{1} \text{ or } 40$$

How you use them

You would use a gearbox when you need to change the operating characteristics of a motor to suit it to its intended application. A gearbox can change:

- the direction of rotation
- the velocity of rotation
- the amount of available torque or turning force.

You can decide what type of gears to use and how many you will need in the gearbox by applying the relevant formulae from above.

However, these formulae take account of only some of the variables, or things that affect, the overall operation of the gearbox. Other variables will also affect the operation of the system as a whole, for example friction in the gearbox, the condition, size and voltage of the batteries, the amount of load that the output shaft must move, and so on.

In practical terms it is not necessary to consider all of these variables. You could spend many hours doing very complex calculations and still not cover everything, nor arrive at an exact answer. So designing gearboxes tends to be concerned with only the major variables and then some experiments!

If you need to use a gearbox then you can either use one of the many cheaply available kits or build your own. Building your own gearbox can take some practice, as you will have to work very accurately to make sure that all the gears are correctly spaced to mesh together. However, with care it is possible to build very effective gearboxes that match your requirements exactly.

See

- Robotic arm, page 209
- Micro-rover, page 211
- Automaton, page 236

■ Linear actuators

What they look like

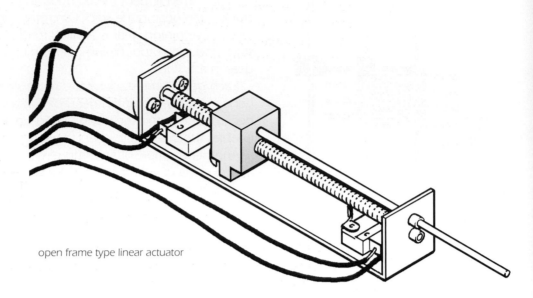

open frame type linear actuator

What they are used for

Linear actuators are electromechanical devices that are used to move things in a **straight line**. They can be used in the same applications as hydraulic and pneumatic cylinders but with the advantage that they do not need supplies of pressurised fluids and can be controlled directly from an electronic control system. They tend to be used in applications that require the movement of smaller loads, than those moved by hydraulic and pneumatic systems.

What they are made of

A linear actuator is made from a wide range of different materials and components that include a DC motor, a steel 'lead screw', a brass, bronze or steel 'captive' nut, various polymers (polythene, nylon, polystyrene, ABS) for casings and bearings, and limit switches which are all mounted on an aluminium or steel chassis or frame.

How they work

The illustration shows an **open frame** type of linear actuator. You can see that the lead screw is driven by the DC motor. It engages with a brass captive nut that is set into a polythene block which also accommodates a metal push rod. The end of the lead screw is supported in a nylon bearing at one end of the aluminium frame and above this is an identical bearing providing support for the push rod.

If the motor is connected to a power supply it will turn the lead screw and cause the nut to run to one end of the frame. If the polarity of the power supply is reversed then the nut will run to the opposite end of the frame. This linear actuator also contains two microswitches which are used as limit switches. The limit switches are connected so that the motor supply is switched off before the nut reaches the very end of its travel. This prevents the nut from becoming jammed at one end.

How you use them

For manual operation of the actuator, the limit switches are connected to a DPDT (double pole, double throw) switch as shown below. When the actuator reaches the end of its travel, limit switch L1 will open and cut the supply to the motor. If the DPDT switch is moved to the other position the actuator will drive to the opposite end. Limit switch L1 will close again and L2 will open, which cuts the supply to the motor again.

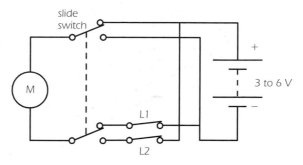

See

- Shape memory actuator, page 230

The actuator can be controlled electronically by using a DPDT relay to switch the supply to the motor. This allows the position of the actuator to be controlled from a wide variety of input devices or sensors.

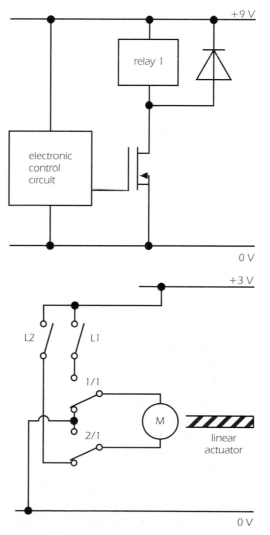

using a DPDT relay to control a linear actuator from an electronic control circuit

■ Piezo transducers

What they look like

polymer transducer   disc type transducer on brass plate   general symbol for piezo electric transducer

What they are used for

A **transducer** is any device that can change one form of energy into another. **Piezo transducers** can change electrical energy into mechanical energy and mechanical energy into electrical energy. They can be made very small so they are often used as miniature speakers in electronic devices. In this kind of application they are known as **piezo sounders**. However, the sound quality is not as good as that from a conventional speaker, so piezo sounders tend to be used in devices that go 'beep', such as digital watches and smoke alarms.

They are also used in a wide variety of sensing applications where the system needs to respond to a surface being hit. They can be made to produce very high voltages when mechanical energy is applied, usually by striking them. The voltage can be high enough to cause a spark to jump between two electrodes. This type of piezo transducer is often used for igniting gas, as in a cooker.

What they are made of

Piezo transducers can be made from minerals, ceramics or polymers. Naturally occurring minerals such as quartz exhibit the **piezo electric** effect. Many polymers also exhibit the piezo electric effect. The piezo electric material is normally made into a thin film which is coated with metal on either side. Wire connections are then made to the metal coating.

How you use them

A commonly available type is the **disc transducer**. This is about the same diameter as, and about a quarter of the thickness of, a two pence piece. It has two connecting wires already attached to it. It can be used as either a sounder or a sensor. The diagrams show it in two example applications.

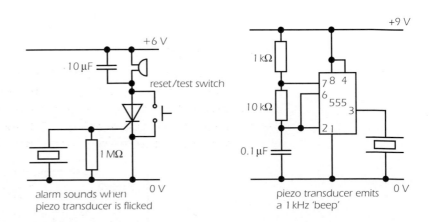

alarm sounds when piezo transducer is flicked   piezo transducer emits a 1 kHz 'beep'

Piezo transducers also come as part of a **piezo buzzer** device. The package contains a piezo transducer and an electronic oscillator. When the correct voltage is applied a high-pitched, and quite loud, sound is emitted. These devices are very useful in warning and alarm systems.

■ Thermochromic film

What it looks like

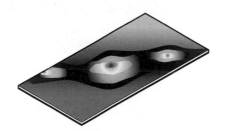

What it is used for

Liquid crystal is a very unusual material which responds to electronic signals. Many products such as calculators, digital watches and laptop computers show information using **liquid crystal displays (LCDs)**.

Thermochromic liquid crystal is a special form of liquid crystal that changes colour when heated. It is put into minute capsules by a process known as **microencapsulation** and then made into ink for printing onto plastic or paper. Thermochromic ink has a number of uses which include:

■ Thermometers which change colour along their length according to temperature.
■ Warning patches which show when something, such as a computer chip, is getting too hot.
■ Battery test panels. In this application the thermochromic ink is printed onto material that heats up when a current passes through it. If a battery is in good condition then enough current passes through the strip to heat it up and cause the ink to change colour.

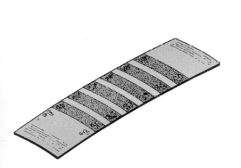

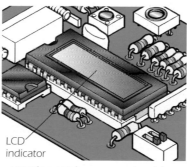

LCD indicator

warning patch on computer chip

What it is made of

Thermochromic film consists of a thin flexible plastic film (called a **substrate**) which has an **adhesive** on one side and **thermochromic ink** on the other. The ink coating is protected by a clear plastic film. The film is normally black but changes colour to a bright blue at 27 °C. If you touch this material for a few seconds the heat from your finger will cause it to change colour.

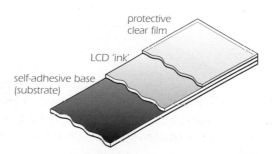

protective clear film

LCD 'ink'

self-adhesive base (substrate)

How it works

The film changes colour only at 27 °C. If your hand is cold or the sheet is stuck to a good thermal conductor such as metal, it will not change colour because the heat will be conducted away. The film should normally be stuck on plastic or card which are both poor conductors of heat. If the application requires it to be fixed to a metal base then an insulating layer (such as foam core board) should be placed between the thermochromic film and the metal.

Thermochromic film takes a little time to warm up, but when the source of heat is removed, the film stays warm for a short time. The bright blue colour then changes slowly to yellow and gradually back to black. Also if you watch the blue area, it continues to spread out slightly after the source of heat is taken away. This is because the heat is conducted through the film and affects the surrounding ink.

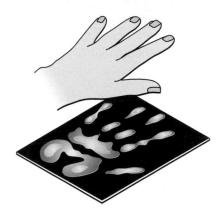

How you use it

You can use thermochromic film in a variety of interesting applications where you need an indication of temperature. Its advantages are that it requires no power, has no moving parts and does not wear out.

Another interesting use for the material is in electronically controlled displays. In this application the source of heat is a length of **nichrome** resistance wire. This wire will heat up when a current flows through it. As a general guide a 100 mm length of 0.3 mm diameter nichrome wire will heat up sufficiently with a 3 V power source.

If you lay a length of nichrome wire on the sticky back of thermochromic film, it will stay in place until the protective paper backing sheet is replaced. When the wire is heated up using a battery, the film will change colour along the pathway of the wire. The longer the wire is heated the more the blue colour will spread out. It will continue to spread out slightly after the battery has been disconnected.

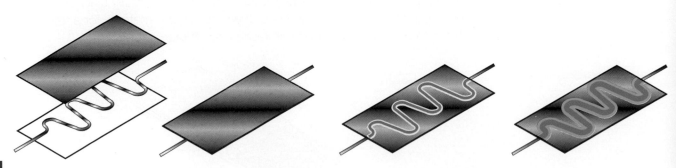

trap wire between adhesive and backing paper   pass current to show effect

You can make more complex designs with the wire such as words or logos. Fixing the film down with masking tape can help when you are positioning the wire. However, the wire should never be allowed to cross over itself as this will cause a short circuit. If your design requires a wire to cross then you should insulate the crossing point with a small piece of paper or insulating tape.

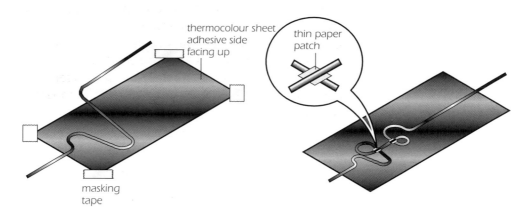

thermocolour sheet adhesive side facing up — thin paper patch — masking tape

You can control the display in a variety of ways:

- manually from a simple switch
- automatically from an electronic control circuit that responds to inputs from sensors
- with a flashing display from a 555 timer or programmable microcontroller.

Note that the on/off time from the control circuit in this application should be no greater than about 20 s. If it is any quicker than this, the display will not have time to cool down.

See

- Thermochromic indicator/display, page 233

Thermochromic film

3 Construction materials

Adhesives

What they are used for

Adhesives are used to form permanent **joints** between two pieces of material and, as there are many different types of material available, there is a correspondingly large number of adhesives that have been developed to join them together.

Adhesives have an advantage over mechanical joining methods (nuts, bolts, screws, rivets, and so on) as they perform better under **fatigue** (prolonged dynamic stress and strain), since the stress is spread across the whole of the join area instead of being concentrated at the fixing points or holes. However, the strength of a join made with an adhesive is limited by:

- The **area** of the join – a larger area gives a stronger join.
- The physical **strength** of the adhesive when set – this may be different from that of the materials being joined.
- The strength of the **bond** between the adhesive and the material to be joined – this can generally be improved by making sure that the material is clean and that non-porous materials have been roughened to provide a mechanical 'key' for the adhesive.

What they are made of

Adhesives are made from a wide variety of substances which include the following.

- Acrylic resins – *Tensol 12*, *Cascamite*, cyanocrylates (super glue), and so on.
- Modified phenolic resins – Phenol formaldehyde resin mixed with nylon, neoprene or polyvinyl butyrate. These are thermosetting adhesives that are used in industry to bond metal to metal, metal to wood, and metal to plastic. They are also used extensively in manufactured board materials like plywood, chipboard and MDF. They require both heat and pressure to make them set.
- Epoxy resins – *Araldite*, etc. These adhesives generally come in two parts: an **adhesive** and a **catalyst** or **hardener**. When mixed they set to form a strong joint between most materials.
- Rubber-based adhesives – *Copydex*, etc. These are made from a solution of **rubber** or **latex** in a **solvent**. These adhesives set as the solvent evaporates. They can often be used as a contact adhesive. Both surfaces are coated with the adhesive, which is left to dry. When they are pressed together an instant join is made.
- Polyvinyl acetate (PVA). Made from an emulsion of PVA in water. The adhesive sets when the water evaporates. PVA is an excellent general purpose adhesive. It is the most popular adhesive for woods and is also used in diluted forms to seal or bond concrete and plasters and even to stiffen fabrics.
- Hot melts. Commonly available in the form of a cylindrical 'glue stick' which is used with a glue gun. They are made from a variety of polymers and come in different colours or are transparent. The most common variety is made from atactic polypropylene.
- Solvents. Mainly used to form a 'weld' between two similar plastics, such as polystyrene. The material to be joined is assembled, then the solvent is applied and drawn into the joint by capillary action. The solvent softens the surface of the plastic, which forms a weld.

How you use them

Although there are a large number of adhesives available, many of them contain dangerous and toxic materials. They often require specialist facilities and expertise to use them safely. However, there are still many adhesives that are safe and non-toxic if they are used carefully and correctly.

Whenever you use an adhesive always make sure that it is the correct adhesive for the job and follow any necessary safety precautions detailed in the manufacturer's instructions on the container.

Adhesives available in a school workshop include the following:

- PVA – a good general purpose adhesive for woods, modelling foam and textiles.

- *Cascamite* – a stronger alternative to PVA for woods.

- *Tensol 12* – acrylic dissolved in a solvent. Good general purpose adhesive for acrylic.

- Solvent cement – the best adhesive for polystyrene but can also be used with acrylic.

- *Araldite* – a two-part epoxy resin that will join a very wide variety of materials. Often used to bond dissimilar materials like metal to plastic, and so on.

- *Copydex* – a latex solution adhesive that is good for textiles.

- Hot melt glue – sets very quickly and can be useful in mock-ups and early prototypes. Alternative adhesives are usually used for higher quality work.

- Double-sided sticky tape or pads – come in a variety of forms and strengths. Can be surprisingly strong and robust. Often used in product modelling.

■ Softwood (pine)

What it is used for

Pine has become the most common and popular form of timber for construction, making internal frameworks (carcassing) and general purpose work. It is cheaply and readily available in a wide variety of sizes. All pine now comes from **sustainable**, 'farmed' sources, unlike many hardwoods which take considerably longer to grow and are generally taken from natural sources.

For a resource to be sustainable its supply must meet its demand. This means that new trees must be grown at the same rate that others are being cut down. If demand outstrips supply then the resource will eventually disappear. This can have potentially disastrous consequences, as is happening with the destruction of the rainforests for the supply of tropical hardwoods.

Pine is available in a variety of stock sizes of strips, planks, boards and mouldings and can be purchased either as **rough sawn, planed both sides (PBS)** or **planed all round (PAR)**.

A variety of surface finishes are used to protect and enhance the surface of the material. These include varnishes, stains, paints, waxes, and so on.

■ Chipboard

What it is used for

Chipboard is a cheaply available manufactured board which is very widely used in the furniture industry. Its surface is quite rough and it does not respond well to applied finishes like paint or varnish; it is also not very resistant to moisture. Wet chipboard swells rapidly and loses its strength. To overcome these problems, chipboard is most often covered with a plastic laminate or a wood veneer. Chipboard is quite strong but care must be taken when joining it. Many 'knock-down' fittings have been developed specifically for use with chipboard (see Manufacturing techniques for wood, page 42).

Plastic laminates, knockdown fittings and low cost make chipboard particularly suitable for self-assembly furniture such as kitchen units, bookcases, desks, and so on.

What it is made of

Chipboard is made from wood particles (chips) which are bonded together with a thermosetting phenolic resin-based adhesive. Because the board is made from small particles it will have no grain direction. This makes it equally strong in all directions. The boards are formed by compressing the mixture of wood chips and adhesive in a heated press to form boards of a uniform density, or by rolling the mixture of wood chips and adhesive through a series of heated rollers which forms a 'core board' that is denser on the outside than in the centre.

flat pressed chipboard particles
have a uniform density

rolled 'core board' particles
are denser on the outside

■ Medium density fibreboard (MDF)

What it is used for

MDF is a comparatively new material which has become very popular for a wide variety of domestic construction and furniture uses. It has a smooth surface that is suitable for a wide variety of surface finishes such as stains, varnishes and paints. In its standard form it is not very resistant to moisture. Wet MDF will swell rapidly and lose its strength. However, it is now possible to obtain specially treated varieties which are highly resistant to moisture. This makes the treated variety suitable for use in damp environments, such as bathrooms, or in exterior applications.

What it is made of

MDF is made from wood fibres which are bonded together with a thermosetting phenolic resin-based adhesive. Because the board is made from small fibres it will have no grain direction. This makes it equally strong in all directions. The boards are formed by rolling the mixture of wood fibres and adhesive through a series of heated rollers. The resulting board has a uniform thickness and a very smooth, hard outer surface. However, the core of the board is much softer than the outside.

In most applications this soft core presents no problem, but if the face of the board is shaped by planing or machining then the soft core will be exposed. The soft core will also be exposed at the edge of the board. If a surface finish such as paint is going to be used, the edge of the board should be sealed to prevent excess paint from soaking in and swelling the edge of the board. This will also give a better finish to the edge. A good way to seal the edge is to apply a thin coat of PVA wood glue which is left to dry before painting.

Note that because MDF is made from fine wood fibres it produces large amounts of dust when it is sanded or machined. Most forms of dust are dangerous if inhaled.

Always wear a protective mask when sanding or machining MDF.

■ Plywood

What it is used for

Plywood is available in a variety of thicknesses and qualities. It can be obtained in standard interior or moisture-resistant exterior grades. It is used in a wide variety of applications.

Low quality plywood is cheap and readily available and is often used in temporary applications such as shuttering and boarding up or in packaging.

Medium quality plywood is used for constructional purposes and sometimes in furniture. A surface finish, plastic laminate or veneer is usually applied to improve the appearance of the final product.

High quality plywood, usually made from birch, is often used in furniture construction, either in flat board form or laminated into complex curved forms.

What it is made of

Plywood is made from a number of individual sheets of wood that are **laminated** (stuck together in layers). The adhesive used is a phenolic-based thermosetting resin. The laminae (individual sheets) can be of uniform or different thicknesses and, depending upon the quality of the final board, are cut from a variety of hard and softwoods such as spruce, birch, beech, and so on.

The laminae are arranged so that the grain directions alternate. This makes the finished board equally strong in all directions.

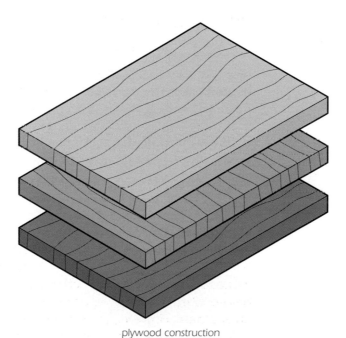

plywood construction

Pre-finished metal

What it is used for

Pre-finished metal has a wide variety of commercial uses which range from architecture and interiors to products and furniture. Example applications include the following.

- 'White goods' – domestic appliances like washing machines, fridges, freezers, tumble dryers and dishwashers.
- Architectural – suspended ceilings, cladding, roofing, cable trunking.
- Transport – under bonnet parts, some vehicle trim, trailer bodies, road signs.
- Other uses – shelving systems, garage doors, furniture.

What it is made of

Pre-finished metal is available in a variety of types. The most common type used commercially is pre-coated steel. This is made from mild steel strip coated in either paint or a polymer film. The coating process is carried out at the steel mill so that the metal is ready to use in the production process. Pre-finished metal removes the need to paint products after they are manufactured. This leads to savings for the manufacturer as they do not need to maintain special painting facilities which are very costly to operate. There are also environmental benefits to using pre-finished metal. The commercial painting process relies upon the use of many dangerous and environmentally damaging solvents. By pre-finishing steel at the mill the process can be very carefully controlled to minimise waste products, and it is a more efficient use of resources than having many different coating facilities at the manufacturers' premises.

Pre-finished steel needs more careful handling by the manufacturer than plain steel, but the coatings are more resistant to damage than many traditionally applied paints. They are particularly suitable for manufacturing products that are made by bending, folding and press-forming techniques.

How you use it

Pre-finished metal may seem like a material that is suitable only for commercial applications. However, it is available in two types, and in relatively small quantities that make it usable in a school workshop. It is possible to obtain pre-appointed steel sheet and anodised aluminium sheet for use in project work. Using pre-finished metal can give a very professional finish to products and you can gain the same benefits as commercial manufacturers.

See
- Desktop furniture, page 242

■ Steel

What it is used for

Steel is available in a wide variety of types and stock sections. The type that you choose will depend on the application that you want to put it to. The following table describes some examples of common steels.

Type	Appearance	Joining	Processing	Properties	Uses
Mild steel	Dull grey. Rusts easily, so must be protected with oil or surface finish such as paint or varnish	Soft solder, silver solder, brazing, welding, mechanical fixings	Turning, milling, forging, bending, grinding and press-forming	Softer than most forms of steel but can be case-hardened. Tough but bends if impact too severe. Fairly malleable, especially available after annealing. Ductile, with high tensile strength	Good general purpose steel because of wide variety of processes
Medium and high carbon steels	Sometimes black on outside surface in stock form, dull grey under surface or after machining. Rusts easily if exposed, so must be protected with oil or surface finish such as paint or varnish	Soft solder, silver solder, brazing, welding, mechanical fixings	Turning, milling, forging, bending, grinding	Harder and tougher than mild steel; less ductile and malleable. Properties can be changed by heat treatment (softening, hardening, tempering)	Medium: garden tools, shafts, wire ropes, axles, springs. High: general low speed (low temperature) toolmaking, e.g. scribers, punches, chisels, knives, shears, some lathe tools, springs, hammers, taps, dies, etc.
Silver steel	Type of high carbon steel supplied as pre-ground stock in accurate sizes. Bright silvery. More resistant to rusting than mild steel, but protection needed in damp conditions	Soft solder, silver solder, brazing, welding, mechanical fixings	Turning, milling, forging, bending, grinding	Properties can be changed by heat treatment (softening, hardening, tempering)	General low speed (low temperature) toolmaking, e.g. scribers, punches, chisels, knives, shears, some lathe tools, springs, hammers, taps, dies, etc.
Tool steel (high speed steel – HSS)	Bright silver colour	Silver solder (rare)	Grinding	Very hard; can be brittle. Low malleability and ductility	High speed (high heat) cutting tools, e.g. lathe tools, milling cutters, twist drills, etc.; cutting tools, e.g. taps, dies and reamers
Stainless steel	Bright silvery colour; very resistant to rusting	Welding and mechanical fixings	Turning, milling, forging, bending, grinding and press-forming	Very hard and tough. Can be heat treated to make it malleable and ductile	Specially suitable for exterior applications, hostile environments, e.g. boat fixtures and fittings, kitchenware. Relatively expensive

What it is made of

The raw material used to make steel is **iron ore**, normally in the form of **iron oxide** in rocks, which is mined or quarried. The iron ore is converted into iron in a **blast furnace**.

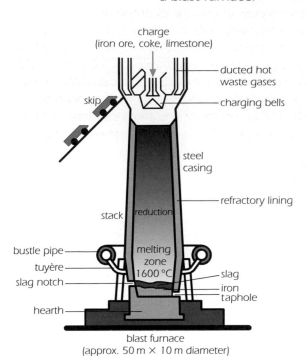

blast furnace
(approx. 50 m × 10 m diameter)

First the iron ore is crushed into small pieces (approx. 10 cm cubes). Further ore is crushed into smaller particles which are mixed with **coke** and heated to form a compound called **sinter**. Then the iron ore and sinter are loaded into the furnace along with **coke** and **limestone**.

Blast furnaces operate continuously until the refractory linings start to burn away. This can take more than 2 years. The raw materials are continuously loaded into the top and the molten iron tapped off at the bottom.

Heated air is blasted in at the bottom of the furnace through tuyères to make the coke burn fiercely at a temperature of about 800 °C. The iron produced is 90 to 95% pure. The iron can be further refined for use in **casting**, or can be further processed into steel. The exact process used will depend upon the type of steel being made, but all steelmaking processes involve removing excess carbon from the iron and adding small amounts of other elements, for example stainless steel contains chromium and nickel.

The oxygen furnace

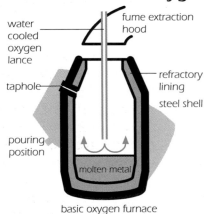

basic oxygen furnace

This method is used for making large quantities of basic steels, such as mild steel. The raw materials used are 70% molten iron and 30% scrap steel. The scrap steel is put into the furnace first and then the molten iron is poured in. Next a water-cooled oxygen 'lance' is positioned just above the surface of the metal. Oxygen is blown into the melt at high speed. It combines with the carbon and other unwanted elements and removes them. The carbon combines with the oxygen to form carbon dioxide and the other unwanted elements form a solid 'slag' which floats to the surface.

The electric arc furnace

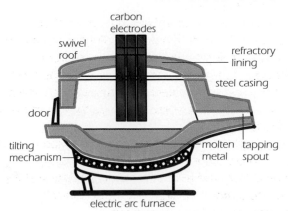

electric arc furnace

This method can be used in the production of standard steels but is very effective in producing special high quality steels. The furnace is loaded with cold scrap steel only. A powerful electric arc is struck between the metal and a series of carbon electrodes. This produces temperatures of over 3000 °C, which melts the metal. Iron oxide, lime and fluorspar are added to combine with any impurities and form a solid 'slag' which floats to the surface. If required, additional elements can be added to produce the desired form of steel.

Aluminium

What it is used for

Aluminium is available in a wide variety of stock sections. It comes in either pure form or can be alloyed with other metals to change its properties.

It is greyish-white in colour and relatively light in weight. It is soft, malleable and highly conductive to heat and electric current. It can be cast, extruded and also machined very well. Aluminium is resistant to corrosion. If left untreated a thin film of inert aluminium oxide forms on the exposed surfaces and protects them from further decay. This process is sometimes artificially enhanced by anodising. The aluminium oxide on the surface of the anodised aluminium is light grey in colour but it can also be dyed using a wide range of colours.

The properties and availability of aluminium make it particularly useful in the school workshop for construction, machining and casting work. It is used commercially in a diverse range of products, from kitchen foil through to jumbo jets!

What it is made of

Aluminium is the most common metal on Earth. However, the process of turning the raw material, **bauxite**, into aluminium is long and complex. Because of this, aluminium did not become widely available until the 1930s.

The first part of the process requires the mined or quarried bauxite to be converted to a white powder of aluminium oxide known as **alumina**. First the bauxite is crushed and dried and then it is mixed with **caustic soda**. This mixture is heated under pressure and the bauxite dissolves. It is then filtered and washed to remove any impurities. Finally it is heated in a kiln to remove moisture.

Alumina is aluminium oxide, which is a combination of aluminium and oxygen. The next part of the process is to separate these two elements. The general name for a reaction of this type is **reduction**. In the case of aluminium the reduction process is achieved by **electrolysis**.

The reduction is carried out in an electrolytic reduction cell, which is a steel box lined with carbon. The carbon lining forms the negative electrode, or **cathode**. A series of carbon **anodes** are suspended in the tank and make contact with the alumina, which is mixed with molten **cryolite** to reduce the melting point of the mixture.

A powerful electric current is then passed through the mixture via the electrodes. The oxygen is liberated from the alumina and rises to the surface, while the aluminium sinks. This is periodically siphoned off and cast into ingots.

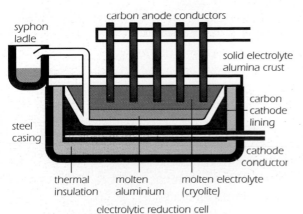

syphon ladle

carbon anode conductors

solid electrolyte alumina crust

carbon cathode lining

steel casing

cathode conductor

thermal insulation   molten aluminium   molten electrolyte (cryolite)

electrolytic reduction cell

■ Acrylic

What it is used for

Acrylic is a transparent thermoplastic material that was originally developed in the late 1940s for making aircraft canopies. Since then it has found its way into a wide variety of products and applications. Acrylic can be coloured with pigments, formed using heat, or spun into fibres for clothing, and can form the base for paints such as artists' acrylics or household emulsion. It is also used in lighting, signs, lenses and furniture.

Acrylic is a hard and stiff plastic which is very durable. It is ten times more resistant to impact than glass, however it does still splinter and scratch easily. It machines very well and can be joined using a variety of mechanical fixings or special adhesives. It is a good electrical insulator and is safe for use with food, for example as kitchen utensils.

As a stock material, acrylic is available in transparent, coloured translucent or coloured opaque sheets, blocks, rods and tubes. It is very useful as a general plastics construction material, particularly for products that are fabricated, heat-formed or machined. The chemical name for acrylic is **polymethyl methacrylate**. There are also many trade names for acrylic, including *Perspex*, *Plexiglass* and *Lucite*.

What it is made of

In common with all modern polymers (plastics), acrylic is made from crude oil. The refining process used in petrochemical plants to extract the useful fuels, such as petrol, paraffin and diesel, also results in by-products. One of these by-products, **naphtha**, is used to make plastics.

Acrylic is completely transparent in its natural state. However, it can be dyed to produce translucent (coloured see-through) material, and it can be pigmented to produce opaque (coloured non-see-through) material.

Polystyrene

What it is used for

Polystyrene is a very commonly used thermoplastic and is available in two main forms. In its natural state it is a fairly stiff and hard plastic. It is more flexible and less brittle than acrylic. It can be coloured with pigments, and a wide range of colours are available. In commercial applications it is processed using either injection moulding, vacuum forming or blow-moulding. It is used in food containers, cutlery, plates, model kits, toys, fridge and freezer linings, the cases of electronic products and many other applications.

Polystyrene is also available as a foam which is often referred to as **expanded polystyrene** or *Styrofoam*. This material is made by adding a 'blowing agent' to the raw polystyrene in the moulding process. The blowing agent releases bubbles of gas into the hot plastic, forming a foam. Expanded polystyrene is very light and buoyant. It absorbs shocks well so is often used for packaging. It is an excellent sound and heat insulator so there are many applications for it in the building industry. However, polystyrene burns very readily, giving off poisonous fumes, so it must be specially flame proofed.

As a stock material, polystyrene is available in transparent, coloured translucent or coloured opaque sheets. However, the most common form is as opaque coloured sheets. It is very useful in product modelling as it is very easy to vacuum form and fabricate into boxes, and it takes spray paint well. It can be machined, but care should be taken as its melting point is quite low. Polystyrene can be joined using a variety of mechanical fixings and solvent adhesives.

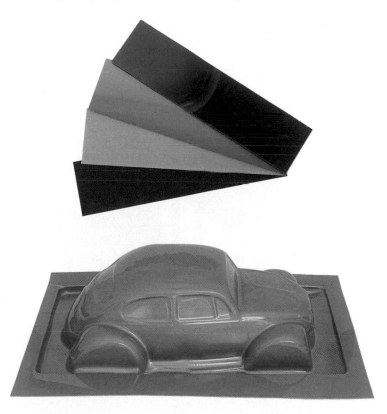

What it is made of

In common with all modern polymers (plastics), polystyrene is made from crude oil. The refining process used in petrochemical plants to extract the useful fuels, such as petrol, paraffin and diesel, also results in by-products. One of these by-products, **naphtha**, is used to make plastics.

■ Acrylonitrile butadiene styrene (ABS)

What it is used for

ABS is a very commonly used thermoplastic in a wide range of commercial applications. It is a fairly stiff and hard plastic that is very resistant to impact. It is quite flexible but it can be given extra structural strength by moulding. ABS is often used in applications that utilise its natural resistance to impact. It can be coloured with pigments and a wide range of colours are available. In commercial applications it is most often processed using injection moulding but it can also be vacuum formed or blow-moulded. It is used in car bumpers and trim, suitcases, the cases of electronic products and many other applications.

As a stock material ABS is most commonly available as a light grey sheet material. It is very useful in product modelling as it is very easy to fabricate into boxes, and it takes spray paint well. In sheet form it often has a textured surface that can be used to give a product model a realistic feel. It can be machined, but care should be taken as its melting point is quite low. ABS can be joined using a variety of mechanical fixings or with solvent adhesives.

What it is made of

In common with all modern polymers (plastics), ABS is made from crude oil. The refining process used in petrochemical plants to extract the useful fuels, such as petrol, paraffin and diesel, also results in by-products. One of these by-products, **naphtha**, is used to make plastics.

SECTION 3

small miracles
of technology

Introduction

We all take everyday products for granted – especially things like drink cans we use or throw away each day. This section asks you to stop and think about just a few examples. 'Throw-away' or 'cheap' does not mean that something is 'simple' either in the way it is designed or in the way it is made. Modern technology has made our consumer society possible, and looking more closely at a few of its products will tell you a lot about the technology that produced them.

As you open your next drink can look carefully at how the top works. Before you crush it in one hand, ask yourself how something so thin can support your entire weight. And, finally, remember that 150 years ago, aluminium was so rare that your can would have been worth four times its weight in gold!

In this section we look closely at a number of everyday articles and ask why they are like they are, how they work, and how they were made. There are a few surprises in store: a throw-away gadget that performs a complex metal-forming operation; something that gets hotter than molten steel – and many more.

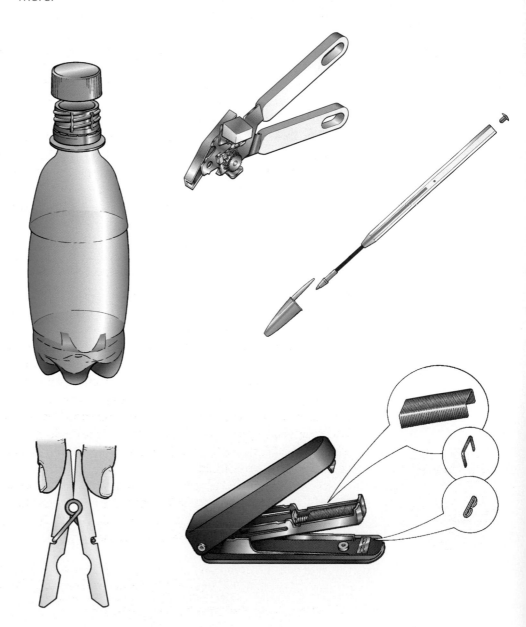

Bottle top

Opening a bottle of sparkling water is the easiest thing to do. Turn the cap to break the seal, unscrew and drink. And then screw down the cap again if there is any water left.

Next time you do this, look closely at the cap (ideally with a magnifying glass). It tells a story of extremely clever design and precision manufacturing, both of which are needed to enable consumers to enjoy cheap and safe-to-drink bottled water which will not go 'flat' waiting on the shelf – or leak if the bottle is shaken and pressure builds up.

The cap is made from **polythene** and has a special **lining** which seals to the top of the bottle and is safe in contact with the contents. (Some plastics are slightly porous to gas, and not all can be allowed to come into direct contact with food and drink.) The polythene top is moulded in a single piece. When it is fitted to the bottle, the edge is folded in on itself to lock on the bottle. (See Manufacturing techniques for plastics, page 39.) This forms a tight **security seal** which can be broken only when you begin to unscrew the cap. The lower part of the cap is joined to the top by a **hinge** and a series of very thin **connectors**. When the cap is turned, it rises up the screw thread on the bottle and the small connectors break one by one. When the cap is fully unscrewed it is attached only by the hinge. Despite their small size, it would be impossible to break the connectors all at once; even just one would be difficult to break normally. The fact that you can do it at all relies on the screw thread. Imagine that your hand and arm is a lever. Providing that you can grip the bottle top firmly, this 'lever' exerts a large turning force like a spanner on a nut. (See Levers in Mechanical control, page 54.) As it turns, the bottle top screw converts this into a much larger force pulling each connector apart in turn. This normally happens so quickly that you think they all break at once.

When the connectors are broken and the top fully unscrewed, the top and bottom of the cap stay attached through a hinge at one point. If you look inside the cap, you will see the sealing material and the screw thread inside. A closer look will show that the thread has a number of **gaps** moulded in. These allow any built-up gas to escape safely as the top is unscrewed. If shaken, pressure in a part-filled bottle can rise to more than the air pressure in a car tyre and it could make the cap jump off (into an eye) if it is not released during turning.

What seemed at first glance like a simple piece of plastic proves to be rather more complicated! The story really starts at the design stage. The idea for the cap then has to be turned into an actual product which in this example calls for precision engineering. Bottle caps are **injection moulded**. (See Manufacturing techniques for plastics, page 39.) Fused plastic is forced into a mould under high pressure; when the plastic has cooled, the mould is opened and the cap ejected. The connecting pieces on the cap are roughly 300 microns in diameter (about three times the diameter of a hair) so channels of this diameter have to be machined into the mould.

Screw bottle caps can be made using a two-part mould but the cap has to be ejected while it is still quite soft. If not, the cap would be effectively screwed on to the mould. It will only 'pop' off if it is still warm. The alternative is to use a special mould that turns while ejecting the cap.

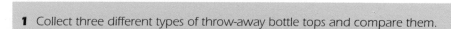

1 Collect three different types of throw-away bottle tops and compare them.

2 List the design features they have in common.

Can openers

Some can opener facts

■ The containers used in the earliest 'tinned' food were soldered together and opened with a hammer and chisel. The lead solder contaminated the food and probably led to deaths on early polar expeditions.

■ A large proportion of domestic accidents leading to hospital treatment are due to people attempting to open tins of food.

■ A tin of 'Parry's Roasted Veal' from 1824 was found, opened and examined 114 years later and the contents found to be in excellent condition.

One of the major methods of storing food is in steel cans, commonly referred to as 'tins' because they are tin plated to protect the contents and prevent rusting. For almost 100 years, cans have been manufactured with a top (and often also a bottom) joined to the sides by folding. This leaves a **rim**.

There have been many inventions for opening cans which take advantage of the rim. The earliest, and perhaps the most dangerous, was the single-blade opener. This had to be pushed into the top of the can to make a starting hole, and then levered up and down as it was pushed around the can. (See Levers in Mechanical control, page 54.) The edge of this opener followed the rim and so the jagged cut-out went around the edge of the can's top. This type of opener is now rarely seen.

Although designs vary between different manufacturers, there are two main types of can opener in current use. It is interesting to compare the ways these work and how they are made.

Top cutter

This type of can opener has a revolving **cutting wheel**. It is driven into the can's top by a **lever** and driven along by turning a toothed **driving wheel** which grips the underside of the can's lip. In this type of opener there are several mechanisms.

1 The cutting and driving wheels are attached to the ends of two levers pivoted together like scissors. When the cutting wheel is placed on the top of the can and the driving wheel under the rim, the handles of the opener are closed and the wheel pierces the can top. This is easy to do because the handles, acting as levers, provide mechanical advantage, the ends of the handles moving through a greater distance than the cutting and driving wheels. (See Levers in Mechanical control, page 54.)

2 The driving wheel is turned by a handle larger in diameter than the wheel, so making it easier to turn.

3 The cutting and driving wheels are connected by two **gears** so that the cutting wheel is also driven. This gives a greater 'grip' on the can and also uses the whole edge of the cutting wheel, not just one part.

It takes two hands to operate this type of opener. An electric version of it requires just one hand to close a lever. An electric motor then does the work of turning the drive wheel.

Side cutter

A more recent type of can opener cuts into the **side** of the can and removes both the lid and rim. It too has driving and cutting wheels, but these are brought together by a combined **lever** and **cam** action. (See Cams in Mechanical control, page 57.) The driving wheel is turned in the same way as the earlier type, but the cutting wheel is allowed to turn freely.

How do they compare?

Most top cutters are made from metal with plastic handle coverings. Side cutters are made almost entirely from plastics. Top cutters have many more parts than side cutters, including a plastic guard for the cutting wheel which is not required by the side cutter type. There are many other differences, including the fact, for example, that the top cutter often has a built-in crown bottle opener.

How they are made

Top cutters contain metal parts which are stamped out of sheet steel, pressed into shape and then electroplated for protection. The plastic handles are formed by a process called **insert moulding** – a form of injection moulding. The steel (skeleton) handles are placed in a mould and plastic is injected into the surrounding space under high pressure. When it cools, it locks firmly on to the steel. (See Manufacturing techniques for metals and for plastics, pages 30–41.)

Side cutters are made largely by **injection moulding** – forcing fused plastic into a mould under high pressure. The few metal components are stamped out of steel.

---

1 What kind of edge do the two types of can opener leave behind on the cans they open?

2 What type of opener do you think is easier to use? Why?

Dispensers

Most disposable containers are designed for protecting their contents while enabling easy access when needed. Examples include soft drink cans, milk cartons and toothpaste tubes. Some containers need to go one step further – for example, preventing access to children or making it easy to count out exact amounts. Although they seem simple, the mechanisms used in these dispensers are very complex, as the following two examples will show.

Child-proof dispensers

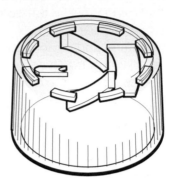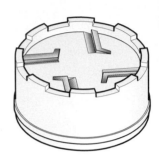

Containers designed for toxic liquids or jars for potentially dangerous pills are made **child-proof** by several methods. In one example (see above), the sides of the bottle cap have to be squeezed together at a certain point before the cap turns to unscrew; in others the cap has to be pushed down while turning (see below). If not, it simply slips around and makes a clicking sound (which itself can be a warning to a parent).

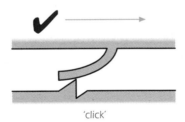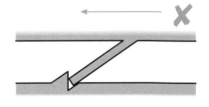

'click'

The **clutch-type** safety cap is the most common child-proof container. It consists of two separate mouldings. One is a screw cap with a series of small raised bumps on its top. The second is an outer cap which fits over the screw cap. It has a similar number of raised bumps on its inside which mesh with those on the screw cap when the two are pushed together. When they are not meshing, the outer cap just turns and the screw cap stays in place. The two cap parts are kept apart by small **springs** moulded on the inside of the outer cap. Unless you push the cap down and turn (anti-clockwise) to open, the inner cap stays firmly screwed down. The springs are specially shaped so that when you screw the cap down (clockwise) they always lock into **grooves** in the inner cap whether or not the outer cap is pushed down. When you turn anti-clockwise, the springs slip over the grooves and make a 'clicking' sound, unless the two caps are pushed together. When something turns only one way like this, it is called a **pawl mechanism**. It is used, for example, in winding up older clocks to stop the spring from turning the winding key backwards.

Sweetener dispensers

Sweetener dispensers come in all shapes and sizes. A popular one is made from three parts: A, B and C. During assembly, parts A and B are pushed together and then slipped into part C like a drawer. Part B can slide up and down by about 5 mm but normally stays in one position because of a moulded-in spring. When the top of part B is pushed down, a single sweetener is released at the bottom of the container. The mechanism for doing this is very clever because it releases only one sweetener at a time. The enlarged illustration shows how this works.

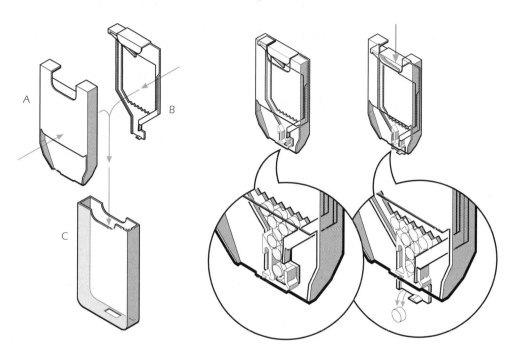

When the dispenser is closed a 'trapdoor' prevents sweeteners coming out. When part B is pushed down, the 'trapdoor' opens and allows the sweetener out – but only one comes out because the width of the channel is also narrowed. When you release the top of part B, it springs back and the whole cycle can be repeated.

1 Why do older people sometimes have problems with child-proof pill bottles?

2 Why are small sweeteners supplied in special dispensers?

Electroluminescent lighting

Some electroluminescent facts

- Electroluminescent (EL) panels are used for lighting on fighter aircraft to assist recognition and formation flying. They are simply stuck on the outside of the aircraft!

- EL panels are used to light up advertisements on some double-decker buses and for emergency lighting (along the floor) in passenger aircraft.

- EL panels do not even get warm and can be used where heat is a problem. They are available in many different colours.

- EL panels require a supply voltage in the region of 60/110 V AC, but the current required for smaller panels is very low. The AC voltage can be generated from batteries using a circuit called an inverter. This circuit can be made using a chip and for small panels will easily fit into a watch.

- EL lighting technology will get cheaper and soon replace bulbs and other types of lighting in many applications in the future.

Electroluminescent lighting is a new technology used in a wide range of consumer goods such as mobile phones, watches and safety clothing. It is also used on a large scale for advertising and emergency lighting. A typical EL panel is flexible and only 0.5 mm in thickness. EL panels have been compared to the surface of fluorescent tubes rolled out flat.

An EL panel consists of a thin (conductive) plastic sheet coated with a layer of **phosphors** and backed by a film of **carbon**. When a suitable power supply is connected to the plastic sheet and carbon layer, the phosphors become excited and emit light. The phosphors used in EL panels are similar to those used in fluorescent tubes and TV tubes. If you expose them to another light source, for example, and then look at them in a totally dark room, they will glow weakly for several minutes as the phosphors release energy absorbed from the light source.

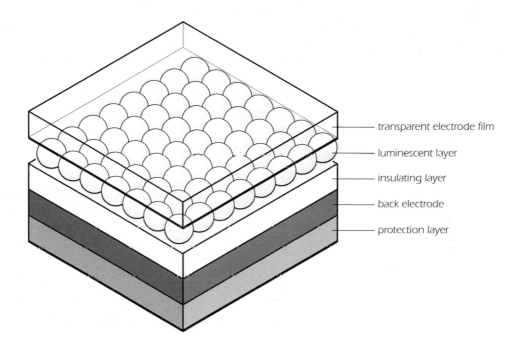

transparent electrode film
luminescent layer
insulating layer
back electrode
protection layer

EL panel material can be cut down from a larger sheet into smaller pieces providing that the cut-down sheet contains electrical connecting strips for both the front and back.

How they are made

EL panels are made by screen printing phosphors onto a plastic sheet which is made conductive by a thin invisible layer of metal. The phosphor material is contained in millions of tiny capsules of clear plastic material (by a process called **microencapsulation**) so that it can be mixed with the printing 'ink'. The capsules protect the phosphors from moisture. The phosphor layer is then **screen printed** with an ink rich in carbon so that it becomes a conductor when dry. EL panels are the only lights made by printing.

1 What is the main type of lamp used in the home?

2 What are its main drawbacks?

Cycle pump

A few years ago there was only one style of cycle pump, which had changed very little over a period of nearly 100 years. This simple, but unsung, design classic is still the cheapest type you can buy. Today, the pump has a plastic rather than a metal body and a rubber piston in place of the earlier leather cup. In other respects, it is almost the same. Amazingly, although the pump is cheap and extremely simple, you can achieve pressures well in excess of the safe pressure for a car tyre!

How do they work?

The basic pump consists of an outer tube (**cylinder**) and a **piston** whose rod is attached to a handle. When the piston is pushed forward the moulded seal in the form of a cup flattens, making contact with the inside wall of the cylinder and preventing any air escape backwards. The compressed air in front of the piston seal is forced into the cycle tyre via a connecting tube. When the piston rod is pulled back, the piston cap seal allows air to pass over it from the rear of the pump ready for the next downward stroke. No air is drawn back from the tyre because of its one-way **valve**. The springs behind the piston of the pump and inside the handle are to cushion the user (and pump) from sudden jarring at the end of each stroke.

When the pump is used, it gets hot because the air heats up when it is compressed. This heat energy comes from the work that you put into pumping. The air temperature in the pump can actually reach the point at which it will set fire to flammable material inside it. This was the principle of the fire tube – one method used for making fire prior to matches. A small piece of flammable tinder (very fine root material) was put into the end of a cylinder about the same size as the cycle pump and a piston rammed down very quickly. The heated air set the tinder alight and it was then quickly taken out to make a fire. Diesel engines ignite their fuel in exactly the same way.

There are many other methods of inflating cycle tyres, including carbon dioxide (CO_2) gas held in small cylinders. But the most popular method is an adaptation of the older-style pump which is larger in diameter (and shorter) and fits directly on to the cycle inner-tube valve. This fitting is similar to the one found on car tyre pumps. The end of the pump contains a tubular rubber seal which fits over the tyre valve. When a locking lever is pushed down, the rubber seal is compressed and fits tightly around the valve stem. A ball within the valve fitting rises and falls to act as a one-way valve.

See
- Air tools, page 213

1 Why does a pump get warm when you use it?

2 Why do racing cycles use higher tyre pressures?

Stapler

Some stapler facts

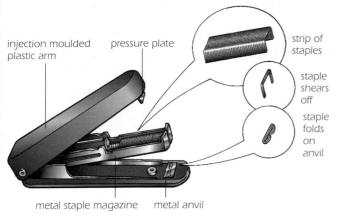

injection moulded plastic arm

pressure plate

strip of staples

staple shears off

staple folds on anvil

metal staple magazine   metal anvil

- The first practical stapling machine was patented in 1868.
- It is estimated that at least 100 billion staples are bought in the UK each year for use in small hand-held staplers.
- When you operate a typical stapler, the pressure applied at the tip of the staple is equivalent to 40 double-decker buses standing on an average person's shoe!
- Stapler users fall into two categories: 'squeezers' and 'bangers'. Hand-held staplers operated by squeezing last longer than those operated by shock loading or 'banging'.

Staples and stapler design

Each time a stapler is used, it performs two precision metal-forming operations: **shearing** and **folding**. The staples are supplied as a continuous steel strip which has been partly 'cut' or weakened so that individual staples can be sheared or broken off in the stapler. When you first operate the stapler, the **pressure plate** whose bottom edge is the width of a single staple applies pressure to and shears off just one staple. Further pressure pushes the staple through the paper or card where its tips meet the **anvil**. It then folds or closes according to the direction of grooves in the anvil.

All hand-held staplers contain at least two **springs**. One of these pushes or feeds the staples in the **magazine** towards the front and the second returns the top arm of the stapler to its open position after use. Even cheap staplers need to operate with precision, and when they go wrong it is usually because the pressure plate fails to strike the staple properly.

How they are made

Most cheap staplers are made from a combination of metal and plastics with the anvil, pressure plate and staple magazine made in steel. These parts are made using similar operations to those the stapler itself performs. Metal **blanks** are stamped out from steel sheet and then formed between **dies** (equivalent to each staple being formed between pressure plate and anvil). (See Manufacturing techniques for metals, page 30.)

The plastic parts are formed by **injection moulding** in which fused plastic is injected under pressure into a mould. (See Manufacturing techniques for plastics, page 39.) Sometimes the metal and plastic parts are snapped together by clever **interference fitting**; sometimes rivets and nuts and bolts are used. Another joining method is called **insert moulding**, in which formed metal parts are partially placed in the plastic injection mould so that the fused plastic flows around and locks on to them.

1 What is the smallest stapler you can buy?

2 Apart from size, how does it differ from a larger one?

Paper-clip

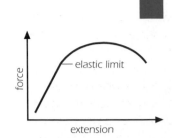

elastic limit

force

extension

Some paper-clip facts

- A paper-clip is a type of spring. The behaviour of springs was described by the English scientist Robert Hooke. Hooke's Law states that the movement of a spring is proportional to the force acting on it – the more force, the greater the movement. Paper-clips obey Hooke's law – but only up to a certain limit, called the elastic limit. (See Elasticity in Why structures fail, page 81.)
- The length of wire needed to make a medium-size common paper-clip, known in the stationery trade as the 'Gem', is 10 cm. A packet of 1000 would total 100 metres and ten packets would stretch 1 kilometre. It is estimated that the wire of all the Gem paper-clips made in a single year would stretch to the moon and back several times over.

The Gem paper-clip has been available for 100 years and sometimes features in special exhibitions as a 'design classic'. It is a unique product because of the huge numbers made and used over the years without significant design change.

Many people have made fortunes from designing and making paper-clips, and others queue up to patent their latest invention, believing that their paper-clip is better than the Gem or any others on the market. Given all this interest, and the fact that billions are sold worldwide, it is worth looking at how the paper-clip works and why it seems difficult to improve on (or is it?).

The Gem clip is made from mild steel wire bent into shape automatically on a machine. High-volume production makes paper-clips very cheap, and many are now coated in different colours. Their size varies to accommodate different thicknesses of paper, but the proportions always stay the same. A very large paper-clip looks like a giant version of the smallest one.

Paper-clips are really flat **springs**. When paper is pushed in, the clip springs open slightly, but it returns to its original shape when the paper is taken out. The correct name for this type of spring is a **torsion spring** because the metal at one end is twisted around (torsion means 'twisting'). (See Torsion in Types of forces, page 73.) If the clip is bent too far – beyond its **elastic limit** (see Stress points and elastic limits, page 80) – it stays bent, but still has enough 'springiness' to hold thicker piles of paper.

The inner loop of a modern Gem paper-clip is slightly raised to allow the clip to slip on more easily. One of the great drawbacks of paper-clips, however, is the fact that in a pile of papers they sometimes get attached to other documents which are then filed away and lost. Also, even a larger Gem clip can hold only a small number of sheets of paper; after that it passes its elastic limit and becomes distorted. Unless the ends of the wire are smoothed or rounded, they can dig into documents and damage them, and eventually may go rusty and discolour them.

Although the Gem clip is by far the best seller, many other designs have come on to the market including, for example, plastic ones. However, you need hardly any tools to make a paper-clip from wire. With imagination and a few trials, you might be able to design a rival to beat the Gem! If you are making several identical clips for trying out, you will need to make a special tool to wrap the wire around. This can be made by drilling holes in a block and fitting in pins.

How they are made

Paper-clips are made on automatic machines that take wire off a spool and wind it round a special tool. The wire is automatically cut after forming. On a typical automatic machine each paper-clip takes less than 0.1 s to make. Coloured paper-clips are made from plastic-coated wire.

See

- Re-inventing the paper-clip, page 245

1 Look out for and draw three different types of paper-clip.

2 Why is the 'Gem' paper-clip still popular after 100 years?

Piezo-igniter

A piezo-electric material is one that produces a **voltage** when it is deformed (for example squeezed) or which makes a small movement when a voltage is applied to it. (See Piezo transducers, page 154.) Naturally occurring quartz crystals exhibit this effect, but synthetic piezo-electric materials are now available and are widely used. Talking greetings cards, books and toys use a thin slice of piezo-electric material as the loudspeaker. When a signal (a varying voltage) is applied to this material, it expands and contracts to produce sound. The same material can be used in reverse as a microphone. Piezo materials are sometimes bonded to windows to act as sensors which produce a voltage if the window is struck.

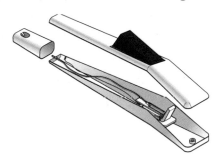

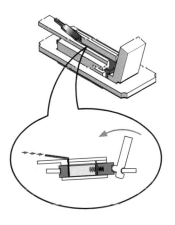

If made in the right way, modern piezo-electric materials produce high enough voltages to make sparks jump across gaps – as much as 10 000 V. This is the principle used for igniting some gas fires and cigarette lighters. General purpose piezo-igniters are now very cheap because they use a cheap piezo element squeezed with a cleverly designed lever system. (See Levers in Mechanical control, page 54.) In a typical piezo-igniter, we find a **piezo element** (usually a small cylinder), a metal frame surrounding it, and a short metal lever connected to the plastic case. When the case is squeezed by hand, the piezo-electric cylinder is compressed and produces a high voltage. This causes a spark to jump across a gap at the end of the igniter. At this moment the piezo-electric material suddenly 'relaxes' to produce a loud click (which most people mistakenly think is a sound made by the spark).

The common piezo-igniter is an interesting example of product design because it uses a wide combination of materials – piezo-electric element, plastics and metals – to produce a spark. In a car engine, producing similar sparks requires special electrical equipment.

Smart materials

Piezo-electric materials of the sort found in the piezo-igniter are among the most important 'smart' materials of the future. Because they can provide a small exact movement when a voltage is applied, they can be used to make electric motors with only one moving part which can be stopped and started with great precision. Piezo-electric motors (PEMs) are replacing some of the conventional motors used in cameras and video recorders. In a simple motor, a number of piezo-electric elements are placed in a cylinder around the revolving part (rotor). (See DC motors, page 131.) When a sequence of electrical signals is applied to the cylinder, the piezo-electric elements change shape to cause an overall 'wriggling' movement which makes the rotor turn. The rotor can be stopped, started and held in position very accurately.

1 What happens when you operate a piezo-igniter next to a radio?

2 Why?

Quartz clock movement

Some quartz clock facts

- A modern quartz movement is as accurate as the best clocks made by John Harrison in the eighteenth century. His clocks were so accurate that they enabled precise navigation at sea during voyages lasting months.
- The quartz crystal in a clock movement vibrates ('ticks') at up to 25 000 000 times per second. If you try to work out how many times an hour this vibrates, you will run out of zeros on your calculator!
- Quartz crystal (before it is made up for use in clocks, etc.) is the most common of minerals.
- Most electronic timers in the world are controlled by quartz crystals using circuits like the quartz clock type.
- If you connect a small pulley to the hour hand spindle of a quartz clock movement, you can use it as a very slow but quite powerful electric motor, for example as a display turntable.
- The motor used in a quartz clock movement is a form of stepper motor (see Stepper motors, page 133). These are normally much larger and move in small steps, but they are a very important form of motor because they can be started and stopped very quickly and made to turn an exact number of times. They are used in computer printers, plotters, photocopiers, robots, and so on.

Quartz clock movements are used in the majority of clocks sold today. Although made by different manufacturers, they have a very similar appearance and use a single AA size battery that can last for up to a year. If a movement is taken apart, it reveals plastic **gears** (see Gearboxes, page 148), similar to the metal ones found in a clockwork movement, and a small **motor** driven by an electronic circuit.

Compared with even the best mechanical clocks of a few years ago, quartz clock movements are incredibly accurate yet they are very cheap. In the 1950s quartz clocks cost many thousands of pounds and were used only in laboratories. So why is it possible to enjoy this sort of accuracy at such low prices? **Precision moulding** of all the mechanical parts in plastic is part of the answer; there are no expensive machining operations needed (see Manufacturing techniques for plastics, page 39). But the cost is really low because the electronic circuit that drives the clock is now made on a single **silicon chip**. (See Integrated circuits, pages 114–122.) An **integrated circuit** (IC) made this way can contain thousands (sometimes millions) of components in a tiny space but cost just a few pence. It is the reason why calculators and computers are every year getting more powerful and at the same time much cheaper. The circuit in a quartz clock movement is about 4 mm × 4 mm and sealed under a 'dot' of plastic for protection.

In a mechanical clock a device called an **escapement** allows the energy stored in a spring to be released in small steps – the familiar 'tick tock' of a clock. In a quartz movement the energy to turn the hands is supplied by a battery. Pulses of current from the circuit cause a small electric motor to turn in steps of 180° (half a circle). This motor turns the hands through the gears. If the pulses of current from the circuit are very regular, the clock will keep good time.

The circuit in a quartz clock creates a series of electric pulses – several million per second. These are fed to a piece of quartz (hence the name) which vibrates and ensures that the pulses are produced at an exact number per second. The number of pulses is too high to drive the motor, and so another part of the circuit converts the pulses to just one per second. The motor consists of a metal frame (called an **armature**) with a **coil** wound on it. Inside this is a magnetised rotor with north and south poles. The pulses of current from the circuit magnetise the coil and frame and cause the rotor to flick around in 180° steps. Because the motor is connected to the second hand through the gears (see Gearboxes, page 148), you will see it moving round the clock face in small jumps. The second hand is connected by more gears to the minute hand, which travels at 1/60th of the speed. This in turn is connected to the hour hand, which travels at 1/60th of the speed of the minute hand.

How they are made

Most of the parts of a quartz clock movement are **injection moulded**. (See Manufacturing techniques for plastics, page 39.) Fused plastic is forced into a mould under high pressure. Although the mould making is expensive, millions of parts can be moulded very quickly at low cost. The **integrated circuit** is made by depositing and removing different materials from a piece of silicon to create conductors, insulators and components all in a single structure. (See Integrated circuits, pages 114–122.) The minute size is achieved by a photographic method. The most expensive parts of the clock are the armature and coil and the quartz crystal, which is visible as a small cylinder connected to the circuit.

See

- Clock, page 237

1 What makes the 'ticking' sound in a quartz clock movement?

2 How many 'ticks' are there for each minute?

Remarkable pencil

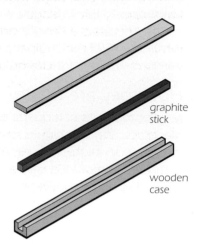

graphite
stick

wooden
case

The pencil as we know it, with a graphite 'lead' running down the middle of a wooden case, dates from the seventeenth century. Early pencils used a thin stick of pure graphite mined from the ground for their 'leads' . Modern pencils use a lead made of graphite and clay baked together – a process developed by a French engineer called Conté in 1795 (the firm still exists, making pencils). Pencils are classified according to the hardness of the lead; the more clay the harder the pencil. Since Conté's time, pencils have not changed much, apart from becoming cheaper as production methods have improved.

The pencil sharpener we are most familiar with today appeared in the 1890s. Before that time pencils were sharpened with a pocket knife, as were quill pens.

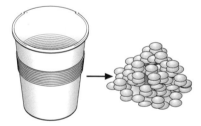

The *Remarkable Pencil* is the first one to be made from *recycled* plastic material – plastic vending machine cups. Instead of heading for landfill sites, each used cup, weighing about 5 g, is washed and reprocessed into granules. These can be used for injection moulding new plastic goods (such as pens made by the Remarkable Pencil Company) or for extrusion into pencils. (See Manufacturing techniques for plastics, page 39.) Each pencil uses the plastic from one cup.

The material for the lead of a *Remarkable Pencil* is a mixture of graphite, recycled plastic and special filler material. It is tougher than usual leads and less likely to break when dropped or when being sharpened. The pencil body is a mixture of recycled plastic and a special filler which makes it strong, lightweight and ideal for resharpening.

The pencils are made by a process called **extrusion**. This is the process of forcing material through a shaped nozzle or die – a bit like squeezing toothpaste from a tube. When hot plastic is extruded through a shaped die, and cooled quickly in water, it retains the cross-sectional shape of the die. Most plastic piping, from water mains to blood transfusion tubing, is made by extrusion.

The *Remarkable Pencils* are made using a slightly more complex process called **co-extrusion**. The lead is first extruded from a die and before cooling is fed into a second die with the surrounding case material. The inner extrusion (the lead) and the outer case bond together and after passing through cooling water are automatically cut to length.

The *Remarkable Pencil* is an excellent example of a 'green' product. The firms who dispose of the original cups can buy back pencils printed with their company logos, thus closing the 'recycling loop'. Unfortunately, many millions of tons of valuable materials are simply lost each year because the original products are thrown away. Examples include aluminium, and steel, drink and food cans, polythene carrier bags and the metal components of batteries. This is both wasteful and potentially harmful to the environment. Although many plastics are now biodegradable, the energy required to make them in the first place is lost.

The *Remarkable Pencil* was awarded Millennium Product status by the Design Council as an innovative and forward-thinking product.

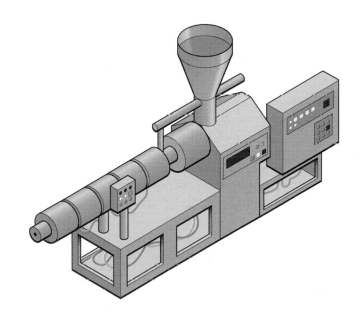

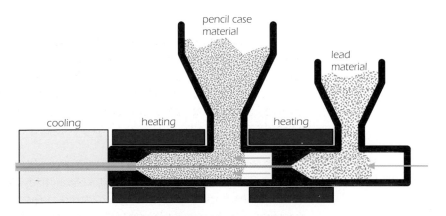

1 How are ordinary pencils made 'hard' or 'soft'?

2 How does a pocket pencil sharpener work and why do pencil leads often break during sharpening?

Springs

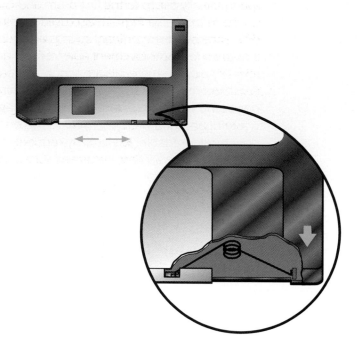

A spring stores energy and tries to return to its original shape if deformed. It is one of the most common mechanical components and is available in thousands of shapes and sizes, ranging from the **coil spring** in car suspension to the **torsion spring** that closes the cover on a floppy disk. These two examples show two important uses of springs: to absorb shocks (car) and to make things return to their original position.

We take return springs for granted until they become weak or break. Other everyday examples of use include clothes pegs, retractable ball-point pens, door handle mechanisms, sweetener dispensers and electronic keyboards.

Springs are sometimes used for storing large amounts of energy to be released over a period of time. Older mechanical clocks and moving toys use springs – hence the term 'clockwork' to describe motors that store energy in springs. An ordinary coil spring produces a varying force as it unwinds – a larger force when wound tight, and a weaker one when almost unwound. This is why cheaper toys such as toy cars run quickly at first and then slow down.

Modern springs, such as the one used in the clockwork radio designed by Trevor Baylis, provide a more constant output force and are called **constant torque** springs (torque is the 'turning power' of the output shaft driven by the spring). This is achieved by unwinding the flat steel spring from one drum on to a second. The spring tries to return to the first drum and exerts a turning force as it does so. Constant torque springs are also used to return tape measures to their cases. The difference between ordinary springs and constant torque springs can be shown on a graph showing movement against force applied. Robert Hooke, the English scientist, discovered that extension or compression is proportional to force. A constant torque spring produces a horizontal line on the movement/force graph compared with an ordinary spring which gives an upward sloping curve.

All materials are springy to a certain extent. A paper-clip, for example, springs back to its original shape if you bend it – but only so far! Beyond a certain limit – the paper-clip's **elastic limit** – it stays deformed. (See Stress points and elastic limits, page 80.)

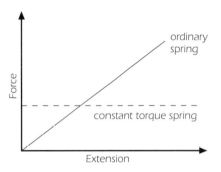

Springs have to be designed for use safely within their elastic limit. They are usually made from steel which is specially hardened and treated, but very often, in plastic goods, springs are cleverly moulded as a part of the product. Plastic clothes pegs are obvious examples; the springs in some sweetener containers are less obvious but all-important.

Spring manufacturers often talk about 'winding' springs, because the most common type are made by winding steel wire round a cylinder or mandrel. In industry this is achieved by automatic machines which take wire continuously from a spool, wind it and cut the completed spring to length. Springs can be hand-made using the same method – on a slowly turning mandrel in a lathe, or entirely by hand. For example, try wrapping thin wire around a pen barrel. The first thing you will notice is that, after winding, the new spring expands outwards. This is just one problem that has to be taken account of when designing and winding springs by machine.

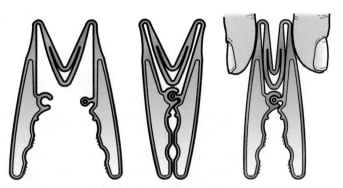

1 List ten products around the home that use one or more springs.

2 How could you use an elastic band to compare the weights of small objects?

Umbrella

Some umbrella facts

- The surface area of a small umbrella is approximately 0.3 square metres (0.3 m²). In a wind of 20 miles per hour, the force on the umbrella held vertically is about the same as a 3 kg mass pulling downwards. This force will move a small boat or accelerate a person on a skateboard to over 10 miles per hour on a smooth surface.
- The average quarter-length umbrella contains over 100 separate manufactured parts.
- A type of umbrella was used in ancient Egypt as a status symbol. Folding umbrellas were used in the eighteenth century for protection against waste thrown out of buildings as well as rain!
- Victorian inventors patented umbrellas with built-in telescopes, lightning conductors, weapons, cameras and handwarmers. This may sound eccentric, but note that some modern umbrellas have built-in torches, drink containers and attack alarms.

Is an umbrella a structure or a mechanism? A modern folding umbrella is both. It unfolds in one movement from a small cylinder 300 mm long into a protective cover up to 0.5 m² in area. When open, it can stand up to forces exerted by winds blowing at up to 30 m.p.h.

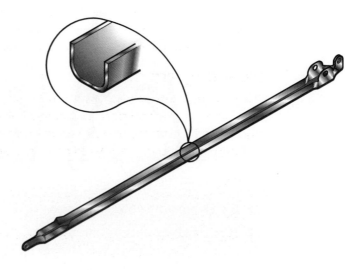

As a structure, an umbrella has a very high **strength to weight ratio**, meaning very high strength for a relatively low weight. As a mechanism, it contains no fewer than 50 moving mechanical parts. Most of these parts are made from 'U' **section steel** which was patented for umbrella making in 1852. This material replaced wood and bone and is what makes the umbrella both strong and light.

How does a folding umbrella work? If you open one slowly, you should be able to work it out and describe it. (A quarter-length umbrella has more parts than a half-length type, and umbrellas are designed in slightly different ways.) The drawings show how just one of the normal eight **rib** mechanisms moves as an umbrella opens. First of all, when you push the **boss** on the umbrella stem, three tubes forming the **stem** extend like a telescope. At almost full height, **struts** attached to the boss start to push open the inner ribs. These ribs are connected to the middle ribs with a **pivot** and **parallel motion** linkage. Each inner rib is connected to the outer rib by a pivot and a wire push rod which forces it to go straight.

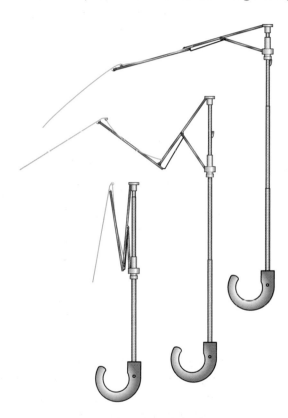

As a structure, all the metal parts of the umbrella are in **compression** or 'squeezed together'. The fabric covering is in **tension** – meaning 'stretched' (see Structures, page 71). It is the tension of the covering and the stiffness of the metal parts that give the umbrella its unique strength.

How they are made

The main mechanical parts of an umbrella are made by stamping out and press-forming the 'U' section steel components. These components are mainly assembled by machine to make up the umbrella frame. The fabric covering is sewn by hand-operated or automated machines and final assembly is done by hand.

1 Unfold an umbrella. Draw a diagram of the mechanism that locks it in the open position.

2 How is the covering held on to the frame of an umbrella?

Zip fastener

Some zip facts

- There are approximately 250 teeth per side in a 66 cm zip used in a typical quilted jacket. It can take just 0.1 s to do up such a zip, which means pairs of teeth coming together at 2500 per second – a very high speed for any mechanical operation.

- When a zip is closed it is immensely strong. If you try to pull it apart sideways you create a shear force (see page 73) on the raised bump of one tooth resting in the hollow of the next. It takes such a high shear force to break or dislodge a large number of teeth that the jacket zip, if held horizontally in a special frame, will not come apart if a small car is hung on it.

- The first recognisable zip was a 'clasp locker or unlocker for shows' patented in 1893 by an American called Whitcomb Judson.

- Just one zip factory in the USA makes several million zip fasteners per day.

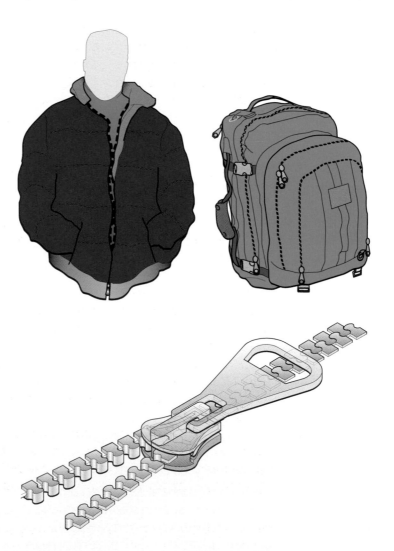

The first successful zip fastener was patented in 1917 and described as a 'separable fastener'. By 1924 the words 'zip' and 'zipper' were in common use. Since that time the zip has become one of the most widely used mechanical fastenings for clothing, luggage, footwear, outdoor equipment and many other everyday objects. It is one of those things most of us use every day but only really notice when it goes wrong!

When zips do fail, they are virtually impossible to repair because they are made with great precision and every single tooth has to be in the right place at the right time.

 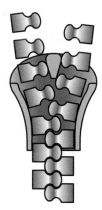

A zip consists of two rows of metal or plastic teeth fastened to fabric strips. Each tooth has a small hollow on one side and a raised bump on the other. When two opposing teeth come together, the bump on one fits into the hollow on the other. A **slider** brings the two sets of teeth together at just the right angle to make them mesh – one on top of the other. When locked normally, they cannot be pulled apart. But if the slider comes off the top of a zip, for example, the teeth will come apart very easily. The strength of a zip depends on all the teeth making perfect contact.

Although most zips use the same basic principle, there are many design differences. To find out more about zips, compare several under a low-power magnifying glass. Some plastic wallets are opened and closed by a completely different type of 'zip'. The plastic sheet is produced with special sections running along the edges. When these come together they lock. This type of 'zip' can be pulled apart quite easily.

How they are made

The teeth of metal zips are made in different ways. The most common is to squeeze a metal wire between two specially shaped tools to create each tooth. The wire is automatically fed into the tool and cut for each tooth. This operation happens many times per second. Plastic teeth are injection moulded (see Manufacturing techniques for plastics, page 39). Fused plastic, usually nylon, is forced into a mould under high pressure. Several teeth are injection moulded in one go.

Finally, the individual teeth are positioned automatically, sewn by the same machine on to fabric strips. Like many other things we take for granted, we have zip fasteners only because of the cleverly designed machinery that makes them so precisely in large numbers and at low cost.

1 Look carefully at a zip opening and closing. Compare it with the enlarged drawing opposite.

2 Where are zips used other than in clothing?

PET fizzy drink bottle

Some PET bottle facts

- A typical 330 ml PET fizzy drink bottle weighs only 10 g.
- A typical PET bottle has a wall thickness of 0.2 mm which is made up of three separate layers or **laminates**.
- When a fizzy drink bottle is shaken, it has to stand up safely to a pressure of approximately 4 bar – twice the pressure in a typical car tyre. If you work out the number of square centimetres on a 330 ml bottle's surface, the total pressure loading on the bottle is approximately 1.5 tons when the internal pressure is 4 bar.
- In tests, a typical PET bottle can withstand pressures of up to 10 bar.
- PET bottles have reduced accidents due to the fact that they are virtually impossible to break.
- It is estimated that 1.5 billion PET bottles are sold and thrown away in the UK each year.

Bottle design and PET

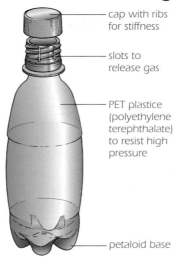

cap with ribs for stiffness

slots to release gas

PET plastice (polyethylene terephthalate) to resist high pressure

petaloid base

balloon base PET bottle with plastic ring on base for stability

Almost all plastic fizzy drink bottles are made from a relatively new plastic material called **PET**. This stands for **polyethylene terephthalate**, which is a mixture (**co-polymer**) of plastics with very special properties. These properties include:

- very high **tensile strength** – resistance to stretching (see Structures, page 71)
- high **impact resistance** – the ability to withstand sudden knocks
- **non-permeability** – resistance to gas under pressure 'leaking' through the material.

Most people take PET bottles for granted and throw them away without much thought. However, great care has gone into their design to make them both cheap and safe.

To withstand high pressures, the shape of a fizzy drink bottle is very important. A good shape is a sphere, which is sometimes used for natural gas containers. It is not a very practical shape for bottles because spheres take up a lot of space in boxes or on shelves. The next best shape is cylindrical, but this presents a problem because of the base. A thin flat base would 'balloon' outwards under pressure and cause the bottle to fall over. Some PET bottles do have a **balloon base** but these bottles also have a **plastic ring** at the bottom to stand on. A majority of PET bottles now have either a **champagne base** or a **petaloid** base to overcome the problem of containing pressure while at the same time enabling them to stand upright.

The champagne base gets its name from glass champagne bottles that have an inverted dome at the bottom. The petaloid base shown in the drawing is so named because it resembles petals on a plant. It is really a number of balloon bases clustered together and, because there are several of them, the bottle stands up. You may think this is an obvious solution to the problem, but it took several years of development work to arrive at.

The screw cap and bottle top are also very special designs. The cap has a built-in (**integral**) seal which gets tighter as it is twisted on to the bottle. Inside the cap, star-shaped **ribbing** helps to keep its top flat under pressure. Without this, the cap tends to balloon out under pressure and cause the seal to break down.

The screw threads on both the bottle top and the screw cap are slotted down their length. This is very important because when you unscrew a bottle top, it is important that any gas pressure build-up is released before the top has been fully unscrewed. Without these slots to release gas, the top could fly off under pressure and cause injury.

How they are made

PET bottles are made by a process called **injection blow moulding**. (See 'Manufacturing techniques for plastics, page 39.) In the first stage of this process, hot fused PET material is injected into a small mould and blown into a shape called a **parison** by the injection of air. This moulding is then transferred to a larger mould and blown into the final shape of the bottle.

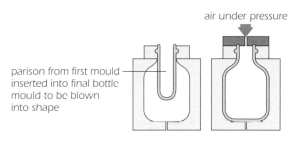

parison from first mould inserted into final bottle mould to be blown into shape

air under pressure

A note on pressure

$$\text{Pressure (in pascals)} = \frac{\text{force (in newtons)}}{\text{area (in square metres)}}$$

The unit of pressure is the **pascal** (Pa for short). 1 Pa = 1 newton per square metre (1 N m^{-2}).

The pressure exerted by the atmosphere (atmospheric pressure) is approximately 100 000 Pa. Atmospheric pressure is also used as a basis for measuring pressure in units called **bars**.

1 bar = atmospheric pressure = 105 000 N m^{-2} = 105 000 Pa
2 bars = twice atmospheric pressure, etc.

Some people still use older imperial units and talk about pounds per square inch (p.s.i.) rather than newtons per square metre. Approximately 14.5 p.s.i. = 1 bar.

---

1 Why does a half-full PET bottle get hard when you shake it?

2 Why does a PET bottle have a very thin wall?

Aluminium drink can

Some aluminium can facts

- A typical aluminium can weighs only 12 g but it takes as much energy to make one as it takes to light a 100 W bulb for 6 h.
- A typical can has a scrap value of approximately 1.5 p.
- A typical aluminium can has a wall thickness in the centre of 0.1 mm – the thickness of good quality paper.
- When standing upright, a typical aluminium can is able to support a load of approximately 115 kg; an empty can will easily support a person standing on it.

scored opening (watch the way the tab tears when you open your next can)

can top flanged and sealed after fitting

paper-thin wall thickness

Can design and aluminium

Almost all ring-pull cans are now made from aluminium (see page 165). Although it is the most abundant metal on the Earth's surface, aluminium requires a lot of expensive electricity to extract the metal from bauxite, its original form. Cans are therefore designed to be as thin and as light as possible. Even though paper-thin, a drink can has to be capable of withstanding a pressure of 6 bar – three times the pressure of a normal car tyre.

The base of an aluminium drink can has an inverted dome shape to resist the internal pressure of fizzy drinks. If the base were flat, it would 'balloon' out under pressure and the can would not stand up properly.

The top of a drink can has to be thicker than the sides to support the **tab-opening** mechanism and it alone accounts for about a quarter of the weight of the entire can. To reduce the amount of metal in the top, its diameter is made smaller and most cans therefore have a distinctive 'neck' shape.

Ring-pull opening mechanisms for metal cans were developed in the 1960s. Earlier cans had detachable ring-pulls which quickly became a health and litter hazard when they were discarded. The modern ring-pull is designed to push the tab inwards where it stays attached to the can top.

When the ring-pull is lifted up, it acts as a **lever** (see page 54) to make an initial break in a line of weakness which is impressed into the top. Even though the metal is very thin along the tear-line, the closure tab does not break off all at once. If you open your next can slowly, you will see that the tear travels (propagates) along the line of weakness.

The stress applied by bending the ring-pull is concentrated on just a tiny amount of metal at the tip of the tear, and the tear propagates along the line of weakness. Normally engineers do everything they can to avoid lines of weakness or surface cracks in metal and other structures, because failure occurs more easily under stress when tears start at the tip of cracks and open up just like the tear in the can top.

The ring-pull is **riveted** to the can top by an ingenious method. (See Manufacturing techniques for metals, page 30.) The rivet itself is formed from the metal of the top as a hollow pressing which is then flattened over the pull tab.

How they are made

The main body of an aluminium can is made by two processes called **drawing** and **ironing** (see Manufacturing techniques for metals, page 30). These are carried out in a combined operation that lasts for about 0.2 s.

- Step 1 – A disc of aluminium sheet 140 mm in diameter is **punched** from a sheet.

- Step 2 – This is formed into a shallow cup using a **punch** and **die**.

- Step 3 – The cup of aluminium is drawn down into a deeper die and as it is pushed down it is thinned by extremely hard **ironing rings** which give it paper-thinness and surface polish.

- Step 4 – The can is printed and given its final neck shape at the top, and the top is attached by folding (**flanging**) as shown in the main drawing opposite.

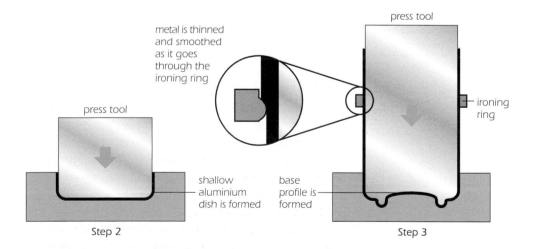

metal is thinned and smoothed as it goes through the ironing ring

press tool

press tool

iroding ring

shallow aluminium dish is formed

base profile is formed

Step 2

Step 3

1   Why can you stand on the end of a can without it crushing, but not on the side?

2   Why is a typical drink can so light in weight?

Disposable ball-point pen

Some ball-point pen facts

- The modern ball-point pen was invented in 1938 by the Hungarian brothers Georg and Ladislao Biro – hence the fact that these pens are sometimes called 'biros'.
- A typical disposable ball-point pen has seven manufactured parts plus the ink but can be bought over the counter for as little as 10 p.
- In use for rapid writing or crossing out, the ball point in a fine-line pen can rotate at a speed of 18 000 r.p.m. (revolutions per minute) – three times the maximum safe speed of most car engines.
- As recently as the 1970s, some people believed that ball-point pens were not 'proper' pens and should not be used, for example, in school exams or on legal documents.

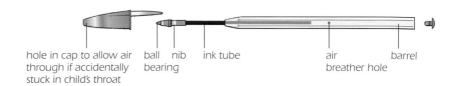

hole in cap to allow air through if accidentally stuck in child's throat   ball bearing   nib   ink tube   air breather hole   barrel

Ball-point pen design

Most disposable ball-point pens are made from different plastics for the **barrel end-plug, cap, ink tube** and **nib holder**. The ball itself is made from steel and rotates in a socket or nib of brass. The ball is ground to an accuracy of 0.013 mm and is identical in type to those used in ball-bearing races for cycles, car engines, and so on. It has to be fitted into the brass nib with the finest engineering fit or tolerance, otherwise either the ball would not turn or the ink would leak out.

Part of the problem of designing a successful ball-point pen was producing a suitable ink. The ink used is thicker (more viscous) and more 'oily' than other inks and actually takes many *years* to dry fully on paper! The ink tube of a disposable pen is open at one end, yet the ink does not run out. This is not simply because it is viscous, but because of surface tension – a 'skin' on the exposed surface of the ink – and the way the ink molecules attach themselves to the plastic tube.

The barrel of the pen has a small **vent hole** in the side so that when the ink at the ball is used up a vacuum does not develop and prevent more ink from flowing. If you block up the vent hole, the pen may stop writing by the time only about 15% of its ink has been used. (Some 'space age' pens have a closed ink tube which is pressurised by gas. These were developed so that, unlike ordinary ball-point pens, they would write upside down.)

The cap of a disposable ball-point pen now has a hole in the end. This is a safety precaution and enables air to pass through if the cap is swallowed by a young child. What stops the cap falling off the pen? Most disposable pen tops fit tightly on to the barrel; this is known as an **interference fit**. The difference between the cap fitting too tightly to pull off, or too loosely to stay on, is very small indeed. Because both the cap and the barrel are moulded to within certain limits, it is not just a question of making the cap 'a little bit smaller'. If you look carefully at the inside of a cap, you will probably see a small moulded-in ring. When the cap is first pushed on to the barrel, it goes on fairly easily, but as the ring passes over the barrel it makes a tighter fit. Because the area of ring in contact with the barrel is so small, the tight-fitting cap can be withdrawn without it sticking.

How they are made

The plastic parts of the pen are made by **injection moulding** (see Manufacturing techniques for plastics, page 39). If you look carefully, the places (**sprue marks**) where the fused plastic is injected can be seen. The ball bearing is made by feeding steel wire between special **skew rollers** which both shape and part off rough spheres of steel. These rough balls are then fed into contact with high-speed grinding wheels which give them an accurate surface finish.

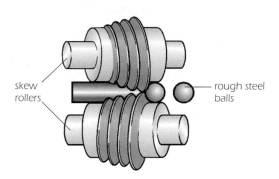

skew rollers

rough steel balls

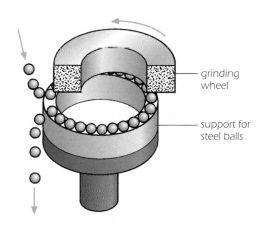

grinding wheel

support for steel balls

See

- Hi-tech pen, page 244

Finally the ball is inserted into the brass nib which is then attached to the ink tube by means of a plastic moulding called the nib holder.

1 What is the main difference between a cheap disposable and an expensive ball pen?

2 Why are some ball pens hexagonal in section?

Torch bulb

Some bulb facts

- The tungsten metal filament of an ordinary bulb gets white hot in operation. Its temperature is around 3000 K which is roughly half the temperature of the Sun.
- The glass envelope of a bulb is evacuated of air which would otherwise cause the hot tungsten to oxidise and the bulb to burn out. Instead of air there is a partial vacuum with traces of inert gases such as argon and nitrogen which prolong filament life.
- Tungsten halogen lamps operate at a higher temperature (3200 K) which is so hot that the tungsten filament starts to evaporate. However, the tungsten vapour combines with the halogen gas and is deposited back again on the filament as metal in a continuous cycle.
- Only a small percentage of the radiation from a filament bulb is actually visible light. Most of the electrical energy is converted into heat. Nevertheless, a typical energised torch bulb (without reflector) is easily visible on a dark night at a distance of one mile.
- There are many different shapes and styles of miniature bulb. The smallest is known as a grain of wheat bulb because it has a similar shape and size to a grain of wheat. These bulbs are roughly the same size as a match head and are used in 'micro-torches' such as keyring fobs.

Bulb design and construction

The type of miniature bulb used for torches is similar in most respects to larger domestic light bulbs but differs in its construction. The **filament** of a typical bulb is actually a coil within a coil of **tungsten** wire. The inner coil is so small that it is hardly visible with the naked eye.

the coil within a coil of a typical filament

In a miniature bulb the filament is connected to two wires which are joined by a tiny **glass bead**. The ends of these wires pass out through the glass **envelope** to be connected to the **terminals** on the lamp base. The base, which is made mainly of brass, is bonded to the glass envelope with a special cement. If this bond breaks down and the glass envelope becomes loose, the bulb will still work providing that the wires coming out of the envelope do not break.

Although they seem very simple things, the bulbs we use in torches have taken many years to evolve into a cheap and reliable form with a long life. In many earlier bulbs, for example, the filament evaporated and darkened the inside of the glass, or the filament broke when the bulb was given a sharp knock. These are now problems of the past. You can now even buy small **halogen** torch bulbs which in the early 1990s were available only for much larger mains-operated equipment. These give out far more light than conventional bulbs and have made torches more effective and cycle lamps much safer.

How they are made

The envelope of a small bulb is made from glass tube which is heated and blown in a mould. The filament assembly is then placed into the open end of the blown 'bubble' and a second length of tubing is fused on to the open end and drawn into a small tip. The last process to complete the envelope is called 'tipping off' and involves pumping out air, introducing **inert gases** and then sealing off the small tip opening by heat. To complete the bulb, the filament leads are connected to the brass cap of the bulb and this is then bonded to the envelope.

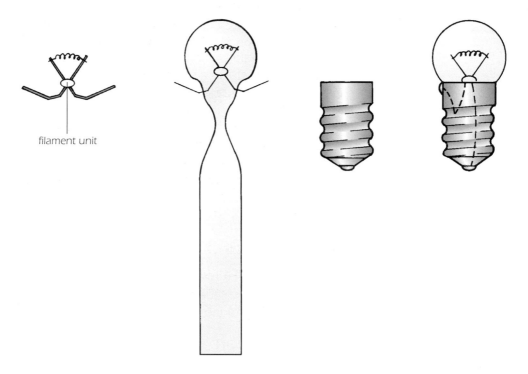

filament unit

Technical notes

The **voltage rating** is normally stamped on the cap of the bulb. If this rating is exceeded, the bulb will glow brighter, but its life will be greatly shortened. A 15% increase in voltage over the stated value could result in a 50% decrease in bulb life.

High-intensity **LEDs** (see page 128) are now being used increasingly to replace or supplement bulbs in rear cycle lamps. Generally, LEDs have a longer life and consume less current than miniature filament bulbs.

See

▪ Light pipe, page 235

1 Why do some small torches use LEDs but most use filament bulbs?

2 What two numbers are marked on a filament bulb?

Tape cassette

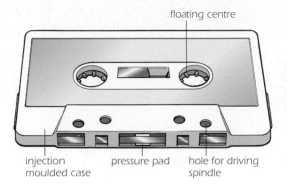

floating centre

injection moulded case   pressure pad   hole for driving spindle

1 μm

particles of the type used in magnetic tape, under high magnification

Some cassette facts

- The tape in a cassette has a thickness of only 12 microns – equivalent in thickness to a typical human hair. A micron (μm) is 1/1000 of a millimetre.
- Cassette tape is coated with billions of metal oxide particles, each of which acts as a tiny magnet. A piece of recorded music consists of billions of these small magnets each having a different state along the length of the tape.
- The playing/recording speed of a cassette tape is 4.76 cm s^{-1} and should not vary from this speed by more than ±0.05%, according to British Standards.
- Cassette tapes are now used mainly for recording sound but were also used before floppy disks to store software. Special cassette tapes continue to be used for software back-up.
- Cassette tape is made as a web about 1 m wide which is then sliced into strips 6.3 mm wide. Video tape is also made this way.

Cassette design

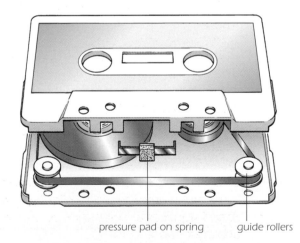

pressure pad on spring   guide rollers

All cassettes are similar in design because they conform to standards to enable them to be used in any player. The claims that manufacturers make for their own cassettes normally concern the **metal oxide** coating and how this affects recording quality. Ordinary tapes use **iron oxide** (Fe_2O_3). More expensive tapes use **chromium dioxide** (CrO_2), for example.

The two tape spools of a cassette have floating centres. This enables them to fit easily into different players and avoids the need for precise bearings in the cassette itself. Bearings within the cassette itself would make it more expensive and probably less reliable.

When playing, tape is not moved across the record/playback head by the two spools. If this were the case, the tape speed would vary as its diameter increased or decreased on the spools (just as it does during fast forward or rewind). The tape is moved by *pinching* it between a rotating **steel spindle** and a **rubber roller** in the player. The steel spindle (the **capstan**) passes through one of the holes in the front of the cassette case.

During playing, slipping belts in the player (and other mechanisms) drive the spools with a very small turning force to keep the tape tensioned. A small **pad** fixed to a beryllium copper **spring** keeps the tape pressed against the recording/playback head.

How they are made

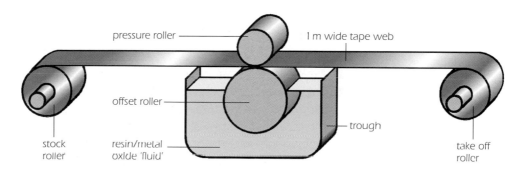

The Mylar plastic tape is made as a wide web which is then coated with the metal oxide. The oxide is mixed with a resin and 'printed' onto the tape by a roller (called an **offset roller**). The speed of this roller is very tightly controlled so that it delivers just the thickness of oxide and resin needed to coat the tape. This is typically just 5 μm! When the resin **cures**, the metal oxide is permanently bonded to the tape surface.

The cassette case and spools are made by **injection moulding** (see Manufacturing techniques for plastics, page 39). For each part needed, fused plastic material is forced under pressure into a precision mould. The parts are then assembled and the two halves of the cassette case bonded together.

Technical note

Many tapes still use **analogue** recording in which sound is converted into a constantly varying electrical signal. This method has always suffered from tape 'hiss' which can be heard in the background when a tape is played. Only electronic circuits (such as *Dolby*) can reduce this. However, the problem is eliminated completely in the **DAT** (digital audio tape) system which stores the sound signal as a digital code on the tape and then re-converts this into an analogue form.

---

1 Estimate the length of tape in a cassette and then measure the actual length in a broken one.

2 Why does the tape have to be strong when pulled?

Lightweight headphones

Some headphone facts

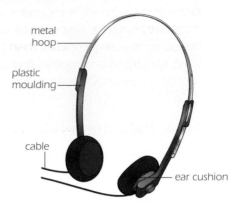

metal hoop

plastic moulding

cable

ear cushion

■ Typical lightweight headphones for a personal stereo weigh just 30 g.
■ These headphones were developed for products like the original Sony *Walkman* which needed a means of reproducing high-quality sound without the bulk and weight of the larger hi-fi headphones then available.
■ Lightweight headphones capable of high-quality sound reproduction depend on a new generation of extremely powerful magnets (e.g. of neodymium) which are also used to make ultra-powerful miniature electric motors.
■ Lightweight headphones are made in such large numbers that some cheaper varieties are available from the manufacturers (to wholesalers) for just 28 p.
■ The thin copper wire coil in each earpiece of a headphone is less than 25 microns thick. A micron (μm) is 1/1000 of a millimetre.

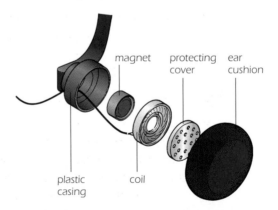

magnet   protecting cover   ear cushion

plastic casing   coil

Headphone principles

Very early headphones, like the ones used with crystal sets in the early days of broadcasting, used a metal disc (diaphragm) placed close to an electromagnet to convert electrical signals into sound. These produced a sound of limited quality and suffered from not being able to reproduce very high ('treble') and very low ('bass') frequencies. The better headphones were also quite heavy.

Modern lightweight headphones are more like a pair of tiny loudspeakers. Each **earpiece** has a moving **cone** whose centre is fixed to a fine **coil** of wire free to move up and down around a powerful **magnet**. When an electrical signal from a cassette recorder (or radio) is supplied to the coil, it moves rapidly up and down in relation to the fixed magnet and drives the cone to produce sound. The cone is made of plastic sheet much thinner than normal paper and has a special pattern moulded around its edge so that it can move more freely.

The main measure of quality for headphones is **frequency response**. This is the extent to which the headphones can turn an electrical signal into the full range of sound it represents. Frequency response is given by specifying the lowest and highest frequencies in **hertz** (Hz) that can be reproduced (1 Hz = 1 cycle per second). Cheaper headphones cannot reproduce very high and very low frequencies and we say that such headphones have a poor frequency response. Nevertheless, even cheaper modern lightweight headphones can do better than some much larger hi-fi models which cost ten times more just a few years ago.

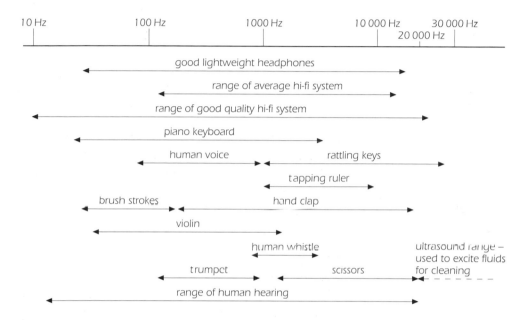

The chart shows the audible frequency range or **spectrum**. Good quality lightweight headphones have a frequency response of 50–15 000 Hz. If the frequency response is, say, only 200–10 000 Hz, all the highest and lowest frequencies will be lost and the overall sound quality will suffer.

How they are made

Lightweight headphones consist of a number of parts made in different ways and then **fabricated** or joined together. The outside casing is made by **injection moulding** in which fused plastic is injected into a mould (see Manufacturing techniques for plastics, page 39). Metal parts such as the headphone 'hoop' are sometimes placed into the same mould so that the plastic solidifies around them to make a metal to plastic joint. This is called **insert moulding**.

The headphone cones are made by various means including **vacuum forming** (see Manufacturing techniques for plastics, page 39). To ensure the highest frequency response, the cone has quite a complex shape when seen in cross-section. Many cones are produced in one operation by heating a large plastic sheet and then drawing it down by means of a vacuum over a number of identical **moulds**. When the sheet cools, it retains the exact shape of each mould and is then cut up into individual cones.

1 What sounds, if any, do you lose when listening to music through small headphones?

2 What gives you the stereo effect using headphones?

SECTION 4

projects

1 Mechanisms

Dispensing system

■ **TASK**   Design and make a dispenser for measuring out sugar, salt or similar granular materials.

dispensing tube

Automatic systems for measuring out quantities of ingredients are used widely in catering. One method for measuring granular materials such as sugar uses the principle of fluidisation. When granules of sugar or salt are piled up, they tend to lock together; if you pour them into a dish they form a cone. If the cone is vibrated, the individual granules move about and the whole mass acts like a fluid, and flattens out.

Sugar fed into a tube with the correct-size holes will stay inside the tube. When it is vibrated the sugar will pour out. The quantity dispensed depends on the length of time the tube is vibrated.

Designing and making a dispenser

You can determine the size of holes that will just keep sugar or similar material in a tube by experiment. The tube can be vibrated using a small motor with an off-centre mass. The dispenser will then need further design work to complete the housing. It may be a sugar dispenser for use near a vending machine, for example.

The measured amount depends on timing and this can be achieved with a simple electronic circuit. When the push-button switch is pressed momentarily, the **capacitor** charges up and keeps the **field effect transistor (FET)** switched on until the capacitor is discharged by the resistor. The time delay depends on the value of both capacitor and **resistor**. A 100 kΩ resistor and 100 µF capacitor will give a vibration time of about 3–4 s.

See

- Field effect transistors (FETs), page 113
- Capacitors, page 123
- DC motors, page 131

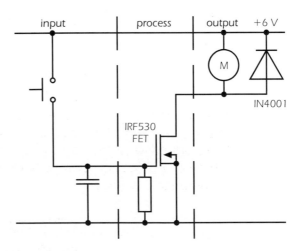

Ball launcher

■ TASK Design and make a table tennis ball launcher for games practice (or elective purpose).

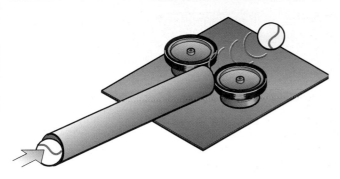

There are several automatic ball launchers for tennis and cricket practice. These use the same basic mechanism to propel a ball. They contain two high-speed spinning wheels with a gap between them slightly smaller than the ball diameter. When a ball is fed between them, energy stored in the spinning wheels is transferred to it, and it moves out at high speed. Very small electric motors driving small plastic wheels can make available enough energy to accelerate a table tennis ball to 30 miles per hour!

See

- DC motors, page 131

Designing and making a ball launcher

The overall size of the launcher is set by the ball diameter and the choice of wheels and motors. Experiments show that two MM12 size miniature motors with plastic wheels of 40 mm diameter (mass 10 g) are a good combination. However, you can do further experiments with different motors and wheels. It is important that the wheels can grip the smooth balls. They normally need a rubber surface to do this, for example an elastic band 'tyre'.

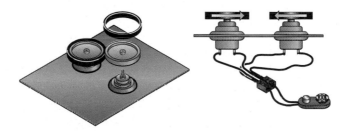

Unless another person is feeding balls by hand, the practice ball launcher requires a method of feeding balls to the wheels. There are two parts to this problem:

■ a hopper or container for the balls
■ a way of releasing the balls one at a time from where the player is standing.

The container could be a tube or ramp providing a gravity feed to the wheels. The release mechanism might be mechanical, such as pulling a cord or even hydraulic. An electrical system would offer more flexibility, but remember that, whatever the method, it has to both release a ball and prevent the next ball rolling on to the wheels.

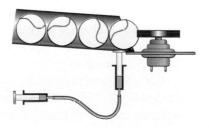

Tumbler unit

Tumbling units, where small parts or materials are tumbled together in a rotating drum, are used widely in industry for surface finishing. Sometimes, for example, they are used to wear away the sharp edges of metal parts, or for polishing hard materials such as low-value 'precious' stones. The parts or materials are placed in the drum with suitable abrasives or polishing materials which take effect over a long period of slow tumbling. Unusual materials have been used in the past, including crushed walnut shells for polishing precision gears!

Designing and making a tumbler

The most common form of small tumbler used for polishing minerals and stones is a drum mounted horizontally on two rollers driven by an **electric motor**. The drum is not fixed but simply rests on the rollers and can easily be replaced by others. A small drum of 100 mm diameter should turn at about 50–80 r.p.m. A faster spin speed will make the contents stick to the drum wall.

See

- Uses of pi, page 6
- DC motors, page 131

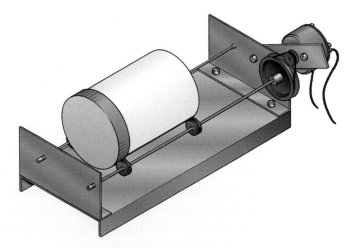

There are many different ways of producing a frame to support two rollers. These might be made from thin rod with wheels for the drum to rest on. The motor might drive one of the **rollers** with **pulleys** and a thin belt as shown. A suitable motor for a small tumbler is a solar motor that can be driven either by battery (expensive) or by an approved **power supply unit (PSU)**.

For a successful product, other problems have to be solved. For example, how will you prevent the drum moving along the rollers? What kind of bearings will you use at the ends of the rollers?

Robotic arm

■ **TASK** Design and make a robotic arm with two axes of movement.

Robots are used increasingly in industry to do repetitive jobs, such as welding or painting in car manufacturing. A complex robotic arm can move just like a human arm; a much simpler robot may have only limited movement in two directions. Industrial robots are usually controlled by computer and are becoming more 'intelligent'. They are usually powered by special electric motors which are able to stop and start with great precision.

> **See**
> - Control, page 50
> - Gearboxes, page 148

Designing and making a model robot arm

Even a simple robot can be very complicated to design and make. An easy starting point is to take two **gearbox** units (with motors attached) and join them together at 90°. The output shaft from one gearbox is joined to a baseplate and the output shaft from the other gearbox is joined to an arm. This gives the arm two directions of movement when the two motors are operated. The gearboxes must be selected for a slow output speed, otherwise the robot will be uncontrollable!

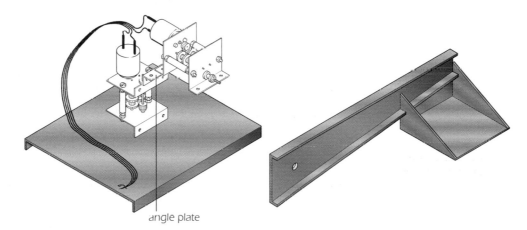

angle plate

It is possible to design the robot to pick and place objects. This involves adding a pick-up or grab to the end of the arm. A very simple solution (for some objects) is a scoop. An alternative is an **electromagnet** for picking up ferrous objects.

To control the robot manually you can use a **double pole double throw (DPDT)** switch with centre 'off' position for each motor. This means that the motors can be stopped or driven in either direction. DPDT slide switches can be wired easily to give this control, or specially made boards can be obtained. The robot can also be programmed to move through a sequence using a computer control package or a self-contained controller such as the **bit-by-bit controller**.

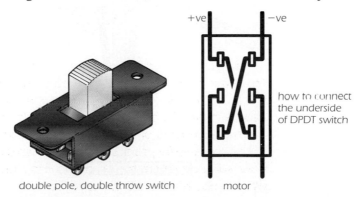

double pole, double throw switch

+ve   −ve

how to connect the underside of DPDT switch

motor

Air muscle mechanism

An air muscle consists of a rubber sac, like a balloon, encased in a woven braid. When the sac is blown up with air, the braid expands outwards and pulls in at both ends. Something attached to the end of an air muscle can be moved when the air muscle is blown up (see page 144). Air muscles are used, for example, in the film industry to animate models. This is called **animatronics**. Air muscles can be used whenever there is a need for force and movement.

Designing and making an air muscle mechanism

> **See**
> ▪ Levers, page 54
> ▪ Air muscles, page 144

Air muscles need to be inflated with air at about 3 bar (three times atmospheric pressure). The air can be supplied directly, for example, from a cycle pump or from a low-pressure system like the one illustrated. This consists of a fizzy drink bottle inflated by a foot pump. A small **three-way valve** is used to supply air to the air muscle and release it again.

air out of muscle

air in

valve closed   valve open

The air muscle is connected to other things by cable ties or rings inserted through the loop at each end. The amount of movement is quite small but the force is quite high (depending on the air pressure). If you are designing something needing larger movements, a **lever** can provide this. The barrier lift shown is an example of an air muscle application that uses a lever – the barrier bar itself – to increase movement of something.

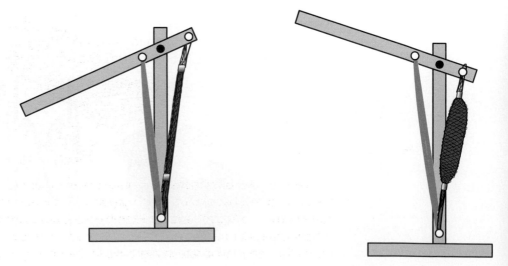

Micro-rover

Design and make a tracked micro-rover vehicle with exploration potential.

Following the example of 'Sojourner' built for Mars exploration, a new generation of smaller 'micro-rovers' are being developed for use here – to explore dangerous places, pick up samples or take pictures. Some of these will be smaller versions of Sojourner, probably with caterpillar tracks to enable them to move over rough ground. They might be manually controlled or programmable, or have the intelligence to explore places without assistance.

Designing and making a micro-rover

See

- Electrical control, page 60
- Gearboxes, page 148

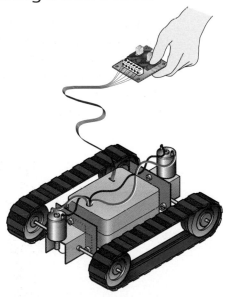

Tracked vehicles offer many advantages over other types when it comes to travelling over obstacles or rough ground. This is equally true when the vehicle is scaled down to 'micro' size, for example 125 mm in length. It is possible to buy rubber caterpillar tracks for models of this size. These normally have a rib running down the centre to locate in a groove in the driving wheels.

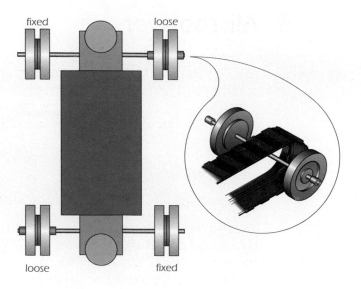

Such vehicles are normally controlled by powering the tracks independently: both tracks moving in the same direction move the vehicle forward, and stopping or slowing one track turns the vehicle. If the two tracks are run in opposite directions, the vehicle can turn around within its own length. One way of achieving independent drives is to use two **motor/gearbox** units at either end of a chassis. In the example shown, the track wheel is fixed at one end of the output shaft and turns loosely at the other. This is repeated for the other gearbox but with the fixed and loose ends reversed. One gearbox drives one track, and vice versa.

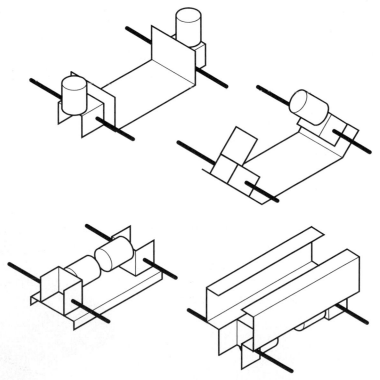

The design of the chassis can range from a simple metal plate to a complex folded unit. Space must be left for any on-board control system and batteries. To control the rover manually you can use a **double pole double throw (DPDT)** switch with centre 'off' position for each motor and gearbox. This means the motors can be stopped or driven in either direction. DPDT slide switches can be wired easily to give this control, or specially made boards are available.

Air tools

Compressed air is used widely in the manufacturing industry to move things and apply forces. **Pneumatic cylinders**, working like a cycle pump in reverse, are supplied with compressed air to cause controlled ram movements for positioning things, holding and moving them around. Pneumatic systems are cheap, flexible and easy to control.

See

- Mechanical control, page 54
- Programmable control, page 68
- Cycle pump, page 178

Designing and making an air system

Commercial air systems work from compressors delivering high (and potentially dangerous) pressures. A simple air supply can be made up using a garden spray compressor or a pump and PET bottle for air storage (TEP system). Either **hand-operated** or **solenoid valves** are then used to feed the air to one or more cylinders. These can be purchased ready made or they can be made up, for example, using the TEP all-plastic system.

The illustration (below centre) shows a complete TEP system using a solenoid valve operated by a **membrane switch**. A programmable system is easily made using a computer control package or a free-standing programmable control unit instead of the switch (such as the bit-by-bit controller, see below right).

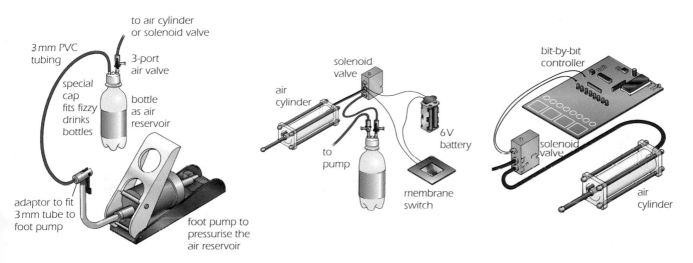

The system can be put to use in various ways. For example, a single cylinder with spring return can be used in a clamping system for someone who needs both hands free to work. With no air, the spring in the cylinder closes the clamp. When supplied with air (for example, via a foot switch) the **ram** moves and opens the clamp.

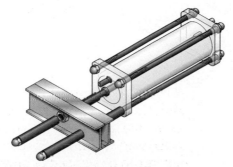

air cylinder actuating jaws of small air-release vice

Paper feeder

■ TASK   Design and make a device for dispensing paper at the press of a button.

See

- Uses of pi, page 6
- Programmable control, page 68

Moving paper in machines such as photocopiers and printers demands clever design and precision engineering. There are many examples that we come across each day, such as cash register receipts, printed tickets and faxes. Behind the scenes – in large printing works, for example – advanced technology is concerned just with moving paper at high speed. It is not the easiest material to get hold of, let alone position precisely when moving at several miles per hour!

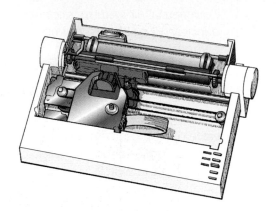

Designing and making a paper feeder

You may have a special dispensing application in mind – for example, sterilised paper towels in a surgery. If so, the dispenser must be designed around the size of the paper. But assuming the paper will be on a roll, a small working prototype can be designed and made around cheap till receipt rolls.

The main problem is gripping the paper. It is normally held between **spring-loaded** rubber rollers, one of which is powered by an electric motor. An easier alternative is to use a single roller and a **pressure plate**. The plate presses the paper against the roller. Paper-feeding rollers often have rubber tyres to reduce contact with the paper surface.

In the example shown below, the tyres are 'O' ring seals. The motor is connected to the roller via a **pulley** and is mounted on a swinging arm for easy adjustment of the drive belt tension. The example is made from folded sheet metal but this design could be made from any other suitable material.

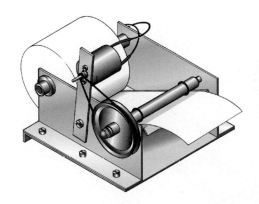

The paper **dispenser** also calls for a means of holding and changing the roll easily and cutting it to size. Fixed lengths of paper can be dispensed by adding a control circuit that keeps the motor running for a fixed length of time after a switch is closed. Examples include a 555 timer circuit, a programmable unit such as the bit-by-bit controller, or a microcontroller programmed via the *Chip Factory*.

2 Control

Electronic timer

Timers are built into many products familiar in the home, including video recorders and microwave ovens. Individual timers are also used, for example, in cooking, photography, and keep-fit activities.

Older clockwork timers and stopwatches are rapidly giving way to electronic ones. Most timer circuits use one or more **integrated circuits** or 'chips'. These are much cheaper to buy and run and at the same time give greater accuracy and performance.

Designing and making an electronic timer

See

- Designing control systems, page 50
- Electrical control, page 60
- Resistors, page 102
- The 555 timer, page 114
- Capacitors, page 123
- Light-emitting diodes (LEDs), page 128

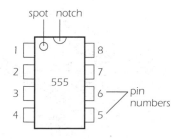

One of the most common integrated circuits for timing is the **555 timer**. This small **eight-pin chip** needs just five additional components to make a complete timer for timing periods from a few seconds to several minutes.

Like most circuits, the timer can be divided into three parts: input, process and output. When the input switch is closed momentarily, the 555 starts timing. When the timed period is up, pin 3 supplies current to energise an **LED** (shown in the figure below) or sound a buzzer if connected.

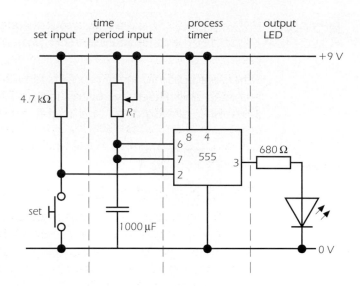

The timed period is set by varying the values of the **resistor** (R_1) and the **capacitor** (shown as 1000 μF). In practice, a **variable resistor** is used to give easy control of the timed interval.

In selecting the variable resistor and capacitor values in the first place, you can use the simple formula:

Timed period in seconds = 1.1 × capacitance in farads × resistance in ohms

For a 1000 μF capacitor and a 1000 ohm (1 kΩ) resistor,

$$\begin{aligned} \text{Timed period} &= 1.1 \times 1000\ \mu\text{F} \times 1000\ \text{ohms} \\ &= 1.1 \times 0.001\ \text{F} \times 1000\ \text{ohms} \\ &= 1.1\ \text{s} \end{aligned}$$

The values can also be found by looking them up on the chart below.

A case has to be designed for the circuit and decisions have to be made about the style and position of the input switch, the variable resistor and the output device – for example, sound or light? Also, you need to decide where the timer will be used. For example, if it will be used in the kitchen you will need to be able to clean the case. The design must also take into account the changing of batteries.

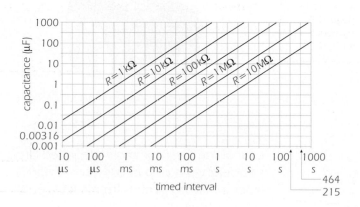

Alarm

■ **TASK**   Design an alarm for the home or to protect a single item.

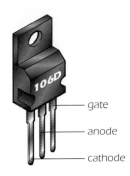
- gate
- anode
- cathode

As people worry increasingly about security, alarm systems in homes, cars and shops have become very common. Most alarms latch on (stay on) when a switch is triggered, if only for a second. Older alarms used **relays** to latch on a bell or other sound device when a switch was momentarily activated. Modern alarms use **electronic circuits**. These are much more reliable and enable many types of input to trigger the alarm. A **thyristor** is a modern component used in alarm systems which latches electronically. When it is triggered, it stays switched on (for example, energising a bell) until the supply to it is cut off or interrupted for a moment.

Designing and making an alarm system

Most circuits can be divided into three parts: input, process and output. A basic alarm circuit consists of one or more switches as the input, connected to doors, under mats, and so on. The process part of the circuit is a 106d thyristor which 'latches on' when the input switch is closed. (It can switch on currents up to 4 A.) The output part of the circuit can be a bulb, buzzer or bell. The alarm can be stopped by temporarily disconnecting the supply or bypassing the thyristor with the switch shown. Either way, the alarm is 'reset'.

See

- Electrical control, page 60
- Thyristors, page 129
- Relays, page 137

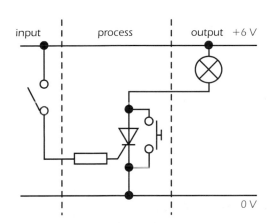

The overall design of the alarm will depend on whether it is part of a larger system or whether, for example, it is designed to protect just one thing such as a picture, an expensive item of clothing or a bag. The use will also determine what type of switch is used at the input. This could be a **pressure mat switch**, a **trembler type** that detects movement, or a **reed switch** which is activated by a passing magnet.

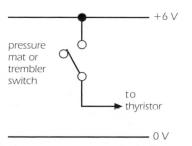

■ Membrane panel switch

Membrane panel switches are the ultra-thin press switches now used for many products, such as credit card calculators and vending machines. They consist of layers of very thin plastic film with printed contacts and connectors. Membrane panels are normally made in three layers. The centre layer is an insulator with a number of holes (or switch sites). When the membrane is pressed over the site of one of these holes two switch contacts come together. Membrane panels have made a big impact on product design. They are cheap and hardwearing and can be brightly printed.

Designing and making a membrane panel

See

- Electrical control, page 60
- Graphics, page 83

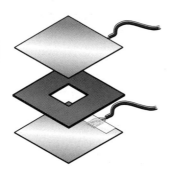

The illustration shows one type of membrane panel using paper or card (instead of plastic) and aluminium foil. It has a conductive foil on the bottom layer, an insulating middle layer with a window, and a top foil layer. The middle layer keeps the top and bottom foils apart until the switch is pressed and they dip through the hole to touch.

The aluminium foil can be stuck down with glue stick adhesive. It is important to use only stranded wire when connecting the switch to other things. It is joined to the *top* of the aluminium with sticky tape.

foil

stranded wire

clear sticky tape

A second type of switch has a complete covering of foil on the top and bottom layers, and one or more windows in the centre. This can be used for a game where players have to guess the position of the switch sites. You can finish a membrane panel switch by adding a fourth top sheet, for example graphics created on a computer.

Auto-shutdown product

■ **TASK** Design a small battery-powered torch which switches off automatically.

Many electrical goods, especially battery-powered ones, automatically shut down after a set time interval. This normally involves an **integrated circuit chip** which times the interval. These circuits are very cheap if produced in large quantities and can now be used in very simple products such as torches and battery-powered fans.

See

- Electrical control, page 60
- Field effect transistors (FETs), page 113
- Capacitors, page 123

Designing and making an auto-shutdown product

A **field-effect transistor (FET)** can be used with a capacitor to give automatic shut-down of a bulb or motor. The FET acts as a switch which is turned 'on' for as long as there is a sufficient voltage at the gate. In the circuit shown below, closing a press switch momentarily charges the **capacitor**. This retains its charge and keeps the FET turned on until discharged by the resistor. The 'on' period depends on the values of the capacitor and **resistor**. A 1 µF capacitor and 1 MΩ resistor will keep a 4.5 V bulb running for approximately 60 s.

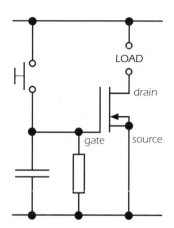

Torches are notorious for flat batteries because they have been left on accidentally when last used. Battery-powered fans are increasingly popular but suffer from the same problem. Can you think of other small products requiring an auto-shutdown circuit to conserve the battery?

When you have identified a product to design, you should allow for a push-to-make switch, the circuit and a means of changing batteries. Push-to-make switches can be bought or they can be made, for example, using card and foil (see Membrane panel switch, page 218).

■ Smartcard application

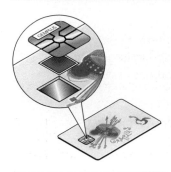

Small lasers are often used to create special lighting effects. The lasers are turned on and off and moved around by a control system which uses a number of stored programs. One way of storing these programs is on **smartcards**. These look like credit cards but contain an **integrated circuit** (chip) which can store information such as 'turn on' and 'turn off' commands. Once a smartcard is programmed, it holds the information until it is re-programmed.

Designing and making a lighting unit

An alternative to small lasers in a lighting unit is ultra-bright **LEDs**. These are available in several colours at much lower costs. They give a wider but focused beam and are effective in a dark room. There are several ways of providing movement for the light such as rotating and flexible mirrors, powered by small electric motors. The LEDs can be turned on and off in a programmed sequence by the smartcard control system and the motors can also be controlled.

See

- Programmable control, page 68
- Light-emitting diodes (LEDs), page 128
- DC motors, page 131

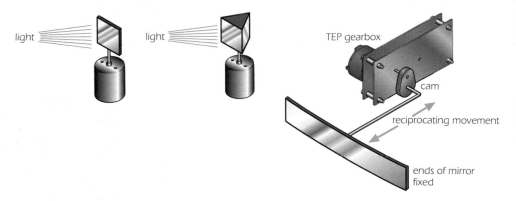

The TEP smartcard system has a separate programming unit and card reader (which becomes part of the project). The card is programmed in a simple programming language to turn up to six outputs on and off. It is then transferred to the reader to run the program. LEDs and suitable motors can be connected directly to the outputs of the smartcard reader.

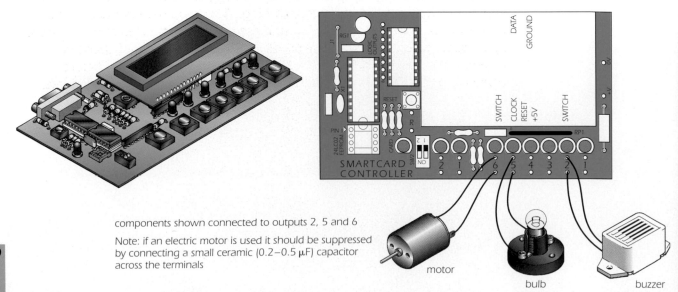

components shown connected to outputs 2, 5 and 6

Note: if an electric motor is used it should be suppressed by connecting a small ceramic (0.2–0.5 µF) capacitor across the terminals

3 Electronics

Decorative lighting

■ **TASK**   Design and make a set of (programmable) decorative lights.

Decorative lights can be used at parties and special occasions; a good example is Christmas-tree lights. These lights used to be strings of small filament bulbs connected together in series and powered from the mains. However, this kind of lighting has caused fires and other accidents, so the trend now is to use **LEDs** powered by a battery. To conserve the battery, the LEDs are made to switch on and off.

See

- Programmable control, page 68
- The 555 timer, page 114
- Light-emitting diodes (LEDs), page 128

Designing and making decorative lights

There are two main parts to a lighting array: the wiring of the lights and the method of controlling them. Several LEDs can be wired in series in just one loop of wire. Several loops of LEDs can be connected to the same battery.

Decorative lights powered by battery usually flash on and off; the 'off' period is longer than the 'on' period, although you may not notice this. This kind of lighting is controlled by a small circuit such as a **555 timer**. Alternatively, you can use a programmer like the one shown below.

Strings of LEDs connected to this can be programmed to come on and off at different intervals. Each loop of LEDs can be programmed differently to give the impression, for example, of random flashing. When you have decided on the number of LEDs in one or more loops, these must be connected to the controller in a suitable case with a switch. The case must provide access for changing the batteries. You should check whether the LEDs need a series resistor before connecting them and make sure that the output of the controller is adequate.

Radio

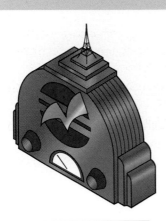

In the early days of broadcasting the shape and size of radios was governed by what was inside them. Early valve radios were large and used a lot of electrical energy. It was only after the **transistor** was invented that radios became much smaller, cheaper and more portable. Most radios today use tiny **integrated circuits** (chips) which means that it is possible to fit the 'works' of a radio into a matchbox! However, in practice the sound quality is usually better with a larger loudspeaker and case, and so at present this often determines its size.

Designing and making a radio

See

- The main groups of materials, page 17
- Graphics, page 83

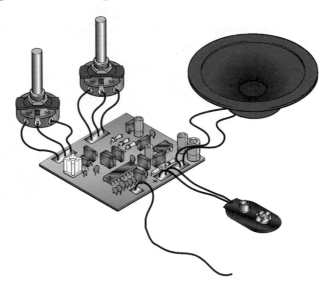

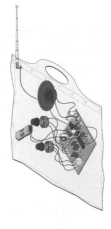

The TEP radio board is a fully working FM radio which simply needs the addition of components such as a **loudspeaker** and **controls** for tuning, volume and 'on/off'. Because the radio is electronically tuned, it has the same type of control – a **variable resistor** – for both tuning and volume. You can design practically any shape for the radio providing it will contain the controls and a loudspeaker. It will normally take the form of a container so that the loudspeaker is fully enclosed. This has a great effect on volume and sound quality. However, the radio does not have to be a box shape or use **resistant materials** such as plastic or wood. Card or fabric can be used, for example. One famous radio from the 1970s was built in a see-through plastic bag.

In designing a radio, you are really spoilt for choice because the inside components no longer dictate what the shape is. The main limitation is your imagination!

Designer chip

■ **TASK**   Design a 'chip' for a chosen use.

Integrated circuits are complex circuits built on a single 'chip' of **silicon** – hence the name 'chip'. They have revolutionised electronics because they are so small and increasingly cheap and powerful. Calculators and mobile phones would simply not be possible without them. In the past, chips were designed and made for set uses. A newer type of chip – the **microcontroller** – can be programmed to do what you want, making it possible for you to design your own chips!

Programming a microcontroller 'chip'

Microcontrollers are 'empty' chips waiting to be programmed to do something, such as turn things on and off in a sequence. The program is held permanently in the chip's memory, but can be wiped by re-programming. Microcontrollers are usually programmed via a PC using an interface link. An easier method is to use the *Chip Factory*. You simply plug in the chip to be programmed and then enter the program using simple instructions. For example, the instruction 'high 1' means turn on output number 1; 'wait 10' means wait for 10 s; 'low 1' means turn off output number 1. The *Chip Factory* does the rest! Once unplugged from the *Chip Factory* the chip will execute your instructions when it is correctly connected to other components. For example, if it contains the above instructions, it will turn on an LED connected to one of its outputs, and this will stay on for 10 s.

The *Chip Factory* comes with an easy-to-follow instruction book and enables you to create simple or complicated programs. You may, for example, want to design and make a micro-rover or automaton that goes through a sequence of movements. You could design a light show where ultra-bright LEDs are switched on and off and reflected from moving mirrors on motors. You might even consider designing and making a small product with 'intelligence'. You do not necessarily need to make the product. Instead, you might simply design the program for the chip and test it out.

See

- Programmable control, page 68
- Light-emitting diodes (LEDs), page 128

4 Structures

Space frame

Many buildings use space frames as part of their structure. These frames often consist of lightweight metal tubes linked together as tetrahedrons (a tetrahedron is a geometrical shape having four identical triangular faces). Space frame structures are very strong for their weight and can support heavy loads over large areas – hence their use for roofs.

Small prototype space frames can be made using tightly rolled paper, sometimes called **roll-tubes**. This turns the paper from a floppy sheet into a stiff tube that resists bending. Roll-tubes can be used in much larger structures but are not as strong as metal or plastic.

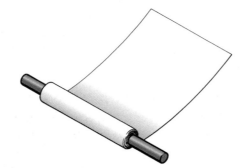

Designing and making a paper space frame

See

- Properties of materials, page 19
- Structures, page 71

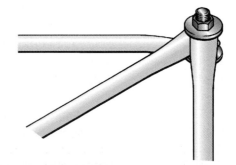

Roll-tubes for paper space frames are rolled over a slotted mandrel and can be glued with glue stick. The ends are punched (and sometimes eyelets are added for strength) so they can be joined with screws and nuts, plastic rivets or other fastenings. A basic space frame element is the tetrahedron which requires six roll-tubes. This can be used, for example, as the basis for an interesting three-dimensional photo or picture frame. You will have to think about how the photo will be attached to the frame. The paper for the space frame can be pre-selected for colour or might be printed along one edge with lettering and graphics. This can be easily reproduced using a photocopier.

Space frame display system

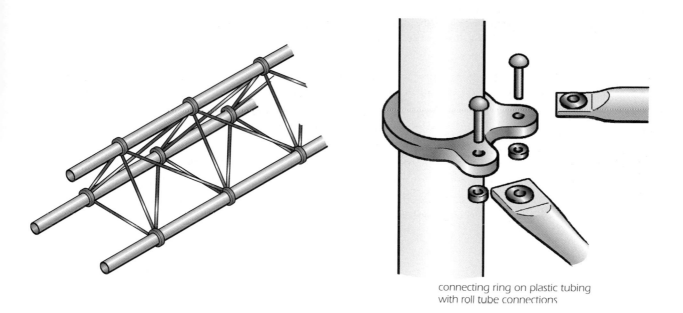

connecting ring on plastic tubing
with roll tube connections

See

- Injection moulding, page 39
- Structures, page 71

Many exhibition display systems use space frames to support panels, and so on. These frames often consist of lightweight metal tubes linked together as tetrahedrons. Space frame structures are very strong for their weight and can support heavy loads, such as lighting, over wide spans.

Large space frames can be made using tightly rolled paper, sometimes called roll-tubes, in combination with metal or plastic tubing. The smaller paper roll-tubes are linked to the larger diameter tubes to make complete units which are then fastened together to make the complete system.

Designing and making a display system

The system is likely to consist of several truss units, each of which has to be designed. For example, a simple exhibition gantry for hanging lights or display boards consists of two upright units and a bridging piece. The most economical truss unit has three larger tubes forming a triangular cross-section. These are joined together with roll-tubes connected at angles for maximum strength. You can make a number of choices about overall design, truss layout and materials to be used.

Inexpensive plastic wastepipe is a possible material for the larger tubes. Special fittings are available for joining the roll-tubes to these. If these are not used, other fittings have to be designed and made. Because of the numbers involved, it would be worth considering designing and making a tool to punch out identical plastic or metal fittings, or making a mould for injection-moulding them.

Fittings also need to be designed and made for joining display boards or other things such as lights. These must take into account the overall strength of the system. For example, foam core board is very light and can be suspended from the trusses using cords.

Hanging shelf system

Shelves are an example of a very simple structure. Some inexpensive shelving systems use fabric or cord as part of the structure.

Sagging of shelves can be a problem. How much of a problem is shown by comparing two nearly identical shelves mathematically, for example shelves 100 cm and 120 cm long. To work out the extra sag of the longer shelf as a percentage increase, raise both lengths to the fourth power and then divide one by the other, for example

$$\frac{120^4}{100^4} = \text{approx. } 200\%$$

This tells us that just a very small increase in length (20 cm) doubles the sag!

Designing and making a shelving system

Many cheaper shelving systems are made with **melamine-coated chipboard**. If this is supported only at each end, it should be kept to shorter lengths because of the above rule and because it 'creeps', that is, it develops a permanent sag over a period of time. The shelf itself can be fabricated (made up) as a stiff box section or, for example, folded from sheet metal.

> **See**
> - Stiffness, page 23
> - Structures, page 71

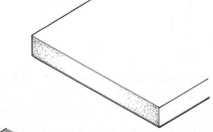 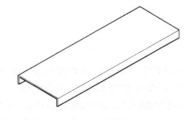

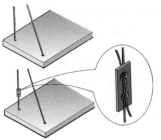

The suspension system might use cord made into a 'ladder' with joining pieces that you design (or simply knot together for a prototype). Another possible method is the creation of a collapsible fabric structure into which shelves are inserted. Much of the design work will probably be in the detail of the system. For example, a single shelf suspended at each end by two cords will need a method of adjusting cord lengths. One solution is a simple 'stay' having two holes as shown. Several identical stays might be needed for one unit.

Packaging for survival

■ TASK Design and make a means of packaging for a selected object (or class of objects) for despatch in the post.

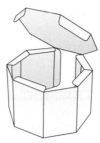 

Millions of pounds worth of goods are destroyed or damaged in the post each year due to inadequate packaging. Packages are always subject to distortion during transit resulting from heavy loads placed on them or shock loading as they are moved around. A good package is one that can resist loading without damage and which absorbs shocks. Many carefully designed packages have built-in crumple zones to protect their contents – a bit like modern cars.

Designing and making a package

Most packages are made from smooth or corrugated card. This is both cheap and tough but becomes useful for packaging only when it is folded. Tightly rolling up card or paper turns a floppy sheet, for example, into a stiff cylinder. Folding paper into a concertina shape makes a stiff platform. Most card packaging takes the form of boxes folded from a net. A traditional chocolate egg box is a good example of a folded box which protects its contents with internal folding of the card sheet.

There are reference books which provide outlines of all the basic styles of carton packaging commonly used in Europe. These are a useful starting point for ideas. A style can be developed, or you might invent an entirely new method of packaging something! Your package might use adhesive to fasten it together or tuck-in joints (or both). Ideally, it should weigh as little for the purpose as possible, and will use material very efficiently.

The prototype package can be tested (against others) by simulating transit conditions, for example by dropping it several times from a standard height. Ultimately, it might actually be sent through the post. If you do this, make sure that the package does not contain any prohibited object. Batteries, for example, should not be sent through the post.

See

- Stiffness, page 23
- Structures, page 71

Kite

Kite flying has become one of the fastest growing of the leisure 'industries'. It has always been a popular hobby, but new materials such as **ripstop nylon** have revolutionised kite design. There are now thousands of kites on the market, many of them designed by engineers.

Designing and making a kite

See

- Structures, page 71

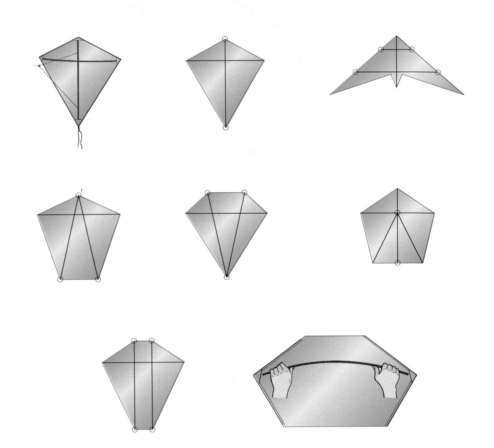

A traditional kite contains **struts** (usually wood or plastic) which support a sail. A diamond-shaped kite has two struts to give shape to the covering. It is flown using a thin cord attached to a bridle. A tail gives the kite stability. There are many other patterns of kite, some of which are shown (the small circles are the bridle attachment points). Once you have decided on the geometry or shape of your kite, you can experiment using very thin **polythene** (such as bin liner material) for the sail and tail, and struts made from wood (such as thin sticks used for garden supports). Sail pockets to hold the struts can be formed using sticky tape.

   The kite can be made in various sizes, but it is a good idea to keep it small to begin with. (The smallest commercial kite is just 11 cm in height!) After experiment, when you are satisfied that the kite flies, you could try using other materials such as ripstop nylon and **composite plastic** struts from a kite specialist shop.

5 Materials

Ergonomic handle

■ **TASK** Design and make a moulded handle for a specific purpose.

We usually take handles for granted, but designers are now giving them a lot of thought so that things are safer and more comfortable to use. A lot of attention is also given to people with special needs, such as those with a weakness who find it difficult to use tools and appliances with ordinary handles.

Designing and making a handle

See

- Materials we use, page 16
- Manufacturing techniques for plastics, page 39
- Ergonomics, page 95

Most plastics, such as nylon, are too hot to mould by hand when they are soft. They are usually **injection moulded**. A new type of plastic called '**polymorph**' softens at just 62 °C and can be moulded like clay or *Plasticine*. When it has cooled to around 30 °C it hardens with similar properties to nylon, including great strength. Granules of 'polymorph' are first softened under hot water and are ready for moulding when they turn from white to clear. Any water is first squeezed out (taking care if it is very hot) and then the mass of plastic is shaped by hand using any suitable tools. It can be kept soft by putting it back into hot water. At room temperatures, 'polymorph' can be cut and machined like other plastics, provided it does not get too hot.

Like most plastics, 'polymorph' shrinks as it cools. If you mould it around something to make a handle, such as a screwdriver or spoon, it locks on tightly as it cools and there is no need to use adhesives. Also, because it is **thermoplastic**, it will soften again when heated.

Shape memory actuator

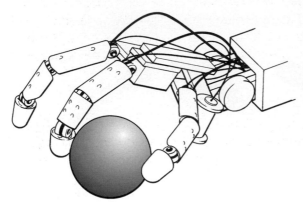

robot hand operated by SMA wire

An actuator is something that causes *straight* movement, for example the actuator in an electric lock that moves the locking bolt backwards and forwards. Actuators are often powered by small electric motors and can be quite complicated. A new metal alloy called **shape memory alloy (SMA)**, sometimes called '**smart wire**', is now being used to replace motors and other parts in small actuators. This alloy is given a 'memory' when it is made, and remembers to change its size at a set temperature. SMA wire made from nickel and titanium 'remembers' that it should be about 5% shorter when heated to 70 °C. It shortens with a useful pulling force. On cooling down again, it returns to its original length.

See

- Levers, page 54
- Shape memory alloy (smart wire), page 146
- Linear actuators, page 152
- Moiré fringe display project, page 241

Designing and making an actuator

SMA actuators can be used for many applications, such as moving small automata, moiré fringe screens, lock bolts, and models (such as a car park barrier). Because SMA wire has a high resistance, it can be heated to change its length by passing a small electric current from a battery through it. (For 100 micron diameter wire allow 3 V per 100 mm of wire.)

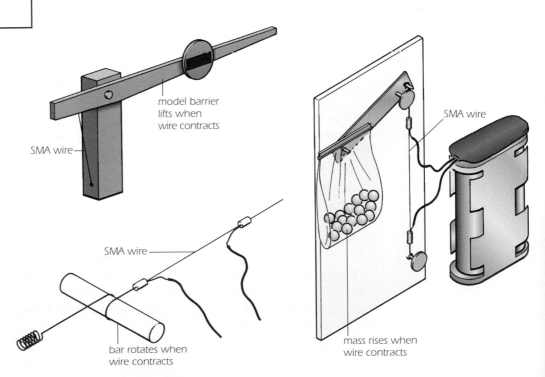

model barrier lifts when wire contracts

SMA wire

SMA wire

bar rotates when wire contracts

SMA wire

mass rises when wire contracts

The length of SMA wire used is worked out from the movement needed. Because it contracts by only about 5% in length, larger movements can be produced with the help of levers. SMA cannot be soldered and is joined to connecting wire by crimps (small metal tubes that can be crushed with pliers). These can also be held in terminal blocks. The illustrations show three examples of simple SMA actuators.

Emergency ice scraper

What seem to be very simple products are often the result of a lot of thinking. A typical car accessory shop sells many products for making life easier in very cold or very hot weather, including tools for scraping ice off windscreens. These tools must have a sharp edge but they must not scratch the glass or damage the rubber seal around the glass.

Designing and making an ice scraper

An emergency tool might be used just once and then discarded. It should be small and easily stored, for example inside a glove compartment, until required. It will need to be cheap and is likely to be made from one material. At the same time it has to be easy to hold and use.

What will be strong enough and at the same time not scratch the window, paintwork (if it slips) or rubber seal? Look-up tables provide hardness figures for metal and plastics. If the edge of the scraper is not to be worn away too quickly you need a hard material but not, for example, steel, which could do damage. Plastic materials might be suitable but polythene, for example, will probably be too soft and not hold an edge. Acrylic or polystyrene seem to fit the bill but, although acrylic is stronger than polystyrene (greater tensile strength), it has less impact resistance and will not stand up very well to knocks. **Polystyrene** (which can be injection moulded) would seem to be a good choice.

Having chosen a material, the design work should produce a prototype so that it can be tested prior to expensive tooling for production. This might be made using flat sheet. Because it is an emergency tool, it could end up looking more like a credit card than a conventional ice scraper with a handle. (Some people use credit cards if they get stuck!)

Polystyrene sheet can be cut with a guillotine or (with care) by scoring and fracturing along the score line. It can also be filed, or even planed with woodworking tools.

Thought should be given to how the tool is stored. You might consider designing a wallet that has a small self-adhesive patch, *Velcro* pad or even a magnet which attaches to a metal part of the car.

See
- Table 1.7 (hardness), page 21
- Table 1.8 (tensile strength), page 22
- Table 1.10 (impact resistance), page 25

■ Cool container

Design and make a container for transporting and keeping cool one or more cans of chilled drink.

During the summer there is often a need to keep drinks and food cool when they come out of the fridge. Modern fridges have become a lot smaller than they used to be because the insulation in the casing is now more effective at keeping the heat out, and so a smaller amount is needed. The same materials, such as **expanded polystyrene**, are used for insulation in portable picnic boxes and in buildings. The most common cool drinks are sold in standard aluminium cans, millions of which are sold each year. The majority are not drunk right away, and need to be kept as cool as possible on a hot day.

See

- Materials we use, page 16

Designing and making a cool container for a drink can

A cool container has two features: a **casing** and **insulation**. The casing has to close around the contents and stand up to handling and knocks. It might be made from an impact-resistant material or even a flexible one such as fabric. The insulation needs to be efficient – a poor **conductor** of heat which takes up as little space as possible. Look-up tables provide information on different materials, and show paper, for example, as a very poor conductor. Paper is especially good in unmoving layers because it traps pockets of air.

The overall size of the container depends on how many cans of drink it will contain and where it will be stored. Will it be free-standing, or is it to fit into something else like a briefcase? If it is free-standing, it will also need a handle or strap. If the insulation is loose (such as shreds of paper or polystyrene chips) it will need a liner as well as an outer container. It will also require an opening, such as a lid, that is as well insulated as the main container.

When a prototype is built, it can be tested. First, measure and plot the rise in temperature of an uninsulated can taken from the fridge. Then measure and plot the same for a can insulated within your prototype. Compare the two results using a datalogger with temperature probe or a surface thermometer whose readings are plotted on a graph against time.

Thermochromic indicator/display

■ TASK Design and make a liquid crystal indicator or display.

Thermochromic film is a plastic sheet covered with a liquid crystal 'ink' which changes colour at a set temperature. The background colour of the film changes from black to a bright colour when you touch it with a finger. This type of material is used in battery test strips. A resistance element under the thermochromic film heats up when connected to the battery (by pushing down at both ends) and changes the colour of the strip, provided the battery is not flat. The same material is also used in thermometers which change to different colours at different temperatures.

See

- Graphics, page 83
- Thermochromic film, page 155

Designing and making a display or indicator

Thermochromic film is available as self-adhesive sheet and can be cut to size with a knife or scissors. If the wax paper backing is peeled off carefully, resistance wire (or very thin copper wire) can be laid on to the sticky side to form a pathway. If the wax paper is replaced, you have a very simple display. When a suitable battery is connected to the wire, it heats up and the surface of the film changes colour along the pathway of the wire.

This principle can be used, for example, to design and make either a battery tester or a display screen which 'spells out' a message or logo. The screen can be switched on and off by a switch or a circuit; 100 mm of 0.3 mm diameter *Nichrome* resistance wire used with a 3 V battery will give good results. Tape the film sticky side upwards on to a surface to lay down the wire. If you need to cross the wire over itself, use a small insulating patch of paper. The resistance wire can be connected to insulated wire with terminal blocks and the display mounted, for example, on foam core board.

Under no circumstances overheat the wire or the film will melt.

6 Product design

Personal organiser

■ **TASK** Design and make a personal organiser.

Despite the fact that the electronic notebooks are now very cheap, many people still prefer using paper-based personal organisers. There are so many different styles (and prices) that some shops specialise in selling them. It is also possible to buy many flat accessories, such as calculators, designed to fit the holes in the organiser spine. The use of translucent plastics such as **polypropylene** has given organisers a new look and makes it very easy to design and make a professional-looking organiser at low cost.

> **See**
> • Graphics, page 83

Designing and making a personal organiser

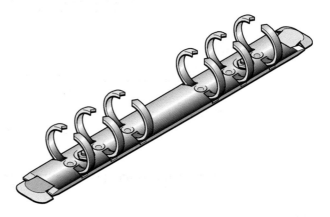

The organiser spine comes as a complete unit which has to be fastened to the cover. The usual method is to use metal rivets but 4 mm screws and nuts can be used. The cover can be made from a range of materials, including card, polypropylene, soft PVC or card-stiffened fabric. Card needs to be marked out and creased prior to bending. Polypropylene should be marked out and folded, if possible in a metal folding unit, to start the bends. It is then folded by hand. Although stiff, a polypropylene 'hinge' can be flexed thousands of times before it breaks. Clear plastic organiser covers are available with pockets front and back for card inserts. These can be printed, for example, using an inkjet printer.

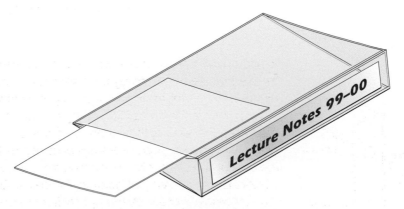

Pages for the personal organiser can be finished with a standard organiser punch. This can also be used to make thin plastic section dividers, polypropylene rulers, and so on.

Light pipe

Optical fibres carry or 'conduct' light over great distances with little loss. They are used in telecommunications for transmitting signals and in surgery for internal examination of patients. An instrument called an endoscope can be used to pass light into the body through optical fibres, and a number of fibres grouped together can be used to see into the same place.

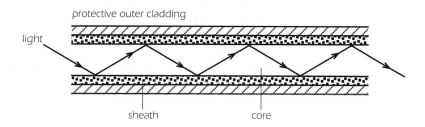

An optical fibre consists of a clear core and outer layer (and sometimes a protective outer sheath). Light entering one end of the fibre is continuously reflected back into the core when it strikes the outer layer and eventually emerges at the other end. Optical fibres are made of glass or plastic (which is cheaper).

Designing and making a light pipe

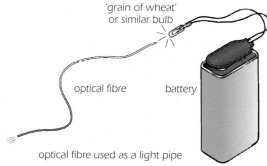

optical fibre used as a light pipe

> ### See
> - Light-emitting diodes (LEDs), page 128
> - Torch bulb, page 198

Plastic optical fibre 1 mm in diameter will transmit a useful amount of light. It can be used, for example, to light up spaces in machinery, locks or car engines where there is not enough space to get a conventional light or torch.

Each end of the optical fibre can be finished after cutting by rubbing on abrasive paper and polishing on dry newspaper. It then has to be fastened close to the light source, such as a small bulb. A small lens can help to focus light into the optical fibre, but this is not absolutely necessary. A tube, turned and drilled on a **lathe**, is a simple way of holding the optical fibre against the light source.

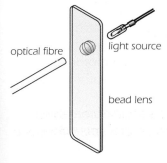

In a complete product, the optical fibre might be fastened into a case holding the batteries and a switch. In use, it should be possible to put the case down and feed the optical fibre to the position required. You might consider, for example, attaching a clip or magnet to the case so that it does not move when in use.

■ Automaton

An automaton is a model that resembles the living thing and imitates some of its movements. The first automata were built for amusement in ancient China, Greece and Rome. In recent years there has been a revival in automata and many people are now designing and making them. They are made for exhibitions and advertising and as examples of craft or art for galleries.

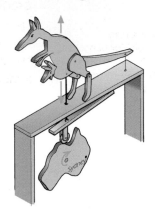

In the 1920s an artist called Alexander Calder made automata simply by bending and connecting pieces of wire. His work is now imitated today.

Designing and making a wire frame automaton

Designing a wire frame automaton is like sketching with wire (which can be bought very cheaply as welding wire and joined using thinner wire). When you have decided on a subject, the wire can be laid out on a board and joined to a thicker wire frame. You will need to experiment because the wire outline may move in unexpected ways when one part is pushed or pulled.

See

- Crank and slider, page 59
- Gearboxes, page 148

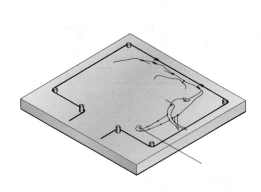
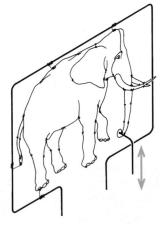
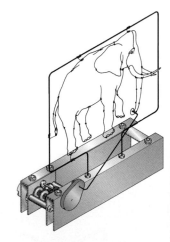

The wire frame automaton can be operated by hand, for example by turning a wire crank handle connected to a rod which moves backwards and forwards. The automaton could also be connected to the output shaft of a **motorised pulley** or **gearbox** so that it moves at the press of a switch. If the automaton is motorised, make sure that the parts move easily by hand first.

Using an electric motor could be the basis for a coin-operated automaton which runs for a short length of time when you insert a coin in a slot. A **555 timer** circuit will give adjustable 'on' times after a switch is closed.

Clock

■ **TASK** Design and make a clock based on a quartz clock movement.

There are two main types of clock: **digital** and **analogue**. Analogue clocks with moving hands are usually based on very accurate **quartz** movements which contain an electronic circuit that 'ticks' millions of times per second! The circuit then drives a small motor to turn the hands.

> **See**
> ▪ Manufacturing techniques for plastics, page 39
> ▪ Quartz clock movement, page 182

Designing and making a clock

There are several clock movements to choose from, but they are very similar in size. They are normally fitted to the clock or clock face by means of a large nut. The hands then just push on. Clocks can be designed and made using just folded sheet material – plastic, card or even paper.

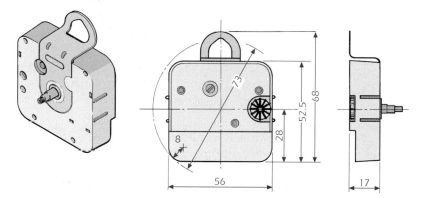

Some clocks are made by **vacuum forming**. In this process a sheet of plastic is heated until softened and then sucked down over a former or mould. This can be shaped from a solid piece of material or built up from parts. As the example below shows, the mould should always have a **draft angle** so that it does not stick to the plastic when it cools.

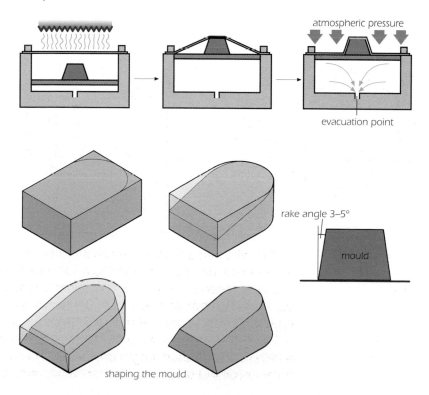

shaping the mould

■ Torch

■ **TASK**   Design and make a thin 'credit card' torch.

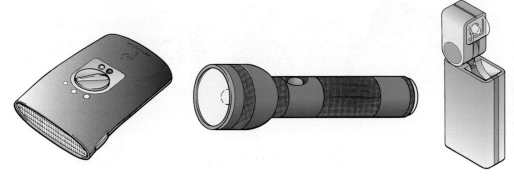

Torches are one of the most common battery-powered products and hundreds of different models are available at any one time. They are normally designed with **injection-moulded** parts. Some torch designs are very unusual and clever. The *Durabeam* torch, for example, has a built-in switch so that the light comes on when the top of the torch is flipped up. Other torches are now being made using mainly paper!

Designing and making a torch

> **See**
>
> - Graphics, page 83
> - Light-emitting diodes (LEDs), page 128

Most torches use a filament bulb and larger batteries, commonly C size. A thin torch needs a different type of battery such as the lithium disc types used in cameras and small calculators. These are extremely small for the amount of energy that they store. Nevertheless, their small size means that filament bulbs would run them down very quickly, so an alternative is a high-intensity **LED** (light-emitting diode).

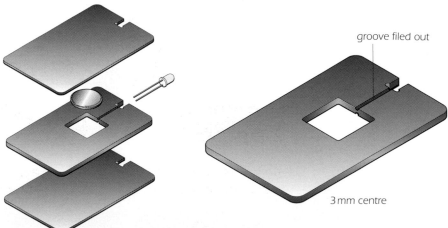

groove filed out

3 mm centre

A combination of LED and **lithium battery** means that you can do away with a separate switch because the legs of the LED can be 'pinched' together against the battery to make contact. They will then spring apart to turn off. The battery has to be housed in card or plastic sheet slightly thicker than itself so that the LED legs are held off the battery until squeezed. The LED's head can be set into the torch body, or it can be left sticking out.

The torch is completed by bonding on thin plastic sides or, for example, affixing self-adhesive paper labels. Such labels give you plenty of scope for graphic design since they can be finished using a colour inkjet printer.

Mirror

We take mirrors for granted because they are so common. Most mirrors used to be made of glass with a metal reflective backing. Now, many 'unbreakable' mirrors are made cheaply from plastic with a reflective metal film on the top, but these mirrors can distort the image if they are slightly bent. It is therefore better to keep them small.

See
- Materials we use, page 16
- The main groups of materials, page 17

Designing and making a mirror

Mirrored plastic can be cut using a guillotine or by scoring and then cracking along the score line. Mirrors made from polystyrene can be finished along the edges by smoothing with a woodworking plane or by using abrasive paper.

First think about the purpose of your mirror and then decide on its size and any special requirements. For example, a vanity mirror usually needs a case to prevent damage to the surface. This might be made from metal or plastic (with a soft lining), welded polythene sheet, or even fabric. A mirror for a cycle or for inspection work will require a special fitting to hold it. This might involve designing and making a universal joint to allow the mirror to rotate.

Two mirrors can be used together to make a periscope. They may be held in a box such as the fold-up card types sold at festivals, or supported by an open frame.

box periscope

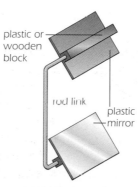

plastic or wooden block

rod link

plastic mirror

open frame periscope

Kaleidoscope

The kaleidoscope was invented in 1818 by the scientist David Brewster. After nearly 200 years, kaleidoscopes are once again popular and made in many shapes and sizes. Anything seen through a kaleidoscope is reflected several times to create a symmetrical image.

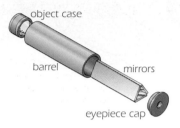

A typical kaleidoscope has three mirrors in a tube or barrel, an eyepiece and an object case. This case contains fragments of plastic or glass beads which produce unique images when the barrel is turned. Some kaleidoscopes use tubes of coloured liquids instead of the object case.

Designing and making a kaleidoscope

Kaleidoscopes can be made using mirrored plastic sheeting which is easily cut on a guillotine or by scoring and cracking. The diameter of a kaleidoscope barrel should be between about 20 mm and 45 mm. There are many types of tubing – card or plastic – within this range. When you have decided on a size, cut three mirrors to make a tight fit. You can work out the mirror widths, for example, by dividing the circular barrel diameter into three using compasses.

See

- Materials we use, page 16
- The main groups of materials, page 17
- Graphics, page 83

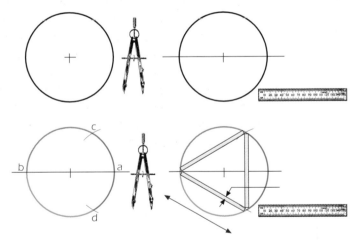

The kaleidoscope does not need an eyepiece, but looking through a small hole improves what you see. This might be made by **drilling** and **turning** on a **lathe**. It should be possible to design and invent entirely new ways of making the image. For example, you can design and make a coloured wheel that turns, or think up a method of passing a strip of printed paper past the end.

Moiré fringe display

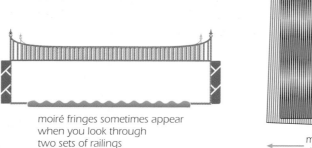

moiré fringes sometimes appear
when you look through
two sets of railings

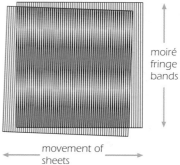

moiré
fringe
bands

movement of
sheets

A moiré fringe is an optical effect that appears when two grid patterns move against one another. You sometimes see it on bridge railings or net curtains. It can be demonstrated by passing a sheet of grid lines printed on acetate over a similar grid printed on paper. Only a very small movement of one sheet against the other produces a very big optical effect. This principle can be exploited in advertising by attracting attention with moving moiré fringes.

See

- Mechanical control, page 54
- Programmable control, page 68
- Shape memory alloy (smart wire), page 146

Designing and making a moiré effect display screen

Printed grids are made in a rub-down form or can be photocopied from some books. If you take a grid and then photocopy it on to both paper and **acetate sheet** (used for overhead projector slides), you have the basic parts for a display. An advertising image might be photocopied on to the paper sheet over the grid lines, or cut out and stuck on. You must then devise a way of moving the printed acetate sheet over the bottom one. It might be fastened with a pin at one corner, for example, or held with two elastic bands. The acetate is then pulled at the bottom to create the effect. In the examples shown, the actual movement is produced by a small length of 'smart wire' which contracts when it is heated by an **electric current**. The acetate could also be moved using an **electric motor** and a **crank mechanism**. Whatever causes the movements should be hidden with a frame.

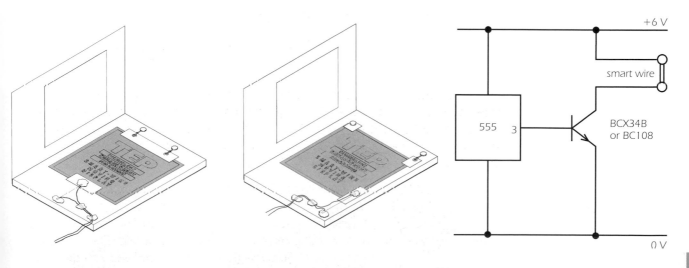

+6 V

smart wire

555   3

BCX34B
or BC108

0 V

Moiré fringe display

7 Manufacturing

Desktop furniture

Desktop furniture is the name given to various items that are used on top of a desk such as pen/pencil trays, notelet holders, paper-clip boxes, disk boxes, calendars, and so on. Shops that specialise in selling pens or personal organisers supply a wide range of desk furniture to cater for a growing market. Appearance matters!

See

- Manufacturing techniques for metals, page 30
- Pre-finished metal, page 162

Designing and making desktop furniture using anodised aluminium

Pre-anodised aluminium is a useful material for making small objects. With the right equipment such as a guillotine, punch and folding unit, it can be made into many shapes and combined with other materials. It does not need finishing after forming because the anodised film offers both protection and a good quality finish. You simply need to be careful not to scratch it (for example, keep it covered in paper).

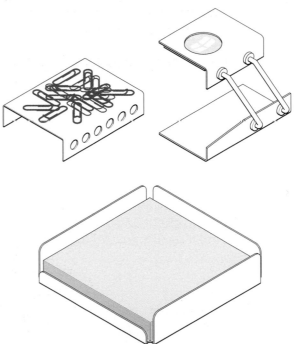

First, do some research in shops and make a list of possible items that need organising on a desk top. When you have chosen one or more items, think about how they can be contained. Because you will be working with sheet metal, the simpler the shape the better when it comes to making it. A simple form will probably look better as well. The illustrations show a few ways of turning anodised aluminium into simple but attractive desktop furniture. There are many more items of furniture that you might consider. Remember that a set of items should match and that you must pay attention to details. For example, metal desk furniture must not scratch a polished surface. How will you prevent this?

Injection-moulded product

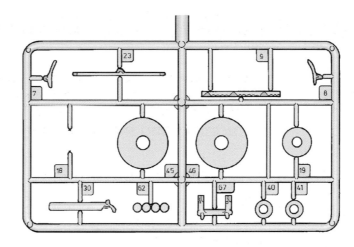

Injection moulding is the most important manufacturing process for plastics. Hot fused plastic is injected under pressure into a mould and allowed to cool. If you look carefully at mouldings in some toys and kits, you will find all the parts still joined together by the channels through which the plastic runs in the mould. Industrial injection moulding machines work automatically, injecting plastic and opening and closing the mould.

Designing and making the product

> **See**
> - Injection moulding, page 39

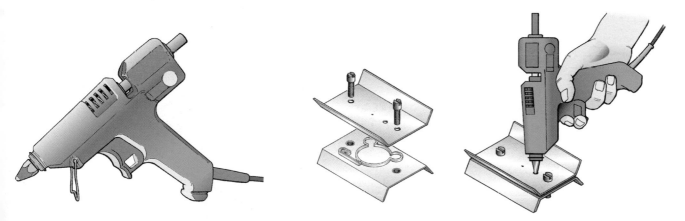

For small mouldings, it is possible to use a **hot melt glue gun** as the injection moulding 'machine'. A mould can be made by forming a length of rectangular wire and trapping it between two metal plates. Alternatively, cut-out metal plates can be stacked together. A special mould case may be used to hold the wire or plates. This is lightly coated with release agent to prevent the glue sticking.

A magnet is moulded into the product by placing a small length of plastic magnetic strip into the mould.

You can work out the volume of plastic required for the product by estimating the area enclosed and using simple maths.

■ Hi-tech pen

■ **TASK** Design and make a pen to house a ball-point refill.

Before the ball-point pen, most people used fountain pens containing a rubber sack for the ink. The ball-point pen was invented by two brothers called Biro (hence the name sometimes used) in 1938. It depends on having a close-fitting ball rotating in a socket, and a special thick ink. Millions of throw-away ball pens are now made every day.

Designing and making a pen

See

- Manufacturing techniques for plastics, page 39
- Disposable ball-point pen, page 196

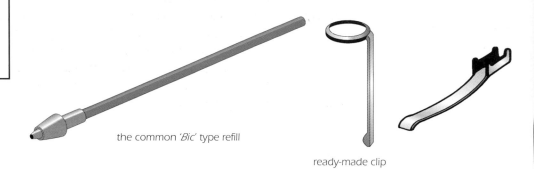

the common *'Bic'* type refill

ready-made clip

You can buy many pen parts ready made, for example the ball-point refills and fittings such as clips. Some of these can also be made. Brightly coloured plastic tubing called **butyrate** is often used for pen making and is available in different diameters. It needs to be cut to length and then faced off, if possible, using a **lathe**.

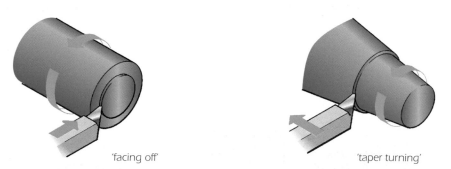

'facing off'

'taper turning'

The ball-point refill will probably not fit directly into any tubing and will need a piece that fits between. This can also be made on the lathe by drilling and turning metal or plastic rod. End caps can be found for the tubing or these can also be turned on the lathe.

If you are making more than one pen, you can use simple gauges to check that the length of each pen barrel is the same. The pen might be packaged by **vacuum forming**.

Re-inventing the paper-clip

■ TASK Design and make a small batch of wire paper-clips to fasten loose sheets of paper together.

There are many problems that designers and inventors return to time and time again. Getting corks out of bottles is one example and holding pieces of paper together is another. The most familiar paper-clip is called the 'Gem' and was designed about 100 years ago. Despite its widespread use, it is still not ideal. It bends easily and can damage paper with its sharp ends.

Designing and making a paper-clip

Stiff wire is a cheap material and can be bought, for example, as welding wire. If you bend wire slightly, it will spring back to its original shape when you let go. Try an experiment with a paper-clip. If you bend it too much (beyond its **elastic limit**) the wire stays bent. The wire also gets harder at the bend which explains why it is so difficult to pull a paper-clip out straight. Both of these things are important in thinking about the paper-clip design.

See

- Properties of materials, page 19
- Paper-clip, page 180

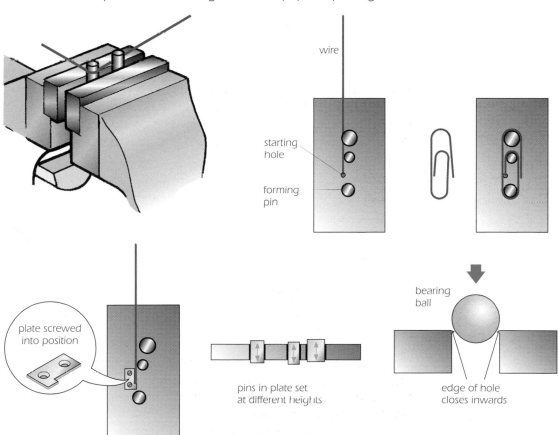

Try making some clips using two metal pins in a **vice**. This makes a very simple **jig** or tool which allows you to repeat shapes. Eventually, you will need a tool that enables you to do all the bending and get each clip exactly the same. The illustrations show a simple **pin tool** for making a Gem-type clip. A better tool has a small plate (or another pin) to hold the starting end of the wire. The pins are set into the tool at different heights through drilled holes. If the pins for the tool are too loose when you try to fit them, a toolmaker's 'trick' is to press in a bearing ball to close the hole up at the edge.

■ Construction system

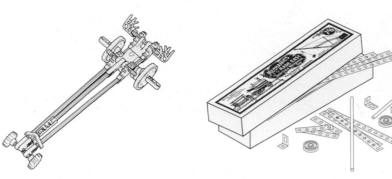

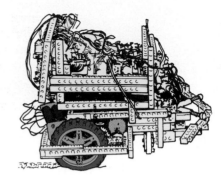

original Meccano set invented by Frank Hornby

Many different construction systems are sold as toys. Some of these, such as *Lego Technic*, started life as aids for engineers to design production lines. Others, such as *Meccano*, have been adapted by engineers for making prototypes, such as some early mechanical computers. Fortunes have been made by inventors of construction systems, an example being Frank Hornby who invented *Meccano*.

<table>
<tr><td>

See

- Manufacturing techniques for metals, page 30
- Manufacturing techniques for plastics, page 39

</td></tr>
</table>

Designing and making a construction system

Many components suitable for construction systems can be bought in shops. These include **nuts** and **bolts**, **plastic rivets** and other **fasteners**. Other components of your construction system can be designed and made using metal or plastic sheet, both of which can be easily cut and formed. Metal parts can be cut out with a guillotine, punched and then folded with a special tool. Plastic parts can be cut with a guillotine, punched and then folded after heating on a strip heater.

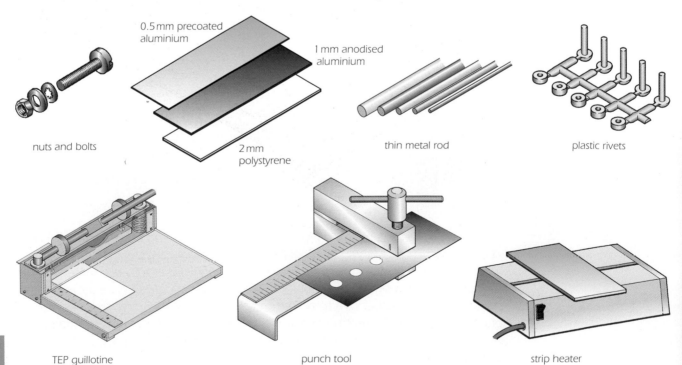

nuts and bolts

0.5 mm precoated aluminium

1 mm anodised aluminium

2 mm polystyrene

thin metal rod

plastic rivets

TEP guillotine

punch tool

strip heater

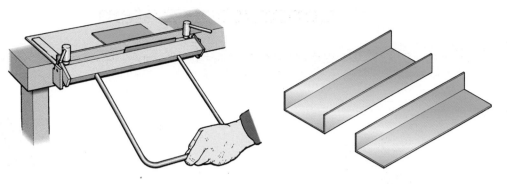

Different parts can be made, for example, by folding thin metal rod using a **jig** or tool. These parts might be used as connecting rods in a working model.

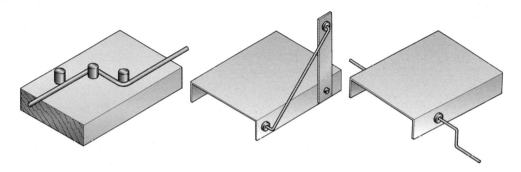

Finally, your construction system will need storing. You might think about a vacuum-formed tray or one cut from foam plastic, for example.

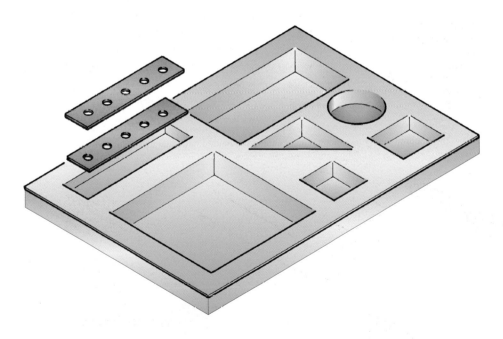

Index